SUPPORTING STUDENTS ON THE AUTISM SPECTRUM IN INCLUSIVE SCHOOLS

Inclusive education has grown as an international movement to not only support students with disabilities but also promote equitable access, participation, and success for all students. This book will transform the capacity of teachers and specialists working with students and families to effectively support an inclusive approach to education for students on the autism spectrum.

This book addresses the urgent need to identify inclusive educational environments and strategies for students on the autism spectrum so that they have the best chance of social, behavioural, and academic success at school. Teachers who include students on the autism spectrum in primary and secondary classrooms require greater knowledge of how they can best support the learning, social, and behavioural needs of their students. Without such knowledge, the consequences can include unsatisfactory learning experiences for all students, and interrupted schooling for the student on the autism spectrum through reduced attendance and retention, lower academic performance, exclusion, disengagement, and pressure on parents to make alternative arrangements for their child's education.

Inclusive education is socially, emotionally, and academically beneficial for all students and positively impacts on respectful attitudes to difference. This book presents innovative, evidence-based practices that will build the capacity of teachers and specialists implementing an inclusive and contextually relevant approach to education that will support students on the autism spectrum and meet the diverse needs of all students in their classrooms.

Suzanne Carrington is a Professor in education at QUT Australia. She has over 25 years of experience working in universities in teaching, research, international development, and senior leadership roles. Suzanne's areas of expertise are in inclusive education, ethical leadership, and disability impacting on policy and practice in Australian and international contexts.

Beth Saggers is an Associate Professor in the School of Early Childhood and Inclusive Education at QUT Australia.

Keely Harper-Hill is the Research Associate for the Enhancing Learning and Teaching education research program of the Autism CRC at QUT Australia.

Michael Whelan is an Associate Professor in the School of Creative Practice at QUT Australia. He is also a writer, musician, and autism advocate.

COVER ART

SUPPORTING STUDENTS ON THE AUTISM
SPECTRUM IN INCLUSIVE SCHOOLS

Tunnel Vision (Oil on Canvas, 40cm x 40cm, © 2016)
In creating this work I was thinking about how, when I focus on something I like, and decide to put 110% into it, I lose track of time, sometimes forgetting to eat, because I am so involved in the project. This painting is about the tunnel vision of focusing on that one thing, and becoming really good at it. It depicts really detailed thoughts in the middle, then blurs towards the edges, and time doesn't exist.

Artist's name – Prue Stevenson (aged 26 years)

SUPPORTING STUDENTS ON THE AUTISM SPECTRUM IN INCLUSIVE SCHOOLS

A Practical Guide to Implementing Evidence-Based Approaches

Suzanne Carrington, Beth Saggers, Keely Harper-Hill, and Michael Whelan

Routledge
Taylor & Francis Group

LONDON AND NEW YORK

First published 2021
by Routledge
2 Park Square, Milton Park, Abingdon, Oxon OX14 4RN

and by Routledge
52 Vanderbilt Avenue, New York, NY 10017

Routledge is an imprint of the Taylor & Francis Group, an informa business

British Library Cataloguing-in-Publication Data
A catalogue record for this book is available from the British Library

Library of Congress Cataloging-in-Publication Data
A catalog record has been requested for this book

ISBN: 978-0-367-50170-9 (hbk)
ISBN: 978-0-367-50174-7 (pbk)
ISBN: 978-1-003-04903-6 (ebk)

Typeset in Bembo
by SPi Global, India

Printed in the UK by Severn, Gloucester on responsibly sourced paper

We dedicate this book to Emeritus Professor Sylvia Rodger AM. Sylvia's leadership in the development of the Autism CRC ensured that our School Years Program research is inclusive, multidisciplinary, and high-quality. Sylvia was passionate about meeting the needs of young people, their families, and educators in order that students are successful at school and beyond. We believe that she would be proud of our collective work.

Emeritus Professor Sylvia Rodger AM

CONTENTS

FIGURES AND TABLES

Figures

Tables

FOREWORD

I am delighted to introduce this publication, *Supporting Students on the Autism Spectrum in Inclusive Schools: A Practical Guide to Implementing Evidence-based Approaches*.

This is one of two volumes written to support researchers, teachers, and specialists working to develop inclusive educational environments and programs for students on the autism spectrum.

This, the *Practice* volume, provides practice guidance and resources for educators and school communities to support students in inclusive school settings, both students on the autism spectrum and, ultimately, all learners. Its companion volume, *Research Approaches to Supporting Students on the Autism Spectrum in Inclusive Schools: Outcomes, Challenges and Impact*, provides an understanding of the challenges inherent in translating research into classroom practice and a framework for inclusive research in education.

In 2013, Autism CRC established the world's first national, cooperative research effort focused on autism across the lifespan – through a formal venture between the research, service, government, and autism community sectors – and supported by the Australian Government's Cooperative Research Centre Program. Our national program of research and its translation to practice and policy spanned the early childhood years, the school years, and adulthood.

In my role as Chief Executive Officer of Autism CRC, it's been my pleasure to see the translation of over six years of research in our School Years Program into evidence-based and research-informed approaches and practices, many of which you will find in this book, the *Practice* volume. Each are designed to support the work of teachers and specialists.

In the average Australian classroom, at least three children have a learning difficulty or neuro-developmental disability. The support and scaffolding these children receive during school can set the trajectory for the rest of their lives, but many teachers don't feel equipped to effectively support the learning of all students in their classrooms.

Autism CRC's School Years Program is built on our foundational research undertaken in Australia's first nationwide needs analysis of the educational needs of autistic students (aged 5–16 years). This study gathered inputs from almost 1,500 school administrators, teachers and specialist support staff, ancillary support staff such as teacher aides, parents, and students.

The School Years Program has directly involved more than 3,000 educators, 7,000 students, and 1,300 parents and carers along with allied health workers, psychologists, and support people in research program design, development, and evaluation. Importantly, teachers have contributed as experts in understanding the classroom context and involved as respected colleagues in co-producing our research and its outputs.

This has resulted in more than 25 research projects conducted on-ground in 300+ state, Catholic and independent schools across Australia, which have developed:

- tools and practices to enhance teaching and the learning experience (classrooms of excellence);
- evidence-based tools and programs for supporting social, emotional, and behavioural needs of children and adolescents;
- a better understanding of the developmental and behavioural trajectories of Australian students on the autism spectrum; and
- the skills and confidence of teachers and support personnel.

In 2020, we released *inclusionED* [inclusioned.edu.au], a major new online professional learning community for educators. The platform provides evidence-based and research-informed teaching practices, videos, printable templates and other resources, designed to support diverse learners in inclusive classrooms. The platform also facilitates a national community of practice, enabling social sharing and educator reviews on the experience of implementing specific teaching practices. You can read more about *inclusionED* in the chapters throughout this book.

Overseeing this vast array of projects and diverse cast of researchers, organisations, education departments, teachers, parents, carers, and students has been Suzanne Carrington, School Years Program Director at Autism CRC and Professor in the Faculty of Education at the Queensland University of Technology. Suzanne and her team of researchers are dedicated to the principles of inclusive education and Universal Design for Learning as an effective framework for providing support for the needs of all students in inclusive schools, including those on the autism spectrum. The team has been driven by a commitment to collaborate with on-ground educators, working out the best way to implement change and improve inclusive education opportunities for all students.

As you read through this book, and its companion *Research* volume, I hope you enjoy the beautiful artwork. In 2014, 2016, and 2018, Autism CRC held an Art Prize inviting people on the autism spectrum to showcase their strengths and interests through art. The response was excellent and some of the wonderful examples are displayed on the cover and throughout the volumes.

I express my sincere thanks to many thousands of students, parents, education, and allied health professionals that have contributed to the outcomes of our School Years Program. My thanks also to the many research team members and the authors of this book for their tireless commitment to our work. I know they join me in dedicating this volume to Emeritus Professor Sylvia Rodger AM, Autism CRC's founder, whose vision and passion continue to inspire us.

For educators reading this book, we hope *Supporting Students on the Autism Spectrum in Inclusive Schools: A Practical Guide to Implementing Evidence-based Approaches* gives you the resources to better support your students and their learning, participation, and engagement in an inclusive education environment.

Andrew Davis
Chief Executive Officer
Autism CRC

ACKNOWLEDGEMENTS

We would like to acknowledge and thank the researchers, our co-authors who have worked with us on the chapters in this book. Our co-authors share our vision for improving the lives of young people on the autism spectrum and supporting inclusive education. Thank you for the collaboration and ongoing professional conversations. We look forward to our future work together.

We would like to acknowledge all of our education partners, schools, the autistic community, students, and parents as this research could not have happened without your great and unwavering support. It has been our privilege to work with you over the past seven years. We hope this book supports our ongoing shared passion and commitment to inclusion.

We would also like to acknowledge Julie Nickerson for her enormous and magnificent contribution to this book. Julie supported our work as authors, co-authors, managed all of the communication with our publisher, managed the internal review processes, the permissions for artwork, communications with the Autism CRC, and was amazing and good fun to work with! Thank you, Julie!!

Finally, we would like to thank Andrew Davis, the Chief Executive Officer, Autism CRC, Therese Conway, the Research Program Manager, Autism CRC, and the review team that she coordinated. Our collective work has been improved after receiving your thoughtful comments and feedback. Thank you!

The artwork featured in this book from 'The Autism CRC Art Prize' (2016) has been provided with permission by:

> Prue Stevenson: *Tunnel Vision* (Oil on Canvas, 40cm x 40cm, © 2016) (Front cover)
> Alarah Gwyn: *We Learn in Different Ways* (Part 1 title page)
> Kai Brelsford: *Threads of the Whole* (Part 2 title page)
> Christopher Chan: *My Autism Strengths* (Part 3 title page)
> Angus Reardon: *Signs* (Part 4 title page)
> Alice Pegler: *Art is My Strength* (Part 5 title page)

The authors kindly thank these artists for the use of their work which has brought the pages to life.

CONTRIBUTORS

Rachel Aberdein has a music background and currently works as a research assistant at Queensland University of Technology. Her research interests centre around inclusive education, particularly regarding students on the autism spectrum. Rachel likes to focus on making research translatable for a range of audiences including people on the autism spectrum. Her research activities include work on a range of educational research projects investigating improving educational outcomes for students on the autism spectrum and supporting the knowledge translation of research findings. She applies extensive knowledge that she has gained from personal experience to research.

Rebecca Armstrong, PhD, is a lecturer in Speech Pathology at the University of Queensland in Australia. Rebecca has worked clinically as a speech pathologist for the Department of Education (Queensland) prior to commencing her academic appointment at the University of Queensland. In the higher education sector, she teaches across the undergraduate and master's speech pathology programs in a range of paediatric areas. Rebecca researches in the areas of language and literacy for school-aged populations, including children on the autism spectrum.

Jill Ashburner's career in the disability sector has spanned over 40 years. Her doctoral study explored the relationship between the sensory processing issues of students on the autism spectrum and their classroom behavioural, emotional, and educational outcomes. As Manager, Research and Development at Autism Queensland for the past 13 years, her research has focused on sensory processing issues, the education of students on the spectrum (including written expression, structured teaching, and bullying), professional development of clinicians, the use of telehealth in early intervention, a post-school transition program, and goal setting for adults and adolescents on the spectrum. She is currently involved in evaluating a program on employment of people on the spectrum.

Wendi Beamish is an Adjunct Senior Lecturer in the School of Education and Professional Studies, Griffith University. She has more than 40 years' experience in the field of special needs education and early childhood intervention. Wendi led the early years stream of the Cooperative Research Centre for Living with Autism (Autism CRC) Project, Models of Practice. Her research interests focus on teacher practice in the areas of educational transitions, autism, positive behavioural support, inclusive education, social-emotional competence, and early intervention.

Yanto Browning is a Lecturer in music at the Queensland University of Technology, and has worked as a music producer and musician, with a focus on the use of technology in music performance and production. With twenty years of studio experience, Yanto has produced several hundred records for a broad range of Australian bands and artists, and has also worked as a composer and producer of music for film, television, and contemporary dance. Yanto has researched, developed, designed and produced several interactive musical spaces, investigating gestural control of electronic instruments and concepts of play, centred around the creation of active musical spaces that incorporate audience participation. This work has included performances and installations at events such as the 2017 Ars Electronica festival. As an educator, Yanto has coordinated the music production program at the Queensland University of Technology for the past several years, while continuing his research and personal practice around technology in music.

Susan Bruck received her PhD in Computer Science from Macquarie University, New South Wales, Australia and holds a BSc(Hons) from the University of Newcastle, New South Wales, Australia. Susan worked as a Senior Research Officer at Autism Spectrum Australia (Aspect) Sydney Australia. Prior to working at Aspect, Susan held research positions at Macquarie University. She holds an academic title, Senior Lecturer, in the School of Medicine, Griffith University, Australia. Susan has published more than 20 original journal articles, book chapters, and reports in fields of autism and the use of technology in education. Her research focus is the development of co-produced, evidence-based inclusive education options for students on the autism spectrum, their educators, and parents.

Suzanne Carrington is a Professor at the Queensland University of Technology, Australia. Her areas of expertise are in inclusive education, disability, and teacher preparation for inclusive schools. She has engaged in research to inform policy and practice in Australian and international education contexts, more recently extending this research to the South Pacific and Asia. She has broad knowledge of education research, and her publication list provides evidence of extensive collaboration with education and health research. Currently she is the Program Director of the School Years Program for the Cooperative Research Centre for Living with Autism (Autism CRC). This is the world's first cooperative research centre focused on autism across the lifespan.

Marina Ciccarelli is an Associate Professor in the School of Occupational Therapy, Social Work, and Speech Pathology at Curtin University, Australia. She has worked as an occupational therapist for over 30 years with a focus on assisting people living with disability to gain employment and facilitating safe return to work of injured workers, by adapting environments to meet individuals' needs. Marina leads research projects at the Cooperative Research Centre for Living with Autism (Autism CRC) focused on assisting young autistic individuals to plan and prepare for what they will do after school and improve their employability. She has a keen curiosity about how emergent technologies can help individuals participate in important everyday activities, and is the co-lead on the *myWAY Employability* online resource to support autistic individuals to plan for their place in society.

Trevor Clark has a comprehensive experience and knowledge of education and research related to autistic students following 30 years in the field. He is currently the National Director, Aspect

Research Centre for Autism Practice (ARCAP), which is the research arm of Autism Spectrum Australia (Aspect), Australia's largest national provider of services for autistic people. He was awarded the international Hollingworth Award (Excellence in the Psychology and Education of Gifted Students) in 1995 for his doctoral thesis proposal, which involved the trial of a differentiated educational curriculum for school-aged students on the autism spectrum who present with twice-exceptional (2e) savant skills. He completed his PhD on this topic in 2001 at the UNSW. He presents nationally and internationally on the Aspect Research Centre for Autism Practice (ARCAP) translational research directed towards improving outcomes for autistic people, and on exceptional skills and autism. Major publications include (i) *Exploring Giftedness and Autism – A Study of a Differentiated Program for Autistic Savants.* London. Routledge (2016), (ii) co-authored *Gifted Students with Disability: Twice-Exceptional Learners* in Exploring Gifted Education. Australian & New Zealand Perspectives. London. Routledge (2018) and (iii) the chapter, *A Curriculum to Support Students with Autism and Special Talents and Abilities,* in The SAGE Handbook of Autism and Education, SAGE (2019). Trevor is an Executive Committee Member of the Australasian Society for Autism Research (ASfAR) and was the past President (2015–2016).

Cerys Downing is a PhD candidate and audiologist within the School of Health and Rehabilitation Sciences at The University of Queensland, Australia. She has worked on research projects across paediatric and educational audiology and has a keen interest in research implementation into clinical practice. At present, Cerys' research focuses on improving diagnostic practices for identifying conductive hearing loss in children.

Emma Gallagher is an autistic researcher, advocate and consultant with Autism Spectrum Australia (Aspect) as well as a registered Early Childhood Teacher in New South Wales. She has an interest in autism research across the lifespan and encouraging research co-production.

Vicki Gibbs is a Clinical Psychologist with specialised training and experience in the diagnosis and support of children and adults on the autism spectrum. She has provided consultation and training in relation to autism to a range of organisations including health and education departments and universities and was key to the development of Launchpad, Autism Spectrum Australia's (Aspect) website assisting young people on the autism spectrum to navigate the transition from school to adult life. Vicki is currently undertaking doctoral studies at Macquarie University. She has presented at national and international conferences and has published several papers in the areas of diagnosis and assessment and the criminal justice system.

Keely Harper-Hill, PhD, is the Research Associate in the education program of research of the Cooperative Research Centre for Living with Autism (Autism CRC) and is based in the Office of Education Research at the Queensland University of Technology. Keely's interest in supporting the educational needs of students on the autism spectrum began in the early 1990s from her clinical work as a speech pathologist in school settings. Her research interests include language processing, educational listening environments, and how students on the autism spectrum are supported to participate in the classroom and access the curriculum.

Megan Hatfield is a Lecturer in the School of Occupational Therapy, Social Work and Speech Pathology at Curtin University, Australia. She developed the Better OutcOmes & Successful Transition for Autism (BOOST-A), an online program that empowers adolescents on the autism spectrum to be successful in the transition out of high school to post-school education, training, and employment. This project was completed with the Cooperative Research Centre for Living with Autism (Autism CRC). Her other research interests include emotional regulation, sensory processing, and spirituality in children. Megan is an occupational therapist who has worked in the disability sector supporting children on the autism spectrum to participate in home, community, and school environments.

Rachel Kelly is a Master of Clinical Psychology student and research officer at the Queensland University of Technology with an interest in the role of connectedness as a protective factor to promote resilience and mental health.

Libby Macdonald completed her PhD with the Cooperative Research Centre for Living with Autism (Autism CRC) and Griffith University. Her doctoral research investigated the use of structured teaching strategies to facilitate the inclusion of students with autism in mainstream educational settings. Libby comes from a background of study in English literature and education and continues to be involved in research in the area of inclusive teaching practices. She is also a parent of a child on the autism spectrum.

Cheryl Mangan is the Manager, Research Translation at the Cooperative Research Centre for Living with Autism (Autism CRC), Australia's first national cooperative research effort focused on autism across the lifespan. Cheryl has over 15 years' experience translating research into evidence-based policy, programs and technology-based solutions, developed in partnership with community. Cheryl is the co-lead for *myWAY Employability*, an initiative supported by Telstra Foundation and the Cooperative Research Centre for Living with Autism (Autism CRC) to translate the outcomes of the Better OutcOmes and Successful Transitions research into a smart web application to help young people on the spectrum to plan and prepare for their working life. Cheryl's research to date has focused on the role of new media in health promotion and community participation in research and program development.

Sofia Mavropoulou is a Senior Lecturer and Study Area Coordinator for Inclusive Education (Master of Education) in the Faculty of Education at Queensland University of Technology. Sofia has extensive teaching experience in preservice, in-service, and postgraduate teacher education programs in universities located in Europe and Australia. Sofia has participated (as chief investigator and associate researcher) in research projects on autism education, with funding from the Greek Government and the European Union. Sofia's current research is focused on educational strategies for students on the autism spectrum in inclusive contexts, and social inequalities and families raising children on the autism spectrum. Sofia is very passionate about creating autism-friendly environments to accommodate the strengths and preferences of persons with autism to promote their inclusion, independence, and wellbeing.

Jayne Orr is a Clinical Psychologist with a Doctorate in Clinical Psychology and works in the private sector with people of all ages (including children, adolescents, and their families) to boost their mental health. Alongside her clinical practice, Jayne is a Senior Research Officer at the Queensland University of Technology and has an interest in research on building resilience and preventing depression in young adolescents. Jayne is the project coordinator for the School Connectedness Project, a project supported by the Cooperative Research Centre for Living with Autism (Autism CRC) to promote resilience and school connectedness for young adolescents on the autism spectrum.

Kelsey Perrykkad is a PhD candidate and teaching associate in the Cognition and Philosophy Lab, School of Philosophical, Historical and International Studies at Monash University, Melbourne, Australia. Kelsey is a cognitive scientist whose research spans the disciplines of psychology, neuroscience, philosophy, and education. She has collected behavioural, cognitive, and physiological data, both in the classroom and in the lab. Much of her work to date focuses on sensory accounts of the cognitive style or architecture associated with a diagnosis of Autism Spectrum Disorder, and how these sensory differences impact self-cognition.

Ainslie Robinson joined Autism Spectrum Australia (Aspect) as an autistic researcher for the Cooperative Research Centre for Living with Autism (Autism CRC) project titled Transition Models of Practice (MoP), which has investigated and developed ways of supporting mainstream teachers of autistic school students in the middle years. Her current work for the Aspect Research Centre for Autism Practice (ARCAP) includes supporting the development and implementation of ARCAP's Exceptional Abilities studies in Australia, China, and the USA.

Beth Saggers is an Associate Professor in the School of Early Childhood and Inclusive Education at Queensland University of Technology, Australia. She currently lectures in autism spectrum, catering for diversity, inclusive practices, and supporting challenging and complex needs, mental health and wellbeing and social emotional support. She has over 30 years of experience working with students on the autism spectrum across a range of age groups and educational settings. She is an active research participant in the Cooperative Research Centre for Living with Autism (Autism CRC). Her research interests include developing supportive learning environments for students on the autism spectrum, the perspectives of key stakeholders, collaborative partnerships, and supporting challenging and complex student needs.

Ian Shochet is a Professor of Clinical Psychology in the School of Psychology and Counselling at Queensland University of Technology, Australia. Ian's area of expertise is in the promotion of mental health and wellbeing in adolescents. In particular, he has done extensive research on the importance of school connectedness on adolescent mental health. He has also developed nationally and internationally recognised school-based interventions that promote connectedness and resilience in adolescence.

Annalise Taylor is a registered special education teacher who completed her doctorate with the Cooperative Research Centre for Living with Autism (Autism CRC) and Griffith University. Her PhD research focused on bridging the research-to-practice gap in relation to the effective and inclusive education of students on the autism spectrum in the first year of school. Her current work focuses on supporting beginning primary and special education teachers via targeted professional learning and training of school-based mentors.

Amanda Webster is currently an Associate Professor and the Academic Program Director for the Master and Graduate Certificate of Autism at the University of Wollongong (UOW). Her research and teaching is focused on creating inclusive learning communities that support individuals on the autism spectrum to exercise agency and achieve their goals. As a community-engaged researcher she is committed to co-production of teaching and research programs that have meaningful social impact for the community. Dr Webster has recently led UOW to become a research partner in the Cooperative Research Centre for Living with Autism (Autism CRC) and has worked with the autistic community in her area to develop the My Life My Decisions

Community of Practice. She has worked actively with education leaders to create systems and strategies to support students on the autism spectrum in Queensland, New South Wales, and Tasmania and has published two books detailing her research with parents and adults on the autism spectrum.

Michael Whelan is an Associate Professor in the School of Creative Practice in the Creative Industries Faculty at Queensland University of Technology in Australia. In addition to his memoir, *The Other Country: A Father's Journey with Autism* which was published by Pan Macmillan in 2008, Michael also wrote the documentary film *What are you doing?* This educational film for school audiences on the topic of social inclusion and autism was distributed to every school in Australia and was screened at the United Nations in New York as part of World Autism Day activities in April, 2013. Michael's current research is focused upon knowledge translation of autism research for application by mainstream teachers of students with diverse learning needs.

Wayne Wilson, PhD, is an Associate Professor and the Head of Audiology at the University of Queensland in Australia. Wayne has over 25 years' experience working as an academic at the Universities of the Witwatersrand, Auckland, and Queensland. His research interests include examining how the brain processes sound, particularly in school-aged populations that include children on the autism spectrum. To date, Wayne has published over 100 scientific papers, book chapters, and patents; given over 300 presentations at scientific conferences; and secured over 35 major, competitive research grants. This research has been cited in white papers and national guidelines both in Australia and around the world.

Astrid Wurfl is based at Queensland University of Technology, Australia as the National and International Coordinator of Training and Program Development of the Resourceful Adolescent Programs (RAP), a resilience intervention to promote positive mental health in teenagers. Astrid has contributed to the development, research, and evaluation of interventions to build resilience across the lifespan. She has been integral in facilitating the widespread national and international up-take and dissemination of the RAP Programs. Astrid has also been a RAP trainer and facilitator for 20 years.

PART 1

Introduction

We Learn in Different Ways (by Alarah Gwyn, aged 8 years)

'Alarah's painting is of an autistic brain in the centre with the message "we learn in different ways". The painting is divided into segments highlighting her interpretation of what the strengths of autism are.'

1

MOVING FROM A SPECIAL EDUCATION MODEL TO AN INCLUSIVE EDUCATION MODEL

Implications for supporting students on the autism spectrum in inclusive settings – An evidence-based approach

Beth Saggers and Suzanne Carrington

The research-supported practices reported on in this book aim to assist educators to have the confidence, knowledge, skills, and partnerships to support all learners in an inclusive environment. The practices also provide a focus on supporting collaboration between specialists and teachers to enable sharing of knowledge and expertise that promotes inclusion and equity in education. To inform practice, a transformational research approach has been taken in this book. It is built on deep reflective practices and a commitment to collaborate with educators in schools to work out how to enact inclusive changes and improve inclusive education for all students. We avoid the use of terms such as 'special education needs' as this perpetuates a 'special' approach. We argue through the chapters in this book that an inclusive approach is good for all. Our work is intended to support educators to design learning environments and programs that are accessible for all students and guide them to set learning goals and plan curriculum, assessment, teaching strategies, and resources to be responsive and supportive of diverse learners in inclusive ways but also support individual needs when necessary. It also highlights the importance of collaborative partnerships with specialised staff, families, and students to ensure appropriate support and inclusive practices are implemented. This chapter will focus on developing a deep understanding of the difference between special education and inclusive education and will present research-informed strategies to support education systems and schools to move to inclusive culture, policy, and practice.

In many countries throughout the world, education systems are trying to move from a special education model to a more inclusive model of practice to support students with a disability in education. This commitment is supported by the signing of international declarations such as the UN *Convention on the Rights of Persons with Disabilities* (CRPD) by countries around the world (UNESCO, 2017; United Nations, 2006). It is clear, however, that many people in education organisations do not understand the difference between special education

> ... *education systems are trying to move from a special education model to a more inclusive model of practice to support students with a disability in education.*

and inclusive education, and do not have the knowledge and practical skills to support this change and develop inclusive culture, policy, and practice in schools.

Inclusive education

An inclusive approach to education is a universal human right and focuses on all children learning and socialising together at the local school. An inclusive approach acknowledges our shared humanity and respects the diversities that exist in ability, culture, gender, language, class, and ethnicity (Carrington et al., 2012; UNESCO, 2017). In 2006, the UN *Convention on the Rights of Persons with Disabilities* (United Nations, 2006) was published and ratified by over 180 countries. *Article 24, General Comment 4*, which followed in 2016, established the authoritative definition of what inclusion is and what it is not:

> Inclusion involves a process of systemic reform embodying changes and modifications in content, teaching methods, approaches, structures and strategies in education to overcome barriers with a vision serving to provide all students of the relevant age range with an equitable and participatory learning experience and environment that best corresponds to their requirements and preferences. Placing students with disabilities within mainstream classes without accompanying structural changes to, for example, organisation, curriculum and teaching and learning strategies, does not constitute inclusion. Furthermore, integration does not automatically guarantee the transition from segregation to inclusion.
>
> (United Nations, 2016, p. 4)

Inclusive education is also a goal in the *2030 Agenda for Sustainable Development* and the *Sustainable Development Goals* (SDGs).[1] The *2030 Agenda for Sustainable Development* is a plan of action for people, our planet, and prosperity and seeks to strengthen universal peace by supporting collaborative partnerships.[2] There are 17 *Sustainable Development Goals* and they build on the *Millennium Development Goals* (United Nations, 2015). The SDGs build on decades of work by the United Nations and emphasise a human rights approach with a particular focus on gender and equity. Education for all is a key priority and the SDG #4 is 'Ensure inclusive and equitable quality education and promote lifelong learning opportunities for all'. This goal focuses on ensuring governments provide equal access to all levels of education including students with disabilities. In addition, this goal supports the provision of inclusive and safe education facilities that are child, disability, and gender sensitive and provide effective learning environments for all students.

Decades of research indicates that inclusive education leads to positive academic and social emotional outcomes for all students, with and without disabilities (Cologon, 2019; Hehir et al., 2016; Ruijs & Peetsma, 2009; Szumski, Smogorzewska, & Karwowski, 2017) and this suggests that governments should be making a clear commitment to inclusion and emphasise the benefits for all children and society at large (UNESCO, 2017). It is expected that as local schools become more inclusive, the need for segregated special schools will diminish.

In an inclusive approach, drawing on the social model of disability (Oliver, 1996), we do not see difference as a problem but value and respect all members (children, teachers, and parents) of the local school community. Teaching and the curriculum is learner-focused with a flexible curriculum and pedagogy to meet students' needs. In an inclusive approach, teachers receive

> *Education leaders need to support staff to develop an understanding of and embrace inclusive education as a transformation of core business rather than an extension of special education.*

support from specialist teachers and allied health professionals to provide successful learning opportunities and outcomes for all children. One of the key challenges in supporting educators to move forward to a more inclusive approach to education is to understand how inclusion is different to special education. Education leaders need to support staff to develop an understanding of and embrace inclusive education as a transformation of core business rather than an extension of special education.

Special education

Special education has historically been dominated by medical and psychological perspectives (Carrington, 2017) and students with disabilities have been viewed as having a problem or having something 'wrong with them that makes it difficult to participate in the normal curriculum of schools' (Ainscow, 1991, pp. 1–2). A special education approach is informed by beliefs that highlight the problem (the disability) as a deficiency in the person and requires 'treatment'. 'The assumption that children and young people who experience disability may be better placed in a "special" education setting and the acceptance of the parallel systems of segregated "special" and "mainstream" education' is an example of how unquestioned ableist beliefs 'subconsciously guide our thoughts, actions and social systems, with considerable implications for the legislation, policy and practice that is consequently accepted' (Cologon, 2019, p. 20). These views and assumptions perpetuate categorisation and separation and result in low expectations due to a focus on deficit within an individual rather than disabling culture and practices in our education systems.

The underlying paradigm and understanding of disability commonly called the 'medical model' has informed the practice associated with special education for years and informs deep beliefs about how difference is viewed in schools.

> *With the emphasis now on moving forward to an inclusive approach, educators need a positive attitude and inclusive values to support school practice.*

The focus is on deficit and how students are seen to be outside the norm. A medical model of diagnosis is based on assessments of individual defects that can be remediated through treatments and interventions that are part of individual education programs. Special placement in segregated settings for children with disabilities has resulted in a marginalised population that has been institutionalised, undereducated, socially rejected, and excluded from society (Biklen, 1988). These types of outcomes are not the result of the disability but are the result of the social, economic, and political actions such as special education. It is clear that the model of special education has a historical basis informed by the beliefs and assumptions of the medical-based paradigm. The beliefs and assumptions may be submerged in the routine of work and thoughts (Carrington, 1999). With the emphasis now on moving forward to an inclusive approach, educators need a positive attitude and inclusive values to support school practice.

Values that support inclusive education

A focus on inclusion in education is based on a commitment to key values such as equity, justice, moral and ethical integrity, an appreciation of diversity, and the importance of contributing to and benefiting from a deeper understanding of other cultures. An inclusive approach to education also assumes that school community members are questioning the status quo and asking how the school can be more inclusive to all (Robinson & Carrington, 2002). Values can be described as fundamental guides that give a sense of direction and underpin actions towards others (Booth, 2011). When seeking to develop an inclusive environment in education, it is important that teachers are clear about the relationship between values and actions, that they make inclusive values explicit, and design educational activities that uphold values of inclusion (Carrington et al., 2012). In doing so, inclusion becomes a philosophy and a way of life that is based on respect for all. However, transitioning to a more inclusive approach to practice will also require changes to school systems and pedagogical approaches, and these will now be discussed.

Moving forward to an inclusive approach

Inclusive education was initially seen as an innovation within special education (Lipsky & Gartner, 1996). However, it is now understood that the development of inclusive schools is much broader than that and requires significant school and system reform drawing on a social-cultural perspective and a social model of disability (Oliver, 1996). Disability can be viewed as just one form of socially constructed difference and different societies react to many kinds of difference. It is the cultural and social constructions of difference and school success and failure that are represented in beliefs, attitudes, and values and shape how teachers and educators interact with students (Carrington, 1999). Diversity in our society is normal and our international and national legal obligations suggest that teachers have a responsibility to teach all of the students in their local community. Inclusion, however, is about much more than what happens in a classroom. It is about respectful and collaborative relationships with parents, students, and the broader school community. As education systems respond to the international and national imperatives and legislation, there is an expectation that segregated and special schools should be diminished over time. There is clear evidence that students who have a disability and who are educated in mainstream settings with non-disabled peers demonstrate better academic and vocational outcomes when compared to students educated in segregated special settings (Cologon, 2019; Hehir et al., 2016). Furthermore, research indicates that supporting the professional growth of educators to enable inclusive education will also support personal satisfaction (Finke, McNaughton, & Drager, 2009) and more confident teachers (Cologon, 2012; Hehir et al., 2016).

Developing an inclusive curriculum that will be accessible for all learners, including students on the autism spectrum, is a focus of an inclusive approach to education. This requires teachers and specialists to work together to implement a flexible curriculum and pedagogy to meet students' needs. Teachers who rely on a rigid approach to the curriculum and assessment will find it difficult to include all students in their classrooms. Cologon (2019) highlights the need to be aware of 'micro-exclusion', 'where a student is present within a "mainstream" setting, but is separated from the group and the curriculum, often through the provision of "inclusion support" that (usually intentionally) isolates the student educationally, socially and even physically' (p. 27). Moving towards inclusion will also require educators to address exclusion wherever it occurs in policy and practice (Booth, 1996).

Evidence-based policy and practice

The last two decades have been 'characterized by the rise of evidence-based policy and practice agendas' (Cooper, Levin, & Campbell, 2009, p. 159) in education. Evidence-based, evidence-informed, or research-informed practices are all phrases commonly used to describe the important focus education now has on knowledge translation or knowledge mobilisation of research outcomes (Cooper et al., 2009; Cordingley, 2004). In the shift from a special education to an inclusive education approach, it is important that there is the development of a strong evidence base and knowledge mobilisation of this evidence in order for educators to be able to successfully support all learners, including those on the autism spectrum, within inclusive contexts. Research around meeting the needs of this particular group of learners in inclusive settings will now be presented.

Inclusive education for students on the autism spectrum

In a special education model, a disability such as autism is commonly viewed through the lens of the medical model with 'treatment' about repair, cure, and correction rather than the focus on support and respect for difference which is seen in inclusive education. Drawing on the social model of disability, inclusive education values and respects difference in all members (children, teachers, and parents) of the local school community. To support the shift to more inclusive ways of working, there is a need therefore for a 'sharpened focus on the question of how to translate what we know about the key elements of inclusive and differentiated practice into reality in classrooms' (Foreman, 2015, p. 31). For students on the autism spectrum, there continues to be a wide gap between research-based findings and school-based interventions (Barry, Holloway, & McMahon, 2020; Brock, Dynia, Dueker, & Barczak, 2020; Guldberg, 2017; Kasari & Smith, 2013). It is therefore essential if we are to promote inclusive outcomes for this group of learners that we successfully mobilise research knowledge into successful and sustainable inclusive practices.

> … knowledge mobilisation of research on inclusion is critical in helping translate appropriate practices into action in inclusive classrooms.

In order to effectively 'facilitate the implementation of inclusive education' (Foreman, 2015, p. 28), knowledge mobilisation of research on inclusion is critical in helping translate appropriate practices into action in inclusive classrooms. According to Cooper et al. (2009), 'Using research evidence should lead to more informed policy, higher-quality decisions, more effective practices, and, in turn, improved outcomes' (p. 160). As a result, there have been growing efforts globally to promote knowledge translation with the formation of the Cooperative Research Centre for Living with Autism (Autism CRC) as just one recent example. Established in 2013, Autism CRC is the world's first national, cooperative research effort focused on autism (Autism CRC, 2020), providing the national capacity to develop and deliver evidence-based outcomes through unique collaborations with the autism community, research organisations, industry, and government (Autism CRC, 2020).

One foundational study within the School Years Program of Autism CRC has been the *Australian Autism Educational Needs Analysis: What are the Needs of Schools, Parents and Students on the Autism Spectrum?* (ASD–ENA; Saggers et al., 2018). This research investigated the needs of school personnel, parents, and students on the spectrum in relation to supporting learning outcomes for students on the spectrum. The purpose of the research was to identify and evaluate on a collective nationwide scale multiple stakeholders' views. The aim being to better inform research in the field and mobilise research knowledge to educational practice that supports learners on the spectrum in educational settings. To support this knowledge mobilisation, the research can help identify and develop:

- A comprehensive profile of the educational support needs of students on the spectrum.
- The needs of educators, professionals, and parents to effectively manage and support students on the spectrum.
- Strategies and models of service delivery required to support students on the spectrum.

These results can also be used to inform professional development and learning for a range of stakeholders that will also support their ability to translate research knowledge by identifying:

- The professional learning needs of different stakeholder groups.
- The most suitable mode of delivery of professional development.
- Barriers to professional learning.

The needs analysis research has offered some useful insights on how to best support students on the spectrum in their learning in relation to academics and learning, behaviour support, sensory, communication, transition needs, promoting school connectedness, supporting student wellbeing, and using technology to support learning.

As part of the needs analysis, educators were asked to rate on a 1–5 Likert scale (1 being strongly disagree, 3 being neither agree nor disagree, and 5 being strongly agree) their confidence in supporting the needs of learners on the autism spectrum. Generally, most educators reported feeling confident to support and teach learners on the spectrum. However, they only marginally agreed in feeling confident in their ability to find, evaluate, and apply these evidence-based practices to meet the needs, support, and teach students on the spectrum. With inclusive education being a global priority, these results highlight the importance of designing, implementing, and translating research that can support teachers to feel confident to mobilise research-informed outcomes into inclusive practice. The needs analysis was a foundational piece of research that has been used to inform the development of a whole body of research in the school years for students on the autism spectrum, educational communities, and families.

These findings have promoted the importance of inclusive practices that support the unique and heterogeneous needs of students on the autism spectrum and promote their social emotional learning and wellbeing, school connectedness, and sense of belonging. In addition, implementing a positive approach to behaviour support and programming that takes into consideration student preferences for learning, as a well as access to a multidisciplinary team, are essential to help mobilise research knowledge into inclusive practice.

The results of this national research also highlight the importance of being able to provide a 'contextual fit' for research outcomes to ensure knowledge can be translated to respond to the needs of the context as well as the individuals in that context. Often considered only related to geographical location, context is so much more and relates to a wider range of elements in the school environment, including:

- Teachers' beliefs and values.
- The teacher's personality and preferred teaching style.
- The relationships that exist and the nature of these relationships.
- The cultural aspects of the environment related to the individual, class, and school environment.
- Peer dynamics.
- The nature of the school and class community.
- The skills, expertise, and experience of the staff.
- The collaborative partnerships that exist.

Effective research considers the 'contextual fit' to ensure outcomes are 'contextually responsive' and allows uptake and mobilisation of knowledge to be as effective as possible (Saggers, Tones, Dunne, & Aberdein, 2019).

It is important to consider strategies for the implementation of these inclusive approaches into the school environment, and this will now be discussed.

Implementing inclusive approaches to practice

It is acknowledged that schools and teachers can often feel challenged to effectively implement an inclusive approach in their context that meets the diverse needs of students on the autism spectrum, especially when social communication issues and repetitive behaviours are present (Denning & Moody, 2013; Roberts & Simpson, 2016). Students may also have heightened stress and anxiety and have different responses to a range of sensory experiences that impact on their success in inclusive education programs (Ashburner, Ziviani, & Rodger, 2008; Hart Barnett & O'Shaughnessy, 2015). If educators are inflexible in their approach to the curriculum and use traditional teaching methods, they may struggle to meet the learning needs of students with disabilities such as autism. If inclusive approaches are to be implemented, it is important for educators to be supported to translate and mobilise research outcomes to practice and have access to specialist knowledge and multidisciplinary collaborations to do this (Saggers et al., 2018).

Partnerships to support all learners in an inclusive environment

Inclusive education has been established as a human right for all school students. We are aware that education can change society (Apple, 2013) and that individuals' participation in inclusive education can have a transformative effect (Carrington, Tangen, & Beutel, 2019). This involves supporting the development and action of inclusive values, policies, and practices in schools. Leaders at all levels within education systems will need to work together to build consensus and commitment to putting inclusive education into practice. It will be helpful if educators and parents can be involved in community meetings that consider issues of equity and inclusion. Some suggestions could include developing a shared understanding of:

- The rationale and purpose of the changes required to move towards a more inclusive approach.
- The value and evidence to support the proposed changes.
- Considerations of the impact of the proposed changes and the implications for educators, parents, and students.
- The importance of communication and action planning to support the various stakeholders.
- The identification of champions to support and drive the change required in the community. (UNESCO, 2017, p. 20)

The research-informed practices in this book highlight the importance of building relationships and working in partnership with students, parents, and educators in schools to support more inclusive practices. The practices also highlight our understanding that inclusive education informs whole-of-life outcomes not only for students on the autism spectrum and their families but also for their peers. Understanding inclusive education and implementing inclusion in practice is the beginning of an ongoing process that is 'one aspect of broader inclusion in society' (Cologon, 2019, p. 2). Inclusive education is the 'beginning not the end point' of the processes of inclusion in society and through whole of life (Cologon, 2019, p. 22). If learners are included without an educational setting developing an understanding of what inclusion is or how it looks in practice or how to transform inclusive values and knowledge into practice, transformative inclusive practices will not occur (Cologon, 2019). It is not just about presence within an educational setting that is inclusion but rather being a valued member of that setting who feels a sense of belonging within it (Cologon, 2019). It is also about implementing contextually fit practices that add value for the student, educators, and families. An inclusive approach values and respects the voice of young people on the spectrum and their families and supports school–family partnerships. It is the families and students who know their needs best. Collaborative partnerships in inclusive settings ensure that:

- Everybody's voice in the partnership is important.
- The 'collective' voice of everyone in the partnership maximises success in inclusive settings.
- The 'best fit' for learning and support is achieved for the learner and contextualised to fit the learning environment.
- Everyone's needs are listened to and met.
- Working partnerships and positive relationships are established that make everyone feel a sense of belonging.
- The 4 Cs are supported – Connections, Communication, Collaboration, Cooperation.

The foundational piece of education research – the ASD–ENA (Saggers et al., 2018) conducted by the Autism CRC – highlighted from the stakeholders' perspective (including educators, specialists, parents, and students) that essential elements of inclusive practice were supporting school connections, establishing positive relationships, and working in partnerships with families, specialist support staff, and students (Saggers et al., 2018). All stakeholders involved in the research identified building rapport, positive and respectful relationships, and open communication as essential elements if effective learning outcomes for this group of students were to occur (Saggers et al., 2018).

The vision for the Autism CRC School Years Program was to have research teams working in real schools/classrooms with school leaders, teachers, specialists, parents, and students to work out together how to teach and support students on the autistic spectrum at school. Our multidisciplinary research teams worked on more than 25 research and development projects with school communities in Queensland, New South Wales, Victoria, Tasmania, and Western Australia in over 300 schools. The outcomes and outputs of the research are shared through an online platform called *inclusionED*.[3] This platform supports a community of practice that enables learning and social sharing about the experience of implementing teaching practices to support diverse learners including students on the autism spectrum. Autism CRC's inclusive approach to working with education partners ensured that *inclusionED*'s teaching practices and site concepts were co-designed with diverse stakeholders including teachers, researchers, inclusive education specialists, principals, policymakers, and students on the autism spectrum. Our aim was to translate research into research-informed, practical teaching strategies and programs.

FIGURE 1.1 *inclusionED* logo.
Source: www.inclusioned.edu.au.

Collaborative partnerships to support knowledge translation

An inclusive approach to education relies on the knowledge and skills of educators who have worked with students with disabilities. The staff in special schools and special classes have an important role to play in sharing their knowledge and experience. Ainscow (2007) suggests that there is a need to encourage cooperation between special and mainstream inclusive schools. In an inclusive approach, teachers receive support from specialist teachers and allied health professionals to provide successful learning opportunities and outcomes for all children (Saggers et al., 2018). A key finding of the ASD–ENA (Saggers et al., 2018) reinforced that for inclusion to be successful it was important for educators to have access to specialist support staff to help develop a comprehensive, strengths-based multidisciplinary approach to support. This multidisciplinary wrap-around approach would include both allied health and specialised education staff. Access to specialist staff and multidisciplinary support has also been recognised as an important characteristic of effective schools, informing not only a whole-school approach but also more individualised supports if needed. Educators identified a lack of access to this type of support as a key challenge to implementing inclusive practices for this group of students.

> *An inclusive approach to education relies on the knowledge and skills of educators who have worked with students with disabilities.*

Teachers face challenges in effectively including students on the spectrum in classes often due to lack of training and resources, and lack of knowledge and understanding of autism (Lindsay, Proulx, Scott, & Thomson, 2014). The ASD–ENA (Saggers et al., 2018) was one of the first research projects invested in by Autism CRC and has helped at a national level to identify a range of different stakeholders' views regarding:

- The educational needs of students on the spectrum.
- The needs of educators, school communities, and education systems in order to support these students' needs.

Conclusion and practitioner reflection

We often think of educators as the carpenters of the education world, armed with the important task of translating the plans of multiple architects and engineers (in this case, researchers and multiple research outcomes) into actionable, workable, and sustainable practices that successfully address the diverse learning needs of the learners in their care. It is important that we support educators in their pivotal and important role of knowledge mobilisation by conducting research that is informed by and responsive to the autism community's needs and the different stakeholders within that community, and ensuring results are translated into user-friendly and digestible ways that are relevant to education contexts and needs. The ASD-ENA (Saggers et al., 2018) identified the need for evidence-based resources and upskilling for educators to provide more inclusive environments for students with diverse learning needs, including those on the spectrum and Autism CRC School Years Program has delivered *inclusionED* to address that need.

The current chapter has focused on developing the reader's deeper understanding of the difference between special education and inclusive education and presented important points drawn from research to support education systems and schools to move to develop a more inclusive culture, policy, and practices. Jordan (2008, p. 13) reminds us that teachers must know

> about the diversity that exists in humankind in the way we learn and understand the world. If educators teach in a way that attains diversity … then more children with different minds will be able to manage in mainstream settings, without needing to have special (and certainly not segregated) support.

Notes

1 https://sustainabledevelopment.un.org/post2015/transformingourworld
2 https://sdgs.un.org/
3 www.inclusioned.edu.au

References

Ainscow, M. (1991). *Effective schools for all*. London: Fulton.

Ainscow, M. (2007). Towards a more inclusive education system: Where next for special schools? In R. Cigman (Ed.), *Included or excluded? The challenge of the mainstream for some SEN children* (pp. 128–139). London: Routledge.

Apple, M. (2013). *Can education change society?* New York, NY: Routledge.

Ashburner, J., Ziviani, J., & Rodger, S. (2008). Sensory processing and classroom emotional, behavioral and educational outcomes in children with autism spectrum disorder. *The American Journal of Occupational Therapy*, 62, 564–573.

Autism CRC. (2020). *Cooperative Research Centre for Living with Autism (Autism CRC): About us*. Retrieved from https://www.autismcrc.com.au/about-us.

Barry, L., Holloway, J., & McMahon, J. (2020). A scoping review of the barriers and facilitators to the implementation of interventions in autism education. *Research in Autism Spectrum Disorders*, 78. doi:10.1016/j.rasd.2020.101617.

Biklen, D. (1988). The myth of clinical judgement. *Journal of Social Issues*, 44, 127–140.

Booth, T. (1996). Stories of exclusion: Natural and unnatural selection. In E. Blyth & J. Milner (Eds.), *Exclusion from school: Interprofessional issues for policy and practice* (pp. 21–36). London: Routledge.

Booth, T. (2011). Curricula from the common school: What shall we tell our children? *Forum*, 53(1), 31–48. doi:10.2304/forum.2011.53.1.31.

Brock, M., Dynia, J., Dueker, S., & Barczak, M. (2020). Teacher-reported priorities and practices for students with autism: Characterizing the research-to-practice gap. *Focus on Autism and Other Developmental Disabilities*, 35(2), 67–78. doi:10.1177/1088357619881217.

Carrington, S. (1999). Inclusion needs a different school culture. *International Journal of Inclusive Education*, 3(3), 257–268.

Carrington, S. (2017). Inclusive education: Two steps forward and one step back. In V. Plows & B. Whitburn (Eds.), *Inclusive education: Making sense of everyday practice* (pp. 233–248). Rotterdam: Sense Publishers.

Carrington, S., MacArthur, J., Kearney, A., Kimber, M., Mercer, L., Morton, M., & Rutherford, G. (2012). Towards an inclusive education for all. In S. Carrington & J. MacArthur (Eds.), *Teaching in inclusive school communities* (pp. 3–38). Brisbane, Australia: John Wiley & Sons.

Carrington, S., Tangen, D., & Beutel, D. (2019). Inclusive education in the Asia Indo-Pacific region. *International Journal of Inclusive Education*, 23(1), 1–6. doi:10.1080/13603116.2018.1514727.

Cologon, K. (2012). Confidence in their own ability: Postgraduate early childhood students examining their attitudes towards inclusive education. *International Journal of Inclusive Education*, 16(11), 1155–1173. doi:10.1080/13603116.2010.548106.

Cologon, K. (2019). *Towards inclusive education: A necessary process of transformation*. Melbourne: Children and Young People with Disability Australia.

Cooper, A., Levin, B., & Campbell, C. (2009). The growing (but still limited) importance of evidence in education policy and practice. *Journal of Educational Change*, 10(2–3), 159–171. doi:10.1007/s10833-009-9107-0.

Cordingley, P. (2004). Teachers using evidence: Using what we know about teaching and learning to reconceptualize evidence-based practice. In G. Thomas & R. Pring (Eds.), *Evidence-based practice in education* (pp. 77–87). Maidenhead: McGraw-Hill Education.

Denning, C. B., & Moody, A. K. (2013). Supporting students with autism spectrum disorders in inclusive settings: Rethinking instruction and design. *Electronic Journal for Inclusive Education*, 3(1). Retrieved from https://corescholar.libraries.wright.edu/ejie/vol3/iss1/6/.

Finke, E. H., McNaughton, D. B., & Drager, K. D. R. (2009). All children can and should have the opportunity to learn: General education teachers' perspectives on including children with autism spectrum disorder who require AAC. *Augmentative and Alternative Communication*, 25(2), 110–122. doi:10.1080/07434610902886206.

Foreman, P. (2015). *Social justice principles, the law, and research, as bases for inclusion: An update*. Melbourne, Australia: Department of Education & Training. Retrieved from https://www.education.vic.gov.au/Documents/about/department/psdlitreview_Socialjusticeprinciples_thelaw_and_research.pdf.

Guldberg, K. (2017). Evidence-based practice in autism educational research: Can we bridge the research and practice gap? *Oxford Review of Education*, 43(2), 149–161. doi:10.1080/03054985.2016.1248818.

Hart Barnett, J. E., & O'Shaughnessy, K. (2015). Enhancing collaboration between occupational therapists and early childhood educators working with children on the autism spectrum. *Early Childhood Education Journal*, 43, 467–472. doi:10.1007/s10643-015-0689-2.

Hehir, T., Grindal, T., Freeman, B., Lamoreau, R., Borquaye, Y., & Burke, S. (2016). *A summary of the evidence on inclusive education*. São Paulo: Alana Institute.

Jordan, R. (2008). Autistic spectrum disorders: A challenge and a model for inclusion in education. *British Journal of Special Education*, 35(1), 11–15.

Kasari, C., & Smith, T. (2013). Interventions in schools for children with autism spectrum disorder: Methods and recommendations. *Autism*, 17(3), 254–267.

Lindsay, S., Proulx, M., Scott, H., & Thomson, N. (2014). Exploring teachers' strategies for including children with autism spectrum disorder in mainstream classrooms. *International Journal of Inclusive Education*, 18(2), 101–122. doi:10.1080/13603116.2012.758320.

Lipsky, D. K., & Gartner, A. (1996). Inclusive education and school restructuring. In W. Stainback & S. Stainback (Eds.), *Controversial issues confronting special education* (2nd ed.) (pp. 3–15). Boston, MA: Allyn & Bacon.

Oliver, M. (1996). *Understanding disability: From theory to practice*. Basingstoke: Macmillan.

Roberts, J., & Simpson, K. (2016). A review of research into stakeholder perspectives on inclusion of students with autism in mainstream schools. *International Journal of Inclusive Education*, 20(10), 1084–1096. doi:10.1080/13603116.2016.1145267.

Robinson, R., & Carrington, S. (2002). Professional development for inclusive schooling. *International Journal of Educational Management*, 16(5), 239–247.

Ruijs, N., & Peetsma, T. T. D. (2009). Effects of inclusion on students with and without special educational needs reviewed. *Educational Research Review*, 4(2), 67–79.

Saggers, B., Klug, D., Harper-Hill, K., Ashburner, J., Costley, D., Clark, T., … Carrington, S. (2018). *Australian autism educational needs analysis: What are the needs of schools, parents and students on the autism spectrum?* Brisbane: Cooperative Research Centre for Living with Autism (Autism CRC).

Saggers, B., Tones, M., Dunne, J., & Aberdein, R. (2019). Tele-classroom consultation: Promoting an inclusive approach to supporting the needs of educators, families and early years learners on the autism spectrum in rural and remote areas in contextually responsive ways. *International Journal of Inclusive Education*. doi:10.1080/13603116.2019.1609103.

Szumski, G., Smogorzewska, J., & Karwowski, M. (2017). Academic achievement of students without special educational needs in inclusive classrooms: A meta-analysis. *Educational Research Review*, 21, 33–54. doi:10.1016/j.edurev.2017.02.004.

UNESCO. (2017). *A guide for ensuring inclusion and equity in education*. Paris: United Nations Educational, Scientific and Cultural Organization.

United Nations. (2006). *Convention on the rights of persons with disabilities*. New York, NY: United Nations.

United Nations. (2015). *The millennium development goals report*. New York, NY: United Nations.

United Nations. (2016). *Convention on the rights of persons with disabilities: General comment no. 4. Article 24: Right to inclusive education*. Geneva: United Nations.

PART 2

Inclusion and school connectedness

A whole-school approach

Threads of the Whole (by Kai Brelsford)

'Interpreting the theme of Autistic Strengths through a personal context, the work draws on ten individual qualities of creativity, courage, logic, determination, problem solving, curiosity, patience, hope, perspective and compassion as "threads of self". Ten patterns emerge that (like the delicate layers of wool and silk worked by hand to create a strong yet soft felt fabric or the wool yarn, hand spun and dyed by the artist that loops back on itself to bind fibres in a beautiful and useful cord) connect, combine and stitch together personal qualities derived from past and present experiences that help to form the artist, the strengths he draws on to live and also touches on the wider context of each individual within a community being a necessary part of the strength of the whole.'

2

SCHOOL CONNECTEDNESS TO SUPPORT STUDENT MENTAL HEALTH AND WELLBEING

Ian Shochet, Astrid Wurfl, Jayne Orr, Rachel Kelly, Beth Saggers and Suzanne Carrington

Early adolescence is a time of increased risk for mental health concerns such as depression to develop. This chapter presents the concept of school connectedness and a sense of belonging and discusses research that highlights the importance of school connectedness as an important protective factor for adolescent mental health and wellbeing. The chapter also highlights that young adolescents on the autism spectrum tend to experience developmental challenges associated with the transition to adolescence as more challenging than their peers, and the characteristics of autism (including difficulties with social skills, communication, emotion regulation, optimism, self-esteem, and transitions) can diminish their sense of school connectedness. The chapter reports on research and practices that promote schools as well-positioned for implementing a widespread approach to promoting school connectedness as an integral part of the curriculum. This approach has the potential to positively influence the academic, social emotional, and behavioural development of all students including young adolescents on the spectrum.

The transition to adolescence leads to several changes in the way adolescents relate to the world. Extra-familial relationships become more important, development of self-identity impacts on self-esteem, and there is an increased risk of mental health problems including depression and anxiety (Chiang & Gau, 2016; Claes, Luyckx, & Bijttebier, 2014; Farrell & Barrett, 2007; Lawrence et al., 2015; Mayes, Calhoun, Murray, & Zahid, 2011). Young adolescents on the autism spectrum tend to experience the developmental challenges associated with the transition to adolescence as more challenging than do their peers (Downs & Smith, 2004; Humphrey & Symes, 2010; White & Roberson-Nay, 2009). School connectedness, or the degree to which students feel valued and included in their school community (Ciani, Middleton, Summers, & Sheldon, 2010; Osterman, 2000), is a significant predictor of future mental health (Shochet, Dadds, Ham, & Montague, 2006) and as such provides an opportunity for schools to have an important role in the mental health and wellbeing of their students.

Increased risk for depression in adolescence

The development of several mental disorders, including depression and anxiety, peaks during adolescence (Kessler et al., 2005). A lifetime prevalence study examining the age of onset for mental health disorders among a cohort of 9,282 American participants identified that half of those who later developed a mental health disorder had started experiencing symptoms by the age of 14 (Kessler et al., 2005). One report on prevalence rates of depression among Australian children and adolescents showed an increase from 1.1% in children aged 4–11 years old to 5% in adolescents aged 12–17 years old (Lawrence et al., 2015). While incidence rates for depression among all young people increase during adolescence, rates of depression among those on the spectrum are often reported as being four times higher than that seen among the rest of the population (Hudson, Hall, & Harkness, 2019; Pezzimenti, Han, Vasa, & Gotham, 2019; Smith & White, 2020). A large percentage of adolescents on the autism spectrum are often diagnosed with a mental health disorder such as depression and anxiety. For example, DeFilippis (2018) reported that approximately 70% of adolescents on the spectrum aged 10–14 years had one mental health disorder and 41% had two or more mental health disorders. At age 13, boys on the spectrum report higher rates of depression than girls on the spectrum of the same age; however, rates of depressive symptoms among young girls on the spectrum significantly increase with age until there is no longer a gender difference among adults on the spectrum (Gotham, Brunwasser, & Lord, 2015; Hudson et al., 2019). A study exploring what depressive symptoms looked like in adolescent males on the spectrum found the profile was characterised by anhedonia (a loss of interest or pleasure), low mood, and suicidal ideation (Bitsika & Sharpley, 2015). Further depressive symptoms that are commonly expressed by those on the spectrum include increased irritability, changes in engagement with their specific interests, exacerbation of repetitive behaviours, and an increase in aggressive behaviour towards themselves and others (Pezzimenti et al., 2019).

> While incidence rates for depression among all young people increase during adolescence, rates of depression among those on the spectrum are often reported as being four times higher than that seen among the rest of the population

Additional risks to mental health for adolescents on the spectrum

Several psychological and social factors are associated with mental health during the transition to adolescence. However, children on the spectrum typically experience additional challenges with social skills, communication, and emotion regulation that can further impact on their transition to adolescence (Sciutto, Richwine, Mentrikoski, & Niedzwiecki, 2012; White & Roberson-Nay, 2009). During this developmental stage, relationships outside the direct family become increasingly important for all young adolescents. For adolescents on the spectrum, difficulties with communication skills and emotion regulation may make the formation and maintenance of peer relationships more challenging. Research by Picci and Scherf (2015) suggests that the increased social pressures experienced during adolescence place additional demands on the social and coping skills of adolescents on the spectrum, which reduces their motivation to build relationships with peers and perpetuates difficulties with maintaining relationships. Developing trusting peer relationships can help to reduce the likelihood of experiencing depression (Bosacki, Dane, Marini, & YLC-CURA, 2007); however, adolescents on the spectrum tend to spend less time with peers and report a greater sense of loneliness than do their peers who are not on the spectrum (Locke, Ishijima, Kasari, & London, 2010). Difficulties with communication and emotion regulation may result in greater peer rejection for adolescents on the spectrum, who are significantly more likely to experience bullying at school, placing them at further risk of developing depression (Foulkes & Blakemore, 2018; Humphrey & Symes, 2010; Sterzing, Shattuck, Narendorf, Wagner, & Cooper, 2012). This in turn reduces their opportunities to develop and practise social and communication skills, maintaining a cycle of isolation (Bauminger, Shulman, & Agam, 2003; White & Roberson-Nay, 2009).

Experiencing depression during adolescence can impact negatively on the social wellbeing of adolescents on the spectrum, reducing the number and quality of relationships with family and friends; increasing social withdrawal or antisocial behaviour; reducing coping skills and self-care; and increasing the risk of self-harm or suicidal ideation (Ghaziuddin, Ghaziuddin, & Greden, 2002; Matson & Nebel-Schwalm, 2007; Stewart, Barnard, Pearson, Hasan, & O'Brien, 2006; White & Roberson-Nay, 2009). Importantly, social support is vital for increasing adolescents' resilience to recurrent and future mental health problems (Rao, Hammen, & Poland, 2010) but difficulties with social and communication skills that adolescents on the spectrum experience, combined with social withdrawal that commonly accompanies lowered mood, intensify the negative impact on their social wellbeing.

In addition to having to develop and navigate complex peer relationships, adolescents also start the process of identity formation (Claes et al., 2014). Social comparisons with peers increase during the transition to high school, with adolescents being particularly sensitive to reductions in their academic success, which in turn impacts how they understand and find value in themselves (Wolff, Wigfield, Möller, Dicke, & Eccles, 2019). The process of identity formation poses another challenge for adolescents on the spectrum, who typically report a lower sense of confidence and feel less capable of rising to new challenges than their peers who are not on the spectrum (Huang et al., 2017). However, research has shown that inclusive settings provide a place for adolescents on the spectrum to recognise themselves as valued members of groups, helping them to incorporate their personality, strengths, and characteristics associated with autism into a positive self-identity (Bottema-Beutel & Smith, 2013) and acknowledge and support the heterogeneity of autistic expression.

> *… inclusive settings provide a place for adolescents on the spectrum to recognise themselves as valued members of groups, helping them to incorporate their personality, strengths, and characteristics associated with autism into a positive self-identity*

Research has shown adolescents who have a higher self-esteem and stronger relationships with schoolmates adjust better with the transition to high school than adolescents with a lower self-esteem and who are isolated (Lim & Lee, 2007; Wigfield, Eccles, Mac Iver, Reuman, & Midgley, 1991). As explored previously, adolescents on the spectrum are at a greater risk of being isolated and developing low self-esteem. Furthermore, the move to secondary school introduces a number of practical changes, including larger schools, multiple classes with multiple teachers, and increased pressure to perform well academically (Benner, 2011). As adolescents on the spectrum may struggle with adapting to these changes to routine, they may require more time and support when adapting to a new high school environment (Huang et al., 2017).

In summary, there are number of psychosocial risk factors for adolescents on the spectrum that are associated with an increase in mental illness. This increased rate of mental illness among adolescents on the spectrum has severe implications for their future development and life prospects. Thus, it is vital to identify and harness protective factors that promote their capacity for resilience, their mental health, and overall wellbeing.

The importance of school connectedness for resilience and mental health

As adolescence is an at-risk time for the development of depression, and adolescents on the spectrum experience depression more frequently and more severely than those not on the spectrum (Bitsika & Sharpley, 2015; Mojtabai, Olfson, & Han, 2016), the prevention and early intervention of mental disorders among this population is an important priority. A wealth of literature has found school connectedness to be an important predictor of current and future mental health, which is being positively associated with resilience and wellbeing, and negatively associated with symptoms of mental illness (Allen, Kern, Vella-Brodrick, Hattie, & Waters, 2018; Arango et al., 2019; Joyce & Early, 2014; Lester, Waters, & Cross, 2013; Oldfield, Stevenson, Ortiz, & Haley, 2018; Parr, Shochet, Cockshaw, & Kelly, 2020; Shochet et al., 2006; Shochet & Smith, 2014; Shochet, Smith, Furlong, & Homel, 2011). Concepts such as school belonging and school connectedness are often used interchangeably but herein refer to the degree to which a student feels accepted, valued, and included in their school environment (Allen et al., 2018; García-Moya, Bunn, Jiménez-Iglesias, Paniagua, & Brooks, 2018; Goodenow, 1993). School connectedness is associated with a range of positive outcomes during adolescence, including academic achievement, a successful transition to high school, prosocial behaviours, and positive mental health (Mahmud, 2019; Slaten, Ferguson, Allen, Brodrick, & Waters, 2016). As school connectedness is one of the strongest predictors of adolescent mental health and wellbeing, a number of school-based prevention and intervention programs have been developed to promote school connectedness (for review, see Chapman, Buckley, Sheehan, & Shochet, 2013).

Students spend approximately 1,100 hours in school every year (Victoria State Government Department of Education and Training, 2019). As such, schools are well-positioned to implement a whole-school approach to promoting school connectedness as an integral part of the curriculum.

> *… schools are well-positioned to implement a whole-school approach to promoting school connectedness as an integral part of the curriculum.*

Curriculum- and school-based preventative intervention programs are valued for their affordability, accessibility, and sustainability, with research establishing school-based interventions as the gold standard intervention for student mental health outcomes (Corrieri et al., 2014). Having an increased sense of belonging is associated with positive schooling experiences and academic success among students on the spectrum (Osborne & Reed, 2011; Sciutto et al., 2012). The Queensland *State Schools Improvement Strategy 2020–2024* outlines the ongoing expectation for schools to promote the academic success and overall wellbeing for all students through inclusive education (Queensland Government Department of Education, 2020). As such, programs promoting school connectedness provide schools with an opportunity to address the academic, social, and emotional needs of adolescents on the spectrum.

Parents and families also play a vital role in promoting the mental health and wellbeing of their children and in promoting the sense of school connectedness. School-Based Family Counselling (SBFC) is a strengths-based, systems-focused approach that integrates school counselling and family engagement to support the child's success at school. It is recognised that families and parents play an important role in this regard (Gerrard, 2008). Parental involvement in schools more broadly influences their child's global sense of self-worth and their academic success (Kaplan Toren, 2013). Parental attachment has consistently been shown to correlate positively with students' sense of school connectedness (Oldfield, Humphrey, &

> *… programs promoting school connectedness provide schools with an opportunity to address the academic, social, and emotional needs of adolescents on the spectrum.*

Hebron, 2016; Shochet, Homel, Cockshaw, & Montgomery, 2008). As such, it is essential to consider the influence of parents and families on interventions promoting school connectedness.

Finally, it is important to recognise that there are intrapersonal components unique to the adolescent that impact on their sense of school connectedness and their mental health. For example, affect regulation, the ability to identify and adapt a response to emotion-triggering experiences, is significantly associated with school connectedness (Swee, Shochet, Cockshaw, & Hides, 2020). Functional forms of emotion regulation, such as cognitive reappraisal and asking for help, are associated with higher degrees of school connectedness (Swee et al., 2020). On the other hand, dysfunctional forms of emotion regulation are associated with a lower sense of school connectedness (Swee et al., 2020). Similarly, research shows that coping styles used by the individual when managing stressors are associated with a sense of connectedness. Students who use more productive forms of coping such as problem solving, positive appraisal, and emotion control experience a greater sense of connectedness, better emotional wellbeing, and greater academic success (Frydenberg, Care, Freeman, & Chan, 2009; Gustems-Carnicer, Calderón, & Calderón-Garrido, 2019). Hence, a range of intrapersonal, interpersonal, and systemic factors influence a student's sense of school connectedness. In line with Bronfenbrenner's (1979) multi-level ecological model, which conceptualises an individual as being supported and influenced by people and organisations at different proximities, there is evidence to support the development of a multi-level intervention working at the individual, parent, teacher, and whole-school levels to promote school connectedness and the wellbeing of the student.

The Autism CRC School Connectedness Project

After identifying school connectedness as a potential mechanism for promoting resilience and mental health among adolescents on the spectrum, the researchers embarked on the Autism CRC School Connectedness Project. The research we conducted was based on an evidence-based, multi-level School Connectedness Conceptual Model (see Figure 2.1). The model demonstrates that the wellbeing and mental health of adolescents on the spectrum can be improved by intervening across three levels: the individual level with the adolescent on the spectrum, the parent level with parents and caregivers, and the whole-school level with teachers, principals, and the school community.

The Autism CRC School Connectedness project developed and conducted a proof-of-concept study of a strength-focused and evidence-based school connectedness program, the Resourceful Adolescent Program (RAP; Shochet, 2002), that had been adapted for students on the spectrum. Originally developed as a universal program for the prevention of depression, RAP incorporates evidence from interpersonal psychotherapy and cognitive behavioural therapy to promote self-esteem, coping skills, affect regulation, and interpersonal skills (Shochet et al., 2001). RAP has over 20 years of empirical support (Mackay, Shochet, & Orr, 2017; Shochet et al., 2006, 2011, 2019; Shochet & Osgarby, 1999) and has been recognised by the Australian Commonwealth as an evidence-based program for the prevention of depression (Shochet & Hoge, 2009). RAP was developed as a multi-level program and is delivered as three group interventions that includes the: i) Resourceful Adolescent Program for Adolescents (RAP-A); ii) Resourceful Adolescent Program for Parents (RAP-P); and iii) R

esourceful Adolescent Program for Teachers (RAP-T). The RAP-T intervention has also been used in conjunction with the *Index for Inclusion*[1] (Booth & Ainscow, 2002) as part of a

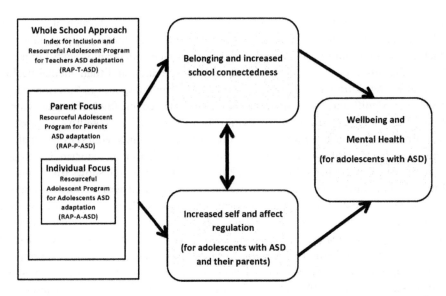

FIGURE 2.1 The conceptual model for promoting mental health and wellbeing among adolescents on the spectrum.
Source: Reprinted by permission from Springer Nature Customer Service Centre GmbH: Springer Nature, *Clinical Child and Family Psychology Review*, The Cooperative Research Centre for Living with Autism (Autism CRC) conceptual model to promote mental health for adolescents with ASD, Shochet et al., © 2016.

whole-school approach implemented to develop a stronger sense of connectedness across school culture, policy, and practice.

The adapted Resourceful Adolescent Program for Adolescents on the Spectrum (RAP-A-ASD; Mackay et al., 2017) had already been developed and piloted as a prevention program aiming to improve resilience and prevent depression among adolescents on the spectrum. The pilot randomised control trial of RAP-A-ASD was delivered one-on-one to adolescents on the spectrum during a 50-minute class within school time over 11 weeks (for details, see Mackay et al., 2017). Results showed promising improvements in coping self-efficacy, self-esteem, and affect regulation; however, no changes were reported by either parents or adolescents on outcomes of depression or mental health. The authors suggested that using a multi-layered intervention that harnesses protective factors at the individual, parent, and whole-school levels may promote more positive mental health among adolescents on the spectrum (Mackay et al., 2017).

The Autism CRC School Connectedness Project adapted the full suite of RAP-A, RAP-P, and RAP-T interventions to meet the needs of early adolescents (aged 11–14 years) on the autism spectrum (for more details, see Mackay et al., 2017). The researchers implemented this multi-level intervention at an individual, parent, and whole-school level in six schools across South-Eastern Queensland to determine the feasibility and impact of the project as a sustainable primary prevention program for adolescents on the spectrum. The study involved 30 adolescents with a diagnosis of autism spectrum disorder, Asperger's disorder, or pervasive developmental disorder not otherwise specified who participated in RAP-A-ASD. Further, 16 teachers and 40 parents or caregivers completed surveys about the adolescents' psychological functioning before, during, and after the RAP-A-ASD program; 31 parents participated in the RAP for Parents of Adolescents on the Spectrum (RAP-P-ASD) workshops; and all teachers, special education teachers, and support staff at participating schools were also invited to attend the two-hour RAP for Teachers of Adolescents on the Spectrum (RAP-T-ASD) workshop. Please see the section on implications for inclusive practice approaches for further details about this program.

The whole-school approach, the RAP-T-ASD, was run concurrently with the *Index for Inclusion*, where the project team and the principal for each participating school created a School Connectedness Committee including other school representatives such as classroom teachers, special education heads, student school captains/vice-captains/leaders, and parents. Together, the committee conceptualised and implemented a project within their school aiming to change school culture and increase school connectedness. This whole-school approach is described in more detail in Chapter 3.

For the young adolescents who participated in RAP-A-ASD, results showed an increase in school connectedness and improved mental wellbeing. Two thirds of participants reported an increase in school connectedness directly after the program, and reliable change calculations on individual scores showed that eight students reported increases that were statistically significant. Of the students with statistically significant increases in school connectedness, half maintained this significant improvement at the 12-month follow-up. Improvements in student-reported measures of anxiety, emotional and behavioural difficulties, sense of school membership, and coping self-efficacy were reported most often. Significant improvements in anxiety, emotional, and behavioural difficulties were stable three months after the RAP-A-ASD program was delivered; however, these high rates of improvement were not maintained by the 12-month follow-up. The improvements from self-report questionnaires were corroborated through qualitative interviews. The following are quotes given by some of the students in the study, reporting how they gained a number of skills for managing school relationships through participating in the RAP-A-ASD program:

- Managing anger or conflict
  [I learned] how to cope with anger and not taking it out on other people
- Problem solving
  [I've learned that] there's more ways to deal with your problems than just one answer …
- Managing stress
  In tests I can think better than I was before … most of the time … my mind just shut down and I couldn't remember simple things … because [of] all the pressure. But now my mind works a little bit and I can remember [because I can calm myself down]
- Social skills
  [The RAP program] has helped me make more friends
- Perspective taking
  It helped me realise … how my parents were seeing things … and other people were seeing things

All of this culminated in the students reporting an increase in self-esteem, greater coping skills, and increased wellbeing:

I've just noticed myself being a bit happier

I was bullied when I was younger and I was put down a little bit by my [younger sibling] … and one of my friends … would metaphorically stab me in the back … but the RAP program helped with boosting self-confidence and identifying what can help … I find laughter and smiling are probably the best things

I [have been] feeling something positive after [completing RAP]

Parents and teachers also observed changes in the students after the RAP-A-ASD program. Parents were more likely than their children to report an immediate improvement in their child's depressive symptoms after the program. On the other hand, teachers were the least likely to report seeing changes in their students. While some student-reported improvements peaked at three months, parent- and teacher-reported improvements were more stable and continued increasing until the final 12-month follow-up.

Parents who participated in RAP-P-ASD reported that feeling isolated and unsupported by existing services motivated their participation and that they valued interacting with other parent participants. The following quotes from parents illustrate how participating in the program helped to develop their sense of connectedness with other parents, improved their relationship with their child, and showed indicators of increasing connectedness they had observed in their child:

- Connectedness with other parents
  - *It allowed us to share experiences that made us feel less isolated*
  - *I wasn't the only parent in that boat … there were other parents [who] had kids in similar situations … so it was connecting … seeing other people are struggling … you never meet those people, never hear about them, so meeting them was great*
  - *I said to [another parent], 'Let's get each other's numbers and try and stay in touch'… we've got something in common … the connectedness and the understanding that comes through shared experience … it might be nice for the kids to meet as well*
- Relationship with their child
  - *It's given us a bit more of a bond … [our relationship] definitely has been improving*
  - *[I've been] picking out the positive things. I think he appreciates that. I'm not always focusing on the negative things*
  - *I think understanding his independence, but also dependence … I hadn't really thought about that too much … kids wanting more independence, but still wanting to be a part of the family*
- Increased connectedness of their child
  - *He's involved with the school musical now as part of the backstage people and he's doing that after school on a Wednesday, and he really, really likes that*
  - *He's spending time on the phone and playing computer games with his friends over the phone*
  - *He's also been developing friendships, which hasn't really happened a great deal in the past*

In addition to the program's impact on their connectedness and that of their child, parents also reported that the program enhanced their wellbeing, parenting efficacy, and increased their ability to parent calmly. For the full analysis of the parent qualitative data and other significant findings, see Shochet et al. (2019).

Schools that implemented the *Index for Inclusion* to improve school connectedness at a whole-school level developed an understanding of school connectedness. Further, they reported an increase in inclusive culture and practice in their schools as a result of the collaboration between school staff and students required for implementation. Results from the whole-school approach are described in more detail in Chapter 3.

The Autism CRC School Connectedness Project provided support for school connectedness acting as a protective factor for the mental health of adolescents on the spectrum. As such, further translational research was conducted to develop a website that would increase the accessibility to resources that promote school connectedness for students on the spectrum across urban, regional, and rural localities. The findings from our implementation of the School Connectedness Program highlighted that parents and schools are desperate for resources to support the mental health of young adolescents on the autism spectrum, and that this is an even greater problem in rural and remote areas. Therefore, with additional funding from the Autism CRC and Positive Partnerships, an Autism Teen Wellbeing website – *Building Connectedness and Wellbeing for Young Adolescents on*

FIGURE 2.2   The Autism Teen Wellbeing website: *Building Connectedness and Wellbeing for Young Adolescents on the Autism Spectrum.*

the Autism Spectrum[2] – was developed. This website was based on the key components of the School Connectedness Program at each level for adolescents, parents, caregivers, teachers, schools, and communities to access resources and strategies to develop school connectedness and build a culture of inclusive education (see Figure 2.1 for a screenshot of the homepage of the website).

As part of the community-based participatory research approach implemented across the whole project (Ahmed & Palermo, 2010), the researchers invited people on the spectrum, parents and caregivers of adolescents on the spectrum, teachers, heads of special education, and school principals to evaluate and provide feedback on the website during its development. Feedback showed that evaluators found that the website provided a range of helpful resources for working with adolescents on the spectrum and addressed a need for additional support for parents and caregivers, teachers and schools, and the wider community regardless of geographical location.

Implications of school connectedness for inclusive practice

An international longitudinal study measuring adolescent wellbeing across 72 countries identified that Australian students have a lower than average sense of school connectedness (Australian Council for Educational Research, 2018). As school connectedness is one of the strongest predictors of current and future mental health and wellbeing (Parr et al., 2020; Shochet et al., 2006), there is a need to engage teachers, principals, and school communities in efforts to promote school connectedness among Australian students. The Autism CRC School Connectedness Project demonstrated that a multi-level resilience building program implemented with students, caregivers, and schools resulted in an improvement in school connectedness and mental health among adolescents on the spectrum.

> *... there is a need to engage teachers, principals, and school communities in efforts to promote school connectedness among Australian students.*

Teachers are ideally placed to continue to build connectedness in their classrooms after the program's completion so that program gains can be maintained. Across the literature, teacher connectedness, or the quality of the relationship between students and their teacher, is considered a key component of school connectedness and is positively associated with student mental health and wellbeing (García-Moya, Brooks, Morgan, & Moreno, 2015; García-Moya et al., 2018). When teachers work on building stronger relationships with students, they also increase connectedness among peers, which has a direct positive effect on adolescent mental health (McLaren, Schurmann, & Jenkins, 2015). Through RAP-T-ASD and the Autism Teen Wellbeing website, teachers are able to explore the importance of the micro-skills of connectedness in the classroom and brainstorm ways of creating a culture of connectedness in the class and across the school. The four micro-skills of connectedness come together to spell the acronym WISE: **W**arm relationships, **I**nclusiveness, **S**trength focus, and **E**quity and fairness (Shochet & Wurfl, 2006).

Warmth and empathy

Providing a warm environment is an essential foundation for building connectedness as it recognises and values all relationships within the school, be they relationships with students, teachers, support workers, administrators, principals, or parents. Empathy is a key mechanism for building relationships and a sense of connectedness with others (Pavlovich & Krahnke, 2012). By using empathy to continually build and maintain warm relationships, teachers can model for students that they are valued and can also value others in the classroom and school environment.

Some ways that teachers can create warmth in classrooms and the school environment include:

- Greeting students by their name and saying hello with a smile.
- Showing respect to all people in the classroom and school environment.
- Spending time completing activities outside the classroom environment, individually and in small and larger groups.
- Welcoming students on their way to class.
- Sharing stories about themselves and their interests.
- Demonstrating random acts of kindness.

Inclusiveness

Promoting inclusiveness involves creating a classroom environment where everyone, including students, teachers, and school staff, feel included. This inclusion can be feeling a sense of belonging to a group during a group task or feeling a sense of belonging in the classroom and/or the whole-school environment. Teachers can promote this inclusion in the classroom and among students and student groups by finding ways to empower all students, modelling acceptance and tolerance, and creating an atmosphere where students can practise inclusion with their peers.

Some ways that teachers can promote inclusiveness in classrooms and the school environment include:

- Creating tasks or roles for all students.
- Creating peer networks such as buddy systems.
- Promoting cultural awareness and tolerance for differences.
- Acknowledging the achievements of the whole class or student groups within the class or school environment across different activities.

- Encouraging students to participate in activities that interest them.
- Making sure activities involve the whole student group involved.

Strength focused

It is important for teachers to employ a strengths-based approach when working with adolescents on the spectrum as doing so promotes engagement, avoids pathologising, and avoids perpetuating stigma (Shochet et al., 2001). A strength focus involves recognising and believing in the individual strengths within all students, and then creating opportunities for students to use those strengths to build their own sense of competence and self-esteem.

Some ways that teachers can promote and cultivate strengths in classrooms and the school environment include:

- Recognising and commenting on students' efforts more than on their achievements.
- Encouraging students to 'have a go'.
- Openly discussing and recognising personal achievements.
- Looking for opportunities to praise students' strengths.
- Showing faith in others.
- Creating opportunities for students to engage in work based on their strengths and interests.

It is equally important for teachers to recognise their own strengths. Teachers need to give themselves a pat on the back whenever they have reached a goal or done something well!

Equity and fairness

Promoting equity and fairness in the classroom is an important task for teachers. While this may involve creating classroom rules that are fair for all students, it is equally important that teachers recognise and cater for differences among the students in order to remove barriers that would reduce some students' chances of succeeding.

Some ways that teachers can promote equity and fairness in classrooms and the school environment include:

- Discussing diversity and embracing differences.
- Establishing group rules and enforcing them consistently.
- Providing equal access for students to resources and support services.
- Acknowledging and accepting differences in opinions or perspectives.
- Treating students in a mature manner and avoid talking down to them.
- Respecting all students and colleagues.

Conclusion and practitioner reflection

The risk of developing depression increases in early adolescence. Young adolescents on the autism spectrum experience developmental challenges associated with the transition to adolescence as more challenging and have a greater risk of developing depression than their peers. School connectedness continues to be one of the most effective protective factors to prevent depression, anxiety, and other mental health difficulties in adolescents. The Autism CRC School Connectedness Project found that a multi-level resilience program led to improvements in school connectedness

> *Using the WISE model to create daily experiences of connectedness within the classroom and within the school community is just one way to promote an overall sense of connectedness in adolescents on the spectrum.*

and mental health in adolescents on the spectrum, and that schools, school staff, and teachers were well positioned to implement school-wide strategies for promoting school connectedness and to develop a culture of inclusive education. All school personnel can work to promote connectedness at the broader level of school culture, policy, and practice. Using the WISE model to create daily experiences of connectedness within the classroom and within the school community is just one way to promote an overall sense of connectedness in adolescents on the spectrum.

While there is a key role that teachers and schools can play in the promotion of school connectedness and mental health among all students, it is equally important for teachers to be provided with ongoing support for their own mental health and sense of connectedness. Teachers and school staff should be encouraged to be part of a culture that develops connectedness among their colleagues at school. A sense of belonging in the workplace is significantly associated with mental health and wellbeing among staff members (Cockshaw, Shochet, & Obst, 2013). Furthermore, research has shown that a teacher's sense of connectedness is directly related to a range of health outcomes among students (Voisin et al., 2005). Therefore, promoting connectedness at the broader level across the whole school culture is important for ensuring mental health and wellbeing for students. In sum, the Autism CRC School Connectedness Project has found that, by promoting connectedness, teachers have a vital role to play in supporting the mental health and wellbeing of all their students, including those on the spectrum.

Notes

1 A version of the *Index for Inclusion* is available here: https://www.eenet.org.uk/resources/docs/Index%20English.pdf
2 www.autismteenwellbeing.com.au

References

Ahmed, S. M., & Palermo, A. G. S. (2010). Community engagement in research: Frameworks for education and peer review. *American Journal of Public Health*, 100(8), 1380–1387. doi:10.2105/AJPH.2009.178137.

Allen, K., Kern, M. L., Vella-Brodrick, D., Hattie, J., & Waters, L. (2018). What schools need to know about fostering school belonging: A meta-analysis. *Educational Psychology Review*, 20(1), 1–34. doi:10.1007/s10648-016-9389-8.

Arango, A., Cole-Lewis, Y., Lindsay, R., Yeguez, C. E., Clark, M., & King, C. (2019). The protective role of connectedness on depression and suicidal ideation among bully victimized youth. *Journal of Clinical Child & Adolescent Psychology*, 48(5), 728–739. doi:10.1080./15374416.2018.1443456.

Australian Council for Educational Research. (2018). *Programme for international student assessment (PISA) Australia in focus number 1: Sense of belonging at school*. Retrieved from https://research.acer.edu.au/ozpisa/30/.

Bauminger, N., Shulman, C., & Agam, G. (2003). Peer interaction and loneliness in high-functioning children with autism. *Journal of Autism and Developmental Disorders*, 33(5), 489–507. doi:10.1023/A:1025827427901.

Benner, A. D. (2011). The transition to high school: Current knowledge, future directions. *Educational Psychology Review*, 23(3), 299–328. doi:10.1007/s10648-011-9152-0.

Bitsika, V., & Sharpley, C. F. (2015). Differences in the prevalence, severity and symptom profiles of depression in boys and adolescents with an autism spectrum disorder versus normally developing controls. *International Journal of Disability, Development and Education*, 62(2), 158–167. doi:10.1080/1034912X.2014.998179.

Booth, T., & Ainscow, M. (2002). *Index for inclusion: Developing learning and participation in schools.* Bristol: Centre for Studies on Inclusive Education.

Bosacki, S., Dane, A., Marini, Z., & YLC-CURA. (2007). Peer relationships and internalizing problems in adolescents: Mediating role of self-esteem. *Emotional and Behavioural Difficulties*, 12(4), 261–282. doi:10.1080/13632750701664293.

Bottema-Beutel, K., & Smith, N. (2013). The interactional construction of identity: An adolescent with autism in interaction with peers. *Linguistics and Education*, 24(2), 197–214. doi:10.1016/j.linged.2012.12.002.

Bronfenbrenner, U. (1979). *The ecology of human development: Experiments by nature and design.* Cambridge, MA: Harvard University Press.

Chapman, R. L., Buckley, L., Sheehan, M., & Shochet, I. (2013). School-based programs for increasing connectedness and reducing risk behavior: A systematic review. *Educational Psychology Review*, 25(1), 95–114. doi:10.1007/s10648-013-9216-4.

Chiang, H., & Gau, S. S. (2016). Comorbid psychiatric conditions as mediators to predict later social adjustment in youths with autism spectrum disorder. *The Journal of Child Psychology and Psychiatry*, 57(1), 103–111. doi:10.1111/jcpp.12450.

Ciani, K. D., Middleton, M. J., Summers, J. J., & Sheldon, K. M. (2010). Buffering against performance classroom goal structures: The importance of autonomy support and classroom community. *Contemporary Educational Psychology*, 35(1), 88–99. doi:10.1016/j.cedpsych.2009.11.001.

Claes, L., Luyckx, K., & Bijttebier, P. (2014). Non-suicidal self-injury in adolescents: Prevalence and associations with identity formation above and beyond depression. *Personality and Individual Differences*, 61, 101–104. doi:10.1016/j.paid.2013.12.019.

Cockshaw, W. D., Shochet, I. M., & Obst, P. L. (2013). General belongingness, workplace belongingness, and depressive symptoms. *Journal of Community and Applied Social Psychology*, 23, 240–251. doi:10.1002/casp.2121.

Corrieri, S., Heider, D., Conrad, I., Blume, A., König, H. H., & Riedel-Heller, S. G. (2014). School-based prevention programs for depression and anxiety in adolescence: A systematic review. *Health Promotion International*, 29(3), 427–441. doi:10.1093/heapro/dat001.

DeFilippis, M. (2018). Depression in children and adolescents with autism spectrum disorder. *Children*, 5(9), 112. doi:10.3390/children5090112.

Downs, A., & Smith, T. (2004). Emotional understanding, cooperation, and social behavior in high-functioning children with autism. *Journal of Autism and Developmental Disorders*, 34, 625–635. doi:10.1007/s10803-004-5284-0.

Farrell, L. J., & Barrett, P. M. (2007). Prevention of childhood emotional disorders: Reducing the burden of suffering associated with anxiety and depression. *Child and Adolescent Mental Health*, 12, 58–65. doi:10.1111/j.1475-3588.2006.00430x.

Foulkes, L., & Blakemore, S. J. (2018). Studying individual differences in human adolescent brain development. *Nature Neuroscience*, 21(3), 315–323. doi:10.1038/s41593-018-0078-4.

Frydenberg, E., Care, E., Freeman, E., & Chan, E. (2009). Interrelationships between coping, school connectedness and wellbeing. *Australian Journal of Education*, 53(3), 261–276. doi:10.1177/000494410905300305.

García-Moya, I., Brooks, F., Morgan, A., & Moreno, C. (2015). Subjective well-being in adolescence and teacher connectedness: A health asset analysis. *Health Education Journal*, 74(6), 641–654. doi:10.1177/0017896914555039.

García-Moya, I., Bunn, F., Jiménez-Iglesias, A., Paniagua, C., & Brooks, F. M. (2018). The conceptualisation of school and teacher connectedness in adolescent research: A scoping review of literature. *Educational Review*, 71(4), 423–444. doi:10.1080/00131911.2018.1424117.

Gerrard, B. (2008). School-Based Family Counseling: Overview, trends, and recommendations for future research. *International Journal for School-Based Family Counseling*, 1(1), 1–30.

Ghaziuddin, M., Ghaziuddin, N., & Greden, J. (2002). Depression in persons with autism: Implications for research and clinical care. *Journal of Autism and Developmental Disorders*, 32(4), 299–306. doi:10.102 3/A:1016330802348.

Goodenow, C. (1993). The psychological sense of school membership among adolescents: Scale development and educational correlates. *Psychology in the Schools*, 30, 79–90. doi:10.1002/1520-6807 (199301)30:1<79::AID-PITS2310300113>3.0.CO;2-X.

Gotham, K., Brunwasser, S. M., & Lord, C. (2015). Depressive and anxiety symptom trajectories from school age through young adulthood in samples with autism spectrum disorder and developmental delay. *Journal of the American Academy of Child & Adolescent Psychiatry*, 54(5), 369–376. doi:10.1016/j.jaac.2015.02.005.

Gustems-Carnicer, J., Calderón, C., & Calderón-Garrido, D. (2019). Stress, coping strategies and academic achievement in teacher education students. *European Journal of Teacher Education*, 42(3), 375–390. doi:10.1080/02619768.2019.1576629.

Huang, A. X., Hughes, T. L., Sutton, L. R., Lawrence, M., Chen, X., Ji, Z., & Zeleke, W. (2017). Understanding the self in individuals with autism spectrum disorders (ASD): A review of literature. *Frontiers in Psychology*, 8, 1422. doi:10.3389/fpsyg.2017.01422.

Hudson, C. C., Hall, L., & Harkness, K. L. (2019). Prevalence of depressive disorders in individuals with autism spectrum disorder: A meta-analysis. *Journal of Abnormal Child Psychology*, 47(1), 165–175. doi:10.1007/s10802-018-0402-1.

Humphrey, N., & Symes, W. (2010). Perceptions of social support and experience of bullying among pupils with autistic spectrum disorders in mainstream secondary schools. *European Journal of Special Needs Education*, 25, 77–91. doi:10.1080/08856250903450855.

Joyce, H. D., & Early, T. J. (2014). The impact of school belonging and teacher support on depressive symptoms in adolescents: A multilevel analysis. *Children and Youth Services Review*, 39, 101–107. doi:10.1016/j.childyouth.2014.02.005.

Kaplan Toren, N. (2013). Multiple dimensions of parental involvement and its links to young adolescent self-evaluation and academic achievement. *Psychology in the Schools*, 50(6), 634–649. doi:10.1002/pits.21698.

Kessler, R. C., Berglund, P., Demler, O., Jin, R., Merikangas, K. R., & Walters, E. E. (2005). Lifetime prevalence and age-of-onset distributions of DSM-IV disorders in the National Comorbidity Survey Replication. *Archives of General Psychiatry*, 62, 593–602. doi:10.1001/archpsyc.62.6.593.

Lawrence, D., Johnson, S., Hafekost, J., Boterhoven De Haan, K., Sawyer, M., Ainley, J., & Zubrick, S. R. (2015). *The mental health of children and adolescents: Report on the second Australian child and adolescent survey of mental health and wellbeing*. Canberra: Department of Health.

Lester, L., Waters, S., & Cross, D. (2013). The relationship between school connectedness and mental health during the transition to secondary school: A path analysis. *Journal of Psychologists and Counsellors in Schools*, 23(2), 157–171. doi:10.1017.jgc.2013.20.

Lim, S. K., & Lee, H. S. (2007). The effects of self-esteem, relationships with parents and peer relationships on adolescents' school adjustment. *Journal of Korean Home Economics Education Association*, 19(3), 169–183.

Locke, J., Ishijima, E. H., Kasari, C., & London, N. (2010). Loneliness, friendship quality and the social networks of adolescents with high-functioning autism in an inclusive school setting. *Journal of Research in Special Educational Needs*, 10(2), 74–81. doi:10.1111/j.1471-3802.2010.01148.x.

Mackay, B. A., Shochet, I. M., & Orr, J. A. (2017). A pilot randomised controlled trial of a school-based resilience intervention to prevent depressive symptoms for young adolescents with autism spectrum disorder: A mixed methods analysis. *Journal of Autism and Developmental Disorders*, 47(11), 3458–3478. doi:10.1007/s10803-017-3263-5.

Mahmud, A. (2019). The role of social and emotional learning during the transition to secondary school: An exploratory study. *Pastoral Care in Education*, 38(1), 23–41. doi:10.1080/02643944.2019.1700546.

Matson, J. L., & Nebel-Schwalm, M. S. (2007). Comorbid psychopathology with autism spectrum disorder in children: An overview. *Research in Developmental Disabilities*, 28, 341–352. doi:10.1016/j.ridd.2005.12.004.

Mayes, S. D., Calhoun, S. L., Murray, M. J., & Zahid, J. (2011). Variables associated with anxiety and depression in children with autism. *Journal of Developmental and Physical Disabilities*, 23, 325–337. doi:10.1007/s10882-011-9231-7.

McLaren, S., Schurmann, J., & Jenkins, M. (2015). The relationships between sense of belonging to a community GLB youth group; school, teacher, and peer connectedness; and depressive symptoms: Testing of a path model. *Journal of Homosexuality*, 62(12), 1688–1702. doi:10.1080/00918369.2015.1078207.

Mojtabai, R., Olfson, M., & Han, B. (2016). National trends in the prevalence and treatment of depression in adolescents and young adults. *Pediatrics*, 138(6), e20161878. doi:10.1542/peds.2016-1878.

Oldfield, J., Humphrey, N., & Hebron, J. (2016). The role of parental and peer attachment relationships and school connectedness in predicting adolescent mental health outcomes. *Child and Adolescent Mental Health*, 21(1), 21–29. doi:10.1111/camh.12108.

Oldfield, J., Stevenson, A., Ortiz, E., & Haley, B. (2018). Promoting or suppressing resilience to mental health outcomes in at risk young people: The role of parental and peer attachment and school connectedness. *Journal of Adolescence*, 64, 13–22. doi:10.1016/j.adolescence.2018.01.002.

Osborne, L., & Reed, P. (2011). School factors associated with mainstream progress in secondary education for included pupils with autism spectrum disorders. *Research in Autism Spectrum Disorders*, 5, 1253–1263. doi:10.1016/j.rasd.2011.01.016.

Osterman, K. F. (2000). Students' need for belonging in the school community. *Review of Educational Research*, 70(3), 323–367. doi:10.2307/1170786.

Parr, E. J., Shochet, I. M., Cockshaw, W. D., & Kelly, R. L. (2020). General belonging is a key predictor of adolescent depressive symptoms and partially mediates school belonging. *School Mental Health*. doi:10.1007/s12310-020-09371-0.

Pavlovich, K., & Krahnke, K. (2012). Empathy, connectedness and organisation. *Journal of Business Ethics*, 105(1), 131–137. doi:10.1007/s10551-011-0961-3.

Pezzimenti, F., Han, G. T., Vasa, R. A., & Gotham, K. (2019). Depression in youth with autism spectrum disorder. *Child and Adolescent Psychiatric Clinics*, 28(3), 397–409. doi:10.1016/j.chc.2019.02.009.

Picci, G., & Scherf, K. S. (2015). A two-hit model of autism: Adolescence as the second hit. *Clinical Psychological Science*, 3(3), 349–371. doi:10.1177/2167702614540646.

Queensland Government Department of Education. (2020). *Every student succeeding: State schools improvement strategy 2020–2024*. Retrieved from https://education.qld.gov.au/curriculums/Documents/state-schools-strategy.PDF.

Rao, U., Hammen, C. L., & Poland, R. E. (2010). Longitudinal course of adolescent depression: Neuroendocrine and psychosocial predictors. *Journal of the American Academy of Child & Adolescent Psychiatry*, 49(2), 141–151. doi:10.1016/j.jaac.2009.09.008.

Sciutto, M., Richwine, S., Mentrikoski, J., & Niedzwiecki, K. (2012). A qualitative analysis of the school experiences of students with Asperger syndrome. *Focus on Autism and Other Developmental Disabilities*, 27, 177–188. doi:10.1177/1088357612450511.

Shochet, I. M. (2002). The Resourceful Adolescent Program (RAP): Building resilience and preventing depression in adolescents through universal school-based interventions. In L. Rowling, G. Martin, & L. Walker (Eds.), *Mental health promotion and young people: Concepts and practice* (pp. 172–184). Sydney: McGraw-Hill.

Shochet, I. M., Dadds, M. R., Ham, D., & Montague, R. (2006). School belonging is an underemphasized parameter in adolescent mental health: Results of a community prediction study. *Journal of Clinical Child and Adolescent Psychology*, 35(2), 170–179. doi:10.1207/s15374424jccp3502_1.

Shochet, I. M., Dadds, M. R., Holland, D., Whitefield, K., Harnett, P. H., & Osgarby, S. M. (2001). The efficacy of a universal school-based program to prevent adolescent depression. *Journal of Clinical Child Psychology*, 30(3), 303–315. doi:10.1207/S15374424JCCP3003_3.

Shochet, I. M., & Hoge, R. (2009). Resourceful adolescent program: A prevention and early intervention program for teenage depression. In E. Essau (Ed.), *Treatment of adolescent depression: Theory and practice* (pp. 123–157). New York, NY: Oxford University Press. doi:10.1093/med:psych/9780199226504.003.0006.

Shochet, I. M., Homel, R., Cockshaw, W. D., & Montgomery, D. T. (2008). How do school connectedness and attachment to parents interrelate in predicting adolescent depressive symptoms? *Journal of Clinical Child & Adolescent Psychology*, 37(3), 676–681. doi:10.1080/15374410802148053.

Shochet, I. M., & Osgarby, S. (1999). The Resourceful Adolescent Project: Building psychological resilience in adolescents and their parents. *The Educational and Developmental Psychologist*, 16(1), 46–65. doi:10.1017/S0816512200050069.

Shochet, I. M., Saggers, B. R., Carrington, S. B., Orr, J. A., Wurfl, A. M., & Duncan, B. M. (2019). A strength-focused parenting intervention may be a valuable augmentation to a depression prevention focus for adolescents with autism. *Journal of Autism and Developmental Disorders*, 49(5), 2080–2100. doi:10.1007/s10803-019-03893-6.

Shochet, I. M., Saggers, B. R., Carrington, S. B., Orr, J. A., Wurfl, A. M., Duncan, B. M., & Smith, C. L. (2016). The Cooperative Research Centre for Living with Autism (Autism CRC) conceptual model to promote mental health for adolescents with ASD. *Clinical Child and Family Psychology Review*, 19(2), 94–116. doi:10.1007/s10567-016-0203-4.

Shochet, I. M., & Smith, C. L. (2014). A prospective study investigating the links among classroom environment, school belonging, and depressive symptoms in adolescents. *Psychology in the Schools*, 51(5), 480–492. doi:10.1002/pits.21759.

Shochet, I. M., Smith, C. L., Furlong, M. J., & Homel, R. (2011). A prospective study investigating the impact of school belonging factors on negative affect in adolescents. *Journal of Clinical Child & Adolescent Psychology*, 40(4), 586–595. doi:10.1080/15374416.2011.581616.

Shochet, I. M., & Wurfl, A. (2006). *Resourceful Adolescent Program for Teachers RAP-T: A program for teachers to promote school connectedness in teenagers.* Brisbane: School of Psychology and Counselling, Queensland University of Technology.

Slaten, C. D., Ferguson, J. K., Allen, K. A., Brodrick, D. V., & Waters, L. (2016). School belonging: A review of the history, current trends, and future directions. *The Educational and Developmental Psychologist*, 33(1), 1–15. doi:10.1017/edp.2016.6.

Smith, I. C., & White, S. W. (2020). Socio-emotional determinants of depressive symptoms in adolescents and adults with autism spectrum disorder: A systematic review. *Autism*. doi:10.1177/1362361320908101.

Sterzing, P. R., Shattuck, P. T., Narendorf, S. C., Wagner, M., & Cooper, B. P. (2012). Bullying involvement and autism spectrum disorders: Prevalence and correlates of bullying involvement among adolescents with an autism spectrum disorder. *Archives of Pediatrics and Adolescent Medicine*, 166, 1058–1064. doi:10.1001/archpediatrics.2012.790.

Stewart, M. E., Barnard, L., Pearson, J., Hasan, R., & O'Brien, G. (2006). Presentation of depression in autism and Asperger syndrome: A review. *Autism*, 10, 103–116. doi:10.1177/1362361306062013.

Swee, G., Shochet, I. M., Cockshaw, W. D., & Hides, L. (2020). Emotion regulation as a risk factor for suicide ideation among adolescents and young adults: The mediating role of belongingness. *Journal of Youth and Adolescence*. doi:10.1007/s10964-020-01301-2.

Victoria State Government Department of Education and Training. (2019). *School policy school hours.* Retrieved from https://www.education.vic.gov.au/school/principals/spag/management/Pages/hours.aspx.

Voisin, D. R., Salazar, L. F., Crosby, R., Diclemente, R. J., Yarber, W. L., & Staples-Horne, M. (2005). Teacher connectedness and health-related outcomes among detained adolescents. *Journal of Adolescent Health*, 37(4), 337.e17–337.e23. doi:10.1016/j.jadohealth.2004.11.137.

White, S. W., & Roberson-Nay, R. (2009). Anxiety, social deficits, and loneliness in youth with autism spectrum disorders. *Journal of Autism and Developmental Disorders*, 39(7), 1006–1013. doi:10.1007/s10803-009-0713-8.

Wigfield, A., Eccles, J. S., Mac Iver, D., Reuman, D. A., & Midgley, C. (1991). Transitions during early adolescence: Changes in children's domain-specific self-perceptions and general self-esteem across the transition to junior high school. *Developmental Psychology*, 27(4), 552–565. doi:10.1037/0012-1649.27.4.552.

Wolff, F., Wigfield, A., Möller, J., Dicke, A. L., & Eccles, J. S. (2019). Social, dimensional, and temporal comparisons by students and parents: An investigation of the 2I/E model at the transition from elementary to junior high school. *Journal of Educational Psychology*. doi:10.1037/edu0000440.

3

HOW TO IMPLEMENT A WHOLE-SCHOOL APPROACH TO SCHOOL CONNECTEDNESS

Suzanne Carrington, Beth Saggers, Ian Shochet, Astrid Wurfl and Jayne Orr

This chapter builds on the previous discussion about the concept of school connectedness as an important protective factor for adolescent mental health and wellbeing. We describe a whole-school approach to school connectedness that empowers a school community (including parents, teachers, school leaders, and students) to work together to develop a sense of belonging at school. Our research across five secondary schools trialled an approach where a School Connectedness Committee implemented a review and development process that involved five phases of the *Index for Inclusion*. In this chapter, we explain in detail how the approach worked in schools and we present three outcomes that provide evidence of the success in one particular school. We put forward five propositions that would be useful for schools who want to try this approach to build a sense of community and connectedness for all. This chapter will be useful for educators and school leaders who are interested in implementing a whole-of-school approach that supports inclusion and connectedness.

Young people who feel accepted, respected, and included in their school community are more likely to experience a sense of belonging and connectedness to their school and school community (Carrington et al., 2021). School connectedness is defined as the way that young people feel connected to school that ensures students feel accepted, respected, and included (Goodenow, 1993). Researchers who are interested in how young people are connected to school also talk about constructs such as school climate (Aldridge & McChesney, 2018) and inclusive school culture (Carrington, 1999). There is evidence of strong links between school connectedness (Goodenow, 1993) and a range of beneficial outcomes such as academic success, high self-esteem, mental wellbeing, optimism, life satisfaction, and hope (Bonny, Britto, Klostermann, Hornung, & Slap, 2000; Shochet, Dadds, Ham, & Montague, 2006; You et al., 2008). Further to these positive outcomes, school connectedness has been found to be a major factor that protects against the development of depression while promoting optimal adolescent development (Baumeister & Leary, 1995; Cockshaw & Shochet, 2010; Jose, Ryan, & Pryor, 2012; Lester, Waters, & Cross, 2013; Shochet et al., 2006; Shochet, Homel, Cockshaw, & Montgomery, 2008). There is a clear link between school connectedness and improved academic outcomes, reduced health risk behaviours, delinquency and violence, and of current and future wellbeing (Anderman, 2002; Anderman & Freeman, 2004; Chapman, Buckley, Sheehan, & Shochet, 2013; Dowrick & Crespo, 2005; McDonald & Hayes, 2001; Schmied & Tully, 2009; Shochet et al., 2006, 2008; Shochet & Smith, 2012).

In summary, students who are well connected to their school tend to:

- Do better academically.
- Have fewer mental health problems.
- Be more motivated.
- Have more optimistic expectations for the future.
- Demonstrate delayed initiation of alcohol and other drug use, and reduced drug abuse in later life.
- Exhibit delayed delinquency and engagement in crime, and lower probability of gang membership and violence.
- Exhibit delayed sexual activity and reduced sexual risk behaviour.
- Make teaching them and managing classes easier and a more enjoyable experience for their teachers.

We know that adolescents on the autism spectrum are at increased risk for mental health issues such as depression and anxiety (Chiang & Gau, 2016; Mayes, Calhoun, Murray, & Zahid, 2011), and promoting protective factors such as school connectedness can help protect against this risk, and it is for these reasons the Autism CRC funded the School Connectedness Project. We believe that a school that promotes school connectedness for all students, including students on the autism spectrum, is a school that supports an inclusive school culture. This in turn can be a protective factor against the increased mental health risk some young people such as those on the autism spectrum may experience. School-based programs that support school connectedness and inclusion should operate across a whole school and include multiple levels of support for families, teachers, students, and school system supports (Carrington et al., 2021; Shochet et al., 2016). The school-based model that includes multiple levels of support for school connectedness and promoting mental health and wellbeing in young adolescents on the autism spectrum has been described in Chapter 2. The next section will describe the whole-school approach to school connectedness that was developed and implemented in this project.

Whole-school approach to school connectedness

The whole-school component of the Autism CRC School Connectedness Project utilised the *Index for Inclusion* (Booth & Ainscow, 2016) and aimed to empower the school community – parents/carers, teachers, school leaders, and students – to engage in cycles of review and development for greater school connectedness in the school community. The cycles of review and development involve the school community gathering information about how students are connected and included at school and working out how to make improvements. The *Index for Inclusion* has been used successfully to support schools to develop a more inclusive approach to education (Carrington, Bourke, & Dharan, 2012; Carrington & Robinson, 2004). Considering the links between school connectedness and inclusion, as described earlier in this chapter, it was considered appropriate to use this resource to foster a whole-school approach to school connectedness. Information about accessing and using the *Index for Inclusion* as part of the whole-school approach is available on the website *Building Connectedness and Wellbeing for Young Adolescents on the Autism Spectrum*,[1] as introduced in Chapter 2.

The *Index for Inclusion* (Booth & Ainscow, 2016) is informed by a set of values that support equity and inclusive education for all in the school community. The Index is an accessible and practical resource which can be used to encourage the whole school community to work together in reviewing all aspects of cultures, policies, and practices in their school. The *Index for Inclusion* process is driven by a committee of school community stakeholders in the school that could include school leaders, teachers, parents, and students. The committee helps a school to:

> *The Index is an accessible and practical resource which can be used to encourage the whole school community to work together in reviewing all aspects of cultures, policies, and practices in their school.*

- Put their own framework of values into action.
- Carry out a thorough self-evaluation.
- Produce a detailed school improvement plan.
- Minimise barriers to learning and participation and build a sense of belonging and connectedness by empowering adults and children to voice their ideas.
- Present a cycle of planning and review for school improvement.

Before we explain the details of the whole-school approach, it is necessary to provide an overview of the *Index for Inclusion* that was used to support the development of school connectedness in the project schools.

Index for Inclusion

The Index can support school review across three dimensions:

1. Culture.
2. Policy.
3. Practice.

Each of these dimensions work together. The three dimensions are each divided into two sections which form a planning framework (Booth & Ainscow, 2016) as shown in Figure 3.1 towards the end of this chapter.

The review process can start at any one dimension or include investigations across two or three dimensions. Each section of the Index is divided into a number of indicators. The indicators are statements that can help guide inclusive aspirations for a school. For example:

Dimension A: Creating inclusive cultures
Section A1: Building community

Indicator 1: Everyone is welcomed.
Indicator 2: Staff cooperate.
Indicator 3: Children help each other.
Indicator 4: Staff and children respect one another.
Indicator 5: Staff and parents/carers collaborate.

There are lists of questions under each indicator to encourage thinking about various issues related to inclusive education. The Index 'is like a set of Russian dolls – as you move through the dimensions, sections, indicators and questions you get deeper and deeper into what is going on in every aspect of the school and how you can improve it' (Booth & Ainscow, 2002, p. 9). For example, under the first indicator 'Everyone is welcomed', the following questions could be asked:

- Is the first contact that people have with the school welcoming?
- Do staff, children, and families create a sense of community in the school?
- Is the school welcoming to all parents/carers and other members of its local communities?

The detailed questions ensure that the materials can provoke thought on how young people are connected and included at their school. While the questions do not provide solutions for schools, they disturb *'what is'*, providing opportunities to consider *'what if'*, and dream about *'what could be'*. They give people permission to think differently and to consider all possibilities that can help promote an inclusive culture and school connectedness in their school. With this in mind, the questions can be used in a variety of ways such as through surveys with parents, teachers, and students or in focus group interviews. Through dialogue and problem solving together, schools can develop a more inclusive culture and address issues of how young people can be more connected to their school. The Index provides a framework for sharing of perspectives and issues of concern between parent/community members, staff, school leaders, and students in a way that can facilitate deep learning and understanding about the values of inclusive education (Carrington et al., 2012) and promote a sense of belonging and school connectedness within the school community.

Using the *Index for Inclusion* to support school connectedness

In order to support the use of the Index, a committee made up of school community stakeholders is established in the school to oversee the five phases of the Index:

1. Getting started with the Index.
2. Finding out about the school.
3. Producing a school development plan.
4. Implementing priorities.
5. Reviewing actions and progress.

The website *Building Connectedness and Wellbeing for Young Adolescents on the Autism Spectrum* illustrates how a school community can work together to establish a school committee to implement the five phases of the Index to support the fostering of school connectedness in the school. The website provides clear information about how a school can use the *Index for Inclusion* to support a whole-school approach to school connectedness and includes a range of useful resources that draw on the *Index for Inclusion* dimensions, indicators, and questions. The website aims to support adolescents on the autism spectrum by empowering them, their parents and carers, teachers, schools, and communities to promote a sense of belonging and school connectedness and wellbeing, and to link parents and carers, teachers, schools, and communities to important resources.

The five phases of the Index will now be described in more detail.

Phase 1: Getting started with the Index

The first step is to establish a School Connectedness Committee with a range of different representatives from the school community. This might include the school principal or deputy principal,

> *The first step is to establish a School Connectedness Committee with a range of different representatives from the school community.*

heads of departments, teachers, parents, students, and a critical friend from outside the school. A critical friend could be a university researcher or an education department representative. This outside perspective can provide a different and more critical perspective and help challenge the status quo in culture, policy, and practice at the school. A leader from within the school should chair and lead the School Connectedness Committee. The leader of the committee should model inclusion and support connectedness between the members to ensure that people collaborate, listen to each other, and have a voice. The committee would begin by discussing key priorities in relation to inclusion for the school community and getting to know the Index dimensions: culture, policy, and practice. The first meeting might involve a group discussion about the dimensions and the sections listed above and consideration of how they connect with any school community priorities. These priorities should be summarised so that the committee is clear of how the future phases of the Index process would address areas of concern while acknowledging strengths. The discussion would include the stakeholders in the School Connectedness Committee (parents, teachers, students) sharing their ideas about priorities under the dimensions and sections. It would be helpful if each committee member had a copy of the *Index for Inclusion*[2] and had reviewed the document before the meeting.

The process of using the *Index for Inclusion* involves cycles of review and development and is enacted through experience and participation of people to create knowledge and action that is directly useful to a group of people, in this case a school community (Lawson, Caringi, Pyles, Jurkowski, & Bozlak, 2015; Reason & Bradbury, 2006). The approach assumes collaboration whereby the stakeholders in the School Connectedness Committee are involved in planning, data collection, analysis, and setting agendas. By challenging the status quo, participants interrogate and have the opportunity to alter the arrangements of schooling that perpetuate systemic inequalities for students and staff (Carrington & Holm, 2005). A School Connectedness Committee would normally meet about four to five times a year and their role is to plan and oversee the implementation of the review and development process that is represented in the five phases of the *Index for Inclusion*.

Phase 2: Finding out about the school

Once the School Connectedness Committee identifies a dimension and section that aligns with identified school priorities related to inclusion, the committee considers ways of gathering information (collecting data) from various stakeholders such as parents, teachers, and students. For example, in one high school, the priority identified by the committee was to help promote a sense of connectedness for Year 7s transitioning into the school. As a result, a student group activity was conducted where current students were asked to share their feelings of belonging and acceptance at the school. The activity was designed to find out how students learn about becoming a student in the school. A group of students responded to a set of questions and the students' responses were then displayed on posters on the wall to encourage group discussion. The questions were:

1. What did I expect my school would be like?
2. What sort of person do I want to be when I leave school?
3. How will my school help me to get there?
4. What kind of connection do you think you feel to your school?
    a. What are some of the things about your school that make you feel like that?
    b. What other things would help you feel like you belong at your school?

5.   What is one thing that kids starting in Year 7 need to know about your school?
6.   What are some things you would have liked to know about your school when you started?

There are many ways that the School Connectedness Committee can gather information to find out what is going well in a school and what are the gaps or areas of concern. The *Index for Inclusion* has a range of ideas that include ideas for staff development days, and sample surveys for parents, teachers, and school students. Further to these ideas, there are published examples of *Index for Inclusion* activities and projects in schools that would be useful (Carrington & Robinson, 2004; Robinson & Carrington, 2002), as well as on the website *Building Connectedness and Wellbeing for Young Adolescents on the Autism Spectrum* mentioned previously. It is important to begin with one focus area that the committee believes is a priority rather than thinking that all challenges need to be addressed at once. Once the cycles of data gathering, discussion, and planning begin, it is likely that new areas of priority will emerge.

Phase 3: Producing a school development plan

> *The action plan provides the opportunities to consider 'what if', and facilitates a vision about 'what could be'.*

The School Connectedness Committee will meet to analyse and discuss the information that was gathered in Phase 2. This might involve reading transcripts of de-identified interviews, reviewing results from surveys, or collated information from staff, student, or parent meetings. The discussions about the information will help the committee to understand what is working well in the school and what areas might need development. For example, the committee may need to plan for ways that staff, parents, and students could be more involved in developing a shared set of values in the school. This could involve short-term actions at school staff meetings and parent committee groups, and there may also be a need for ongoing teacher professional development to work on improving teacher–student relationships in the school. The action plan should also consider who will be involved in the implementation and how and when particular actions would occur. This phase is important as it is the conversations that take place about the collected information from Phase 2 that provide opportunities for members of the committee to share values and their vision for the future priorities in the school. Some priorities will impact on culture, policy, and practice in the school and it is efficient for the planning process to include short- and long-term priorities for implementation. The action plan provides the opportunities to consider *'what if'*, and facilitates a vision about *'what could be'*.

Phase 4: Implementing priorities

Once the School Connectedness Committee develops a plan of action, various stakeholders in the school community will be involved in implementing the short-term and long-term plans. The short-term plans may involve changes to policy and practice, such as a review of a school policy, professional development for staff, or changes in how resources are distributed across the school. If a School Connectedness Committee has a plan of action in the dimension of culture, the plan of action will need to extend over a substantial period of time to ensure long-term and sustainable change. These actions might involve school leaders, parents, teachers, and students working together in various ways to develop a shared vision and collective commitment to a set of values that would inform school connectedness and inclusion for all students. A school leader describes how the School Connectedness Committee members at one school implemented the priorities of a plan on the Autism Teen Wellbeing website *Building Connectedness and Wellbeing for Young Adolescents on the Autism Spectrum*.

Phase 5: Reviewing actions and progress

The School Connectedness Committee will review the progress of the plan. This will involve reviewing a range of data that will provide evidence on whether the plan is successful or not. There may need to be modifications made to the plan in the future, or the committee may formulate new priorities for a new cycle of review and development. The committee will reflect on and share the progress of the plan in various forums in the school community. The idea is that the *Index for Inclusion* process is embedded in cycles of school review and development to support the school to continue to strive for greater school connectedness and inclusion.

The next section of this chapter will report on the outcomes of a School Connectedness Project that was implemented in one school that utilised the *Index for Inclusion* to enable a school community to engage in review, development, and change. The project is reported in more detail in a previous publication (Carrington et al., 2021). The findings indicate that a whole-school approach working across the five phases of the *Index for Inclusion* can highlight a shared understanding and commitment to the notion of school connectedness and support collaboration between students and school staff to engage in participatory action research (MacDonald, 2012) to improve inclusive culture and practice in a school.

Project outcomes from one school: Whole-school approach to school connectedness

Outcome 1

The first outcome was about how the approach supported the school to build community. This outcome is linked to the Index Dimension A of Creating Inclusive Cultures which includes Section A1: Building Community (see Figure 3.1). The data collected from the project school indicated that through the engagement in the Index process, there was greater awareness of the broader school community and the connections between families, staff, and students. By listening to the voices in the School Connectedness Committee and analysing the student responses to the questions, the teachers in particular became more aware of the perspectives of the students. In this project, the school explored perceptions about how students were first welcomed to the school and feedback about that process.

Outcome 2

The second outcome was about the impact on the relationships between students and staff. The School Connectedness Committee had many discussions about the mature and considered responses from the students in the Phase 2 activity, finding out about the school, and had a better understanding of how the students felt about their experiences of belonging and being connected to their teachers, classes, and the broader school community. For example, the students spoke about the bonds that they have with teachers, how they appreciated the conversations that they have with teachers, and how a school supports friendships and a feeling of belonging and support. Once the School Connectedness Committee became more aware of these issues, they implemented a plan to develop a social calendar to provide clear information to students, staff, and parents about the social activities at school. This initiative addressed the feedback about the younger children not knowing about social activities or knowing how to access the various opportunities at the school. Further to that new action, the School Connectedness Committee supported new processes where staff and students were involved in planning the future orientation program for the new students. The following quotes from the Head of Special Education (HOSE) describe how this worked:

> It is about the orientation work … so we have the kids come in Grade 6 in two lots, for two full days, and for part of that, the senior students take them out and they do all these activities with them … and the conversation that we were having about like an orientation booklet about what you want to know about high school, and what happens in high school, and it doesn't, you know, you never really get told that. (HOSE, final interview)

> Another initiative that occurred as a result of the Index for Inclusion process involved gathering feedback and ideas from a greater group of students who were new to the school, so that they could talk about their own experience of orientation and how they were welcomed to a new school. These ideas informed a new program that had a much greater involvement from students. (HOSE, final interview)

Outcome 3

The third outcome was about how the Index process influenced student leadership in the school. The School Connectedness Committee in this project included a male and female school captain and these students worked with other students across the school to gather the data/information in Phase 2 of the process, finding out about the school. The opportunities gave the school leaders a chance to engage more broadly with the school community, particularly teachers and heads of departments in various discussions about the work that they were doing. The students also worked with groups of students across the various levels of the school. One of the advantages of this was that the other students appreciated the role modelling of leadership roles in the school and this influenced them to apply for school leadership opportunities. These outcomes are highlighted in the following quote:

> The students involved in that project initially were that senior leadership team, so the five school captains. I think it's allowed them really to focus … They've really thought about that process, and I think it really helped them understand a little bit more about what they wanted to contribute to the school, rather than just going off and buying a painting or doing … they want to do something that's tangible for the school, that will then go on – and that hasn't happened before. (HOSE, final interview)

It was clear that this whole-school approach to school connectedness influenced a greater appreciation and commitment to involving students and a stronger focus on building a school community that valued relationships between staff and students and built a sense of connectedness within the school community. Other outcomes from this project included a transition booklet to support students and parents navigating transition to a new school. This work included the organisation of a parent information evening that was supported by the school teaching community. A junior leaders program was implemented to provide better pastoral support for young people to ensure they are supported and connected to their school community. This also included leadership development programs conducted in collaboration with community organisations to support upcoming student leaders of the future. The final initiative that was implemented by the School Connectedness Committee was a student rewards program that was aligned to four school values: learning, respect, community, and creativity.

Implications for future practice

We suggest five propositions that would support schools who want to engage in a whole-school approach using the *Index for Inclusion* to build a sense of community that supports young people to be more connected to their school.

Proposition 1

The first proposition is that students should be considered as important stakeholders in their school planning and review cycles. Listening to student voice is a well-known initiative in the field of education (Rudduck & Flutter, 2004) and is informed by Article 12 of the UN *Convention on the Rights of the Child* (United Nations, 1989). Meaningful student involvement has been shown to be a powerful and effective force for school improvement (Rudduck & Flutter, 2004). Involving young people as participants in school review and development values their knowledge and skills (Carrington & Holm, 2005).

Proposition 2

The second proposition is that all members of a school community should be valued and have a voice. The *Index for Inclusion* resource is a great tool to facilitate respectful conversations between school leaders, teachers, parents, and students. Involving members across the school community provides opportunity for conversations to share values and priorities from different perspectives and may prompt a greater appreciation of each other. An inclusive approach to education is informed by collaboration and respect for all.

Proposition 3

The third proposition is about resourcing the review and development process. Including a critical friend or an education department colleague as a member of the School Connectedness Committee brings new ideas and resources from outside the school to the discussions about the cycles of planning, implementation, and review. Further to this external support, the process provides an excellent opportunity to draw on the knowledge and experience of the various internal members of the committee.

Proposition 4

The fourth proposition is the need to determine clear, specific aims that can be achieved by the School Connectedness Committee. The initial planning meeting in Phase 1 is an important time for the members of the committee to discuss key priorities in the school and how they connect with the dimensions and sections of the Index. The committee may have a sense about what is working well and what are the challenges or areas of concern. The five phases of the Index process will enable a deeper investigation across the school community and ensure future planning is informed by a community consultation process.

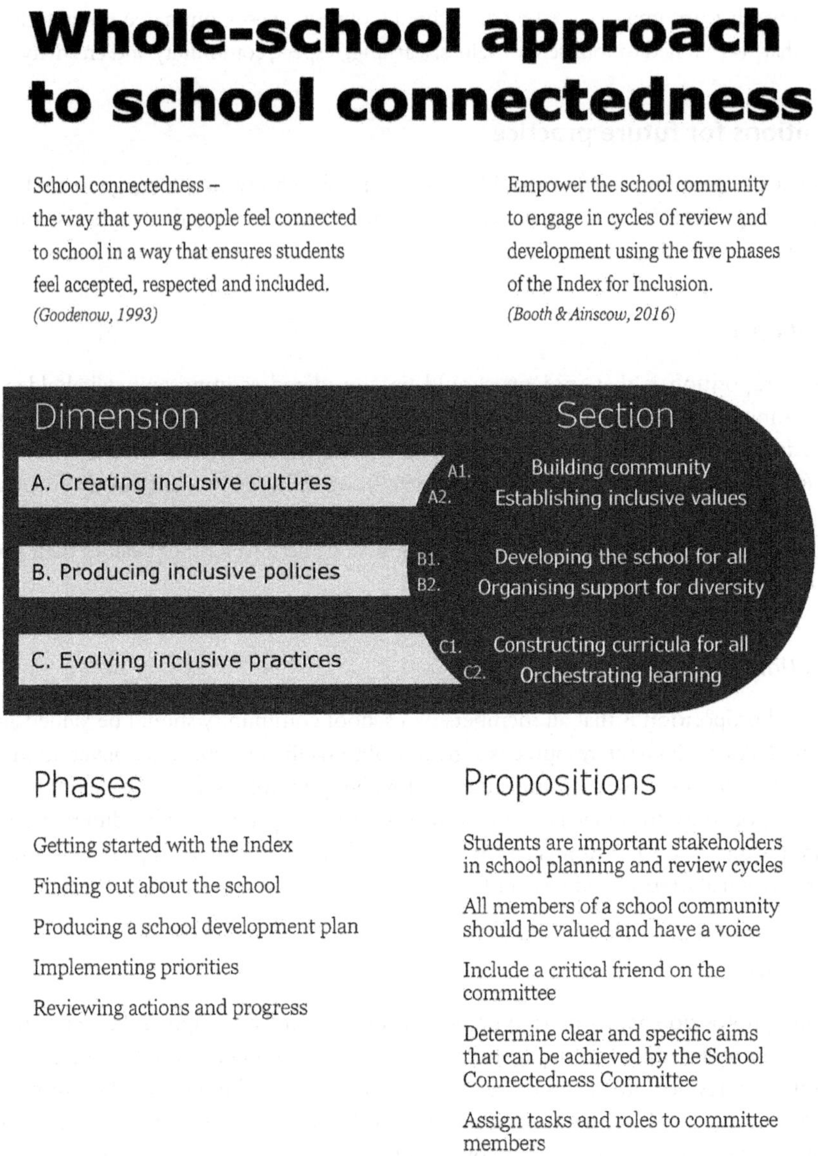

Whole-school approach to school connectedness

School connectedness –
the way that young people feel connected
to school in a way that ensures students
feel accepted, respected and included.
(Goodenow, 1993)

Empower the school community
to engage in cycles of review and
development using the five phases
of the Index for Inclusion.
(Booth & Ainscow, 2016)

Dimension		Section
A. Creating inclusive cultures	A1.	Building community
	A2.	Establishing inclusive values
B. Producing inclusive policies	B1.	Developing the school for all
	B2.	Organising support for diversity
C. Evolving inclusive practices	C1.	Constructing curricula for all
	C2.	Orchestrating learning

Phases

Getting started with the Index

Finding out about the school

Producing a school development plan

Implementing priorities

Reviewing actions and progress

Propositions

Students are important stakeholders
in school planning and review cycles

All members of a school community
should be valued and have a voice

Include a critical friend on the
committee

Determine clear and specific aims
that can be achieved by the School
Connectedness Committee

Assign tasks and roles to committee
members

FIGURE 3.1 Planning framework for the *Index for Inclusion* and propositions.

Proposition 5

The final proposition is to assign roles and tasks to the various members of the committee. Carrington et al. (2021) suggest that the committee needs a leader who will take responsibility for arranging meetings, organising resources, liaising with senior staff, school councils, etc. There may be a person on the committee who provides mentoring support for the student leaders as they take up their work in the various phases of the process. Different members, including students, may lead particular actions that include gathering data/information, communicating results to various forums in the school, and organising and checking on timelines. The important point is that building a sense of community that supports young people to be more connected to their school should become embedded in the ongoing cycles of review and development in a school.

Conclusion

We believe that the model of using the *Index for Inclusion* as part of a whole-school approach to school connectedness that we describe in this chapter can be utilised in any school. The website *Building Connectedness and Wellbeing for Young Adolescents on the Autism Spectrum* is a great resource that can be used to support this process. The website presents a range of strategies for promoting school connectedness and highlights how a multi-level model can be utilised in a school community to increase school connectedness not only for students on the autism spectrum and their families but for all in the school community.

Notes

1 www.autismteenwellbeing.com.au
2 A version of the *Index for Inclusion* is available here: https://www.eenet.org.uk/resources/docs/Index%20English.pdf

References

Aldridge, J. M., & McChesney, K. (2018). The relationship between school climate and adolescent mental health and wellbeing: A systematic literature review. *International Journal of Educational Research*, 88, 121–145.

Anderman, E. M. (2002). School effects on psychological outcomes during adolescence. *Journal of Educational Psychology*, 94, 795–809. doi:10.1037//0022-0663.94.4.795.

Anderman, L. H., & Freeman, T. M. (2004). Students' sense of belonging in school. *Advances in Motivation and Achievement, 13*, 27–63.

Baumeister, R. F., & Leary, M. R. (1995). The need to belong: Desire for interpersonal attachments as a fundamental human motivation. *Psychological Bulletin*, 117, 497–529.

Bonny, A. E., Britto, M. T., Klostermann, B. K., Hornung, R. W., & Slap, G. B. (2000). School disconnectedness: Identifying adolescents at risk. *Pediatrics*, 106, 1017–1021.

Booth, T., & Ainscow, M. (2002). *Index for inclusion: Developing learning and participation in schools*. Bristol: Centre for Studies on Inclusive Education.

Booth, T., & Ainscow, M. (2016). *Index for inclusion: A guide to school development led by inclusive values* (4th ed.). Cambridge: Index for Inclusion Network Limited.

Carrington, S. B. (1999). Inclusion needs a different school culture. *International Journal of Inclusive Education*, 3(3), 257–268.

Carrington, S. B., Bourke, R., & Dharan, V. (2012). Using the Index for Inclusion to develop inclusive school communities. In S. B. Carrington & J. MacArthur (Eds.), *Teaching in inclusive school communities* (pp. 341–366). Brisbane: John Wiley & Sons.

Carrington, S., & Holm, K. (2005). Students direct inclusive school development in an Australian secondary school: An example of student empowerment. *Australasian Journal of Special Education*, 29(2), 155–171.

Carrington, S., & Robinson, R. (2004). A case study of inclusive school development: A journey of learning. *International Journal of Inclusive Education*, 8(2), 141–153.

Carrington, S. B., Saggers, B. R., Shochet, I. M., Orr, J. A., Wurfl, A. M., Vanelli, J., & Nickerson, J. (2021). Researching a whole school approach to school connectedness. *International Journal of Inclusive Education*. doi:10.1080/13603116.2021.1878298

Chapman, R. L., Buckley, L., Sheehan, M., & Shochet, I. M. (2013). School-based programs for increasing connectedness and reducing risk behavior: A systematic review. *Educational Psychology Review*, 25, 95–114. doi:10.1007/s10648-013-9216-4.

Chiang, H., & Gau, S. S. (2016). Comorbid psychiatric conditions as mediators to predict later social adjustment in youths with autism spectrum disorder. *The Journal of Child Psychology and Psychiatry*, 57(1), 103–111. doi:10.1111/jcpp.12450.

Cockshaw, W. D., & Shochet, I. (2010). The link between belongingness and depressive symptoms: An exploration in the workplace interpersonal context. *Australian Psychologist*, 45, 283–289.

Dowrick, P. W., & Crespo, N. (2005). School failure. In T. P. Gullotta & G. R. Adams (Eds.), *Handbook of adolescent behavioral problems: Evidence-based approaches to prevention and treatment* (pp. 589–610). New York, NY: Springer.

Goodenow, C. (1993). The psychological sense of school membership among adolescents: Scale development and educational correlates. *Psychology in the Schools*, 30, 79–90.

Jose, P. E., Ryan, N., & Pryor, J. (2012). Does social connectedness lead to a greater sense of well-being in adolescence? *Journal of Research on Adolescence*, 22, 235–251. doi:10.1111/j.1532-7795.2012.00783.x.

Lawson, H. A., Caringi, J. C., Pyles, L., Jurkowski, J. M., & Bozlak, C. T. (2015). *Participatory action research*. New York, NY: Oxford University Press.

Lester, L., Waters, S., & Cross, D. (2013). The relationship between school connectedness and mental health during the transition to secondary school: A path analysis. *Australian Journal of Guidance and Counselling*, 23, 157–171. doi:10.1017/jgc.2013.20.

MacDonald, C. (2012). Understanding participatory action research: A qualitative research methodology option. *Canadian Journal of Action Research*, 13(2), 34–50.

Mayes, S. D., Calhoun, S. L., Murray, M. J., & Zahid, J. (2011). Variables associated with anxiety and depression in children with autism. *Journal of Developmental and Physical Disabilities*, 23, 325–337. doi:10.1007/s10882-011-9231-7.

McDonald, J., & Hayes, L. (2001). Strengthening welfare services for young people: The vision and the challenge. *Youth Studies Australia*, 20(1), 37–42.

Reason, P., & Bradbury, H. (2006). *A handbook of action research*. Thousand Oaks, CA: Sage.

Robinson, R., & Carrington, S. B. (2002). Professional development for inclusive schooling. *International Journal of Educational Management*, 16(5), 239–247.

Rudduck, J., & Flutter, J. (2004). *How to improve your school: Giving pupils a voice*. London: Bloomsbury Publishing.

Schmied, V., & Tully, L. (2009). *Effective strategies and interventions for adolescents in a child protection context: Literature review*. Sydney: New South Wales Department of Community Services.

Shochet, I. M., Dadds, M. R., Ham, D., & Montague, R. (2006). School connectedness is an underemphasized parameter in adolescent mental health: Results of a community prediction study. *Journal of Clinical Child and Adolescent Psychology*, 35, 170–179. doi:10.1207/s15374424jccp3502_1.

Shochet, I. M., Homel, R., Cockshaw, W., & Montgomery, D. (2008). How do school connectedness and attachment to parents interrelate in predicting adolescent depressive symptoms? *Journal of Clinical Child and Adolescent Psychology*, 37, 676–681. doi:10.1080/15374410802148053.

Shochet, I. M., Saggers, B. R., Carrington, S. B., Orr, J. A., Wurfl, A. M., Duncan, B., & Smith, C. L. (2016). The Cooperative Research Centre for Living with Autism (Autism CRC) conceptual model to promote mental health for adolescents with ASD. *Clinical Child and Family Psychology Review*, 19(2), 94–116.

Shochet, I. M., & Smith, C. L. (2012). Enhancing school connectedness to prevent violence and promote wellbeing. In S. R. Jimerson, A. B. Nickerson, M. J. Mayer & M. J. Furlong (Eds.), *Handbook of school violence and school safety: International research and practice* (pp. 475–486). London: Routledge.

United Nations. (1989). *Convention on the rights of the child*. Geneva: United Nations.

You, S., Furlong, M. J., Felix, E., Sharkey, J. D., Green, J. G., & Tanigawa, D. (2008). Relations among school connectedness, hope, life satisfaction, and bully victimization. *Psychology in the Schools*, 45, 446–460.

PART 3

Enhancing teaching and the learning experience in the classroom

Impact on educational practice for students on the autism spectrum

My Autism Strengths (by Christopher Chan, aged 18 years)

'As an autistic person, I am visual and artistic with exceptional memory. I am able to focus on any task of my choice. I find it hard to lie (I am truthful) and I am happy to lead a simple (not complex) lifestyle.'

4

INCLUSIVE TEACHING FOR STUDENTS ON THE AUTISM SPECTRUM

Amanda Webster, Beth Saggers and Suzanne Carrington

This is the first chapter in Part 3 that focuses on enhancing teaching and the learning experience in classrooms. Teachers require the knowledge, skills, and confidence to effectively teach the diversity of students in their classrooms; a belief that all students can be successful if supported to do so in their own ways; the skill of using inclusive pedagogies and practices that emphasise strengths and build on interests; and support from school leaders. This chapter provides an overview of the current research on the factors and practices that enable teachers to address both the unique needs of students on the autism spectrum and the needs of students with other diverse needs in today's inclusive classrooms and curriculum. School leaders, teachers, and specialists who collaborate to support an inclusive approach for all students will find this chapter has information about quality and evidence-based and evidence-informed practice that can be implemented in a range of school settings. This chapter provides a broad introduction to the following chapters that have more detailed information about strategies and models of practice for teachers.

The move to an inclusive model of practice for students on the autism spectrum can be viewed by educators as presenting both challenges and opportunities. While some teachers may view inclusive practice as additional strategies they must learn to support specific students, others will embrace the opportunity to transform their practice for all students. An inclusive approach to education requires educators to be prepared to teach all students in their classroom and to demonstrate a positive attitude, knowledge, and skills in inclusive practice. In turn, educators are supported by a context in which education systems, researchers, school leaders, and teachers work together to transform policy and practice.

Inclusion in practice

A substantial body of evidence demonstrates that an inclusive approach to education results in more positive social, academic, and post-school outcomes for students with disability and benefits all students (Hehir et al., 2016; Szumski, Smogorzewska, & Karwowski, 2017). Although inclusion and inclusive philosophy are represented in policies guiding education communities and systems, there is often a knowledge-to-practice gap cited between the ideas represented in policy and the practices in schools, particularly for students on the autism spectrum (Segall & Campbell, 2012). In contrast, inclusive practices are those actions which embody the belief of a particular system or school and are used by the system or school to support the needs of all students in their care. Researchers note that often the practices enacted in schools are in contradiction with inclusive education policies and vision statements (Anderson & Boyle, 2015; Makoelle, 2014a). Transforming these practices requires schools to take a critical approach to the ways that they support successful learning

> ... an inclusive approach to education results in more positive social, academic, and post-school outcomes for students with disability and benefits all students

and engagement including creating student-centred pedagogy, which demonstrates a value on learner diversity and high expectations for all learners.

According to Child Australia (2017), pedagogy is 'an encompassing term concerned with what a teacher does to influence learning in others' (p. 1). Quality pedagogies help educators to improve outcomes for all learners. Inclusive pedagogies are those instructional practices and strategies implemented by educators to create a supportive learning environment in which all students can successfully participate, engage, learn, and achieve (Makoelle, 2014b). This means that teaching and learning processes must be flexible and utilise a range of options rather than a one-size-fits-all approach aimed at the perceived 'typical' student (Saggers et al., 2018).

Inclusive pedagogy emphasises the interaction between learner and teacher and views students as active constructors rather than passive recipients of learning. This type of approach supports the learning of all students, including those on the autism spectrum, and encompasses the teaching methods, curriculum, and beliefs that facilitate students' participation in learning. Rather than merely adapting their practice, teachers must change their teaching pedagogies to incorporate more inclusive ways of working. More importantly, if teachers are to enhance the learning of all students, they must first understand how their students learn.

Perspectives of individuals on the autism spectrum

Listening to student voices (Makoelle, 2014a) is essential to an inclusive approach to pedagogy. Individuals on the autism spectrum have identified practices and strategies that support them in inclusive school settings (e.g., Ashby & Causton-Theoharis, 2009; Carrington et al., 2017; Mayton, 2005; Saggers, 2015; Sciutto, Richwine, Mentrikoski, & Niedzwiecki, 2012). These include incorporating and building on students' interests, providing them with choice and responsibility, providing a sense of safety from stressors, and adding structure.

> Underlying all of these strategies and pedagogies is the presumption of competence.

Underlying all of these strategies and pedagogies is the presumption of competence. This is particularly important for individuals who may utilise alternative forms of communication (Biklen & Burke, 2006) and who often have not been provided with equal opportunities to engage in curriculum.

In addition to helpful strategies, individuals on the autism spectrum have reflected on the particular challenges they experience in school settings, noting difficulties with managing stress, anxiety, and sensory demands (Saggers, 2015), discerning hidden expectations, and coping with assessments (Humphrey & Lewis, 2008). Dealing with bullying is another commonly reported issue (Humphrey & Symes, 2010), while social support and friendships with peers are linked to more positive experiences of inclusion. As a result, students on the autism spectrum emphasise their need for support to connect and form relationships with others in their environment (Humphrey & Lewis, 2008). Moreover, Australian students on the autism spectrum recently highlighted their needs in social emotional learning, self-regulation, executive functioning, sensory, behavioural, and communication domains (Saggers et al., 2018). Other needs included handwriting and support to organise time and manage steps to complete tasks. These findings emphasise that inclusive pedagogies need to go beyond support for academic needs but also encompass instruction and practices that support a broader range of social and personal management skills.

Influences and challenges

School leaders' and teachers' implementation of inclusive pedagogies is greatly influenced by: the attitudes and beliefs that they have about students with diverse needs including those on the autism spectrum; the knowledge and experience they have of pedagogies and practices that support these students' needs; and the education history, skills, networks, and needs demonstrated by the specific students at the school at given points in time.

Leadership

Leaders play a critical role in establishing a culture and context to support inclusive pedagogies and practice (Bays & Crockett, 2007). Creating inclusive school cultures requires an ethical approach to leadership (Ehrich & Carrington, 2018), which is underpinned by an ethic of care, justice, and critique (Starratt, 2012). Ethical leadership also involves an ethic of community (Ehrich & Carrington, 2018). This requires school leaders to listen to students' and parents' voices and ensure there is time and space for school communities to work together for long-term commitment and change.

> *Leaders play a critical role in establishing a culture and context to support inclusive pedagogies and practice*

Leadership for inclusive practice includes leaders working at different levels. At the systems level, leaders generate supportive policies and system-level priorities. School leaders work with the school community to create a unified vision, establish a sense of coherence among multiple priorities, and develop supportive structures and supports for staff to implement quality pedagogies and practices (Webster, 2018). To enact inclusive practice, school leaders must help their staff to explore their beliefs and attitudes and create a shared vision that clearly communicates to all community members a presumption of competence of all students including those on the autism spectrum. In addition, principals need to establish a system of shared leadership and responsibility for students on the autism spectrum; play an active role in professional learning to enhance knowledge of effective pedagogies; lead staff in enacting inclusive and specialised curriculum and practice to support learning across a range of areas; manipulate and create resources and structures to establish conditions for learning; and facilitate meaningful collaborations to draw upon expertise of families and professionals supporting students on the autism spectrum (Webster, 2016). The degree to which school leaders are able to implement these actions, however, is influenced by a number of factors which include:

- The principal's belief that students on the autism spectrum can, and should, successfully participate and achieve in mainstream school curriculum and environments (see Horrocks, White, & Roberts, 2008).
- The principal's attitude towards inclusion, as leaders with more positive attitudes are more likely to create structures and supports to facilitate inclusive pedagogies across the school.
- Engagement with other school leaders around instruction for students with diverse needs. These collaborations can directly influence a principal's capacity to lead inclusive practice by supplementing their personal knowledge of effective practices for students with specific needs such as those on the autism spectrum. For example, partnerships between principals and special education leaders can greatly impact the degree to which a school is able to implement a school-wide approach to inclusive practice for students on the autism spectrum (Webster & Roberts, 2020).

Beliefs and attitudes of teachers

Teachers' attitudes towards students on the autism spectrum and their self-efficacy to support these students also influence their ability to implement inclusive pedagogies. Rouse (2010) suggests that implementation of inclusive practice entails more than developing knowledge and skills but requires educators to challenge their assumptions about difference and learning so they can transform their practice for all students. In essence, inclusive practice for students on the autism spectrum centres on teachers' 'knowing, doing and believing' (Rouse, 2010, p. 49). However, Buehl and Beck (2015) offer that a teacher's belief and knowledge may not always align with their practice, highlighting a common knowledge-to-practice gap as educators fail to translate their knowledge of inclusive policy into daily practice for students with diverse needs. Factors which may prevent teachers from translating their knowledge into practice include: teacher's experience, perception of support from school leaders, perceived alignment or conflict with other school priorities and pedagogies, and confidence that they have the knowledge and skills to implement practice and support the needs of students on the spectrum within the overall demands of the class. Over time, the combination of these factors contributes to teachers' self-efficacy to implement inclusive pedagogies to support students on the autism spectrum.

Elements of inclusive practice

In order to enact inclusive practices, it is important to reflect on critical elements that form the basis of inclusive practice, which include:

- Students with and without identified needs are able to access and benefit from the expertise and input of both general and special educators.
- Teachers employ a student-centred approach in which teachers value each student's individual strengths, needs, and accomplishments.
- Schedules and programs cater for the full range of students' needs and no child is educated in ways that disrupt their sense of belonging and peer interactions.
- All students are met with high expectations and have the opportunity to engage with high-quality curriculum, which is used flexibly and individualised to meet the needs of particular students.
- A team approach is used in which educators, support staff, parents, and community services work collaboratively to support student learning.

- The classroom climate fosters social emotional learning, acceptance of diversity, and peer relationships.
(Causton & Theoharis, 2014, pp. 34–35)

McLeskey, Waldron, Spooner, and Algozzine (2014, pp. 4–5) suggest six additional elements of inclusive practice in schools:

- Schools provide comprehensive and ongoing support to students' needs.
- Educators and professionals work collaboratively to provide high-quality instruction and support.
- Students receive their education in natural settings and are supported by effective evidence-based education practice.
- Students have the opportunity to learn together.
- Students are valued members of all classrooms.
- Students are provided with individualised support as needed to meet group and individual outcomes.

These elements demonstrate that inclusive practice challenges teachers to use pedagogies and practices that enable students on the autism spectrum to fully participate and achieve in class curriculum and interactions, and supports their individual needs for skill development (Ravet, 2011). Currently, research on general educators' use of inclusive pedagogies is limited. However, a deeper analysis of the broad knowledge base in this area suggests that inclusive practice for students on the autism spectrum involves three key pedagogies:

1. Utilising evidence-informed or evidence-based practice.
2. Providing multi-tiered systems of support.
3. Engaging in student-centred practice.

Utilising evidence-informed or evidence-based practice

One key pedagogy for schools is that they utilise evidence-based practice to support students on the spectrum. However, a current dilemma for educators is that most research on evidence-based practices for individuals on the autism spectrum has been conducted in clinical or segregated settings, and the effectiveness of many practices have not yet been tested in multiple studies. As a result, a number of practices currently have only a developing or emerging evidence base to support them. Some researchers (Costley, Clark, & Bruck, 2014) have responded to this dilemma by suggesting that use of 'evidence-informed practice' is more appropriate in natural settings such as inclusive schools. Using evidence-informed practice, teachers select the practices with the best evidence that are the best fit given the individual's needs, the knowledge and skills of implementers, and the resources and other programs in the greater environment.

Providing multi-tiered systems of support

Schools must be able to utilise practices and supports at multiple levels (Roberts & Webster, 2020). The pedagogy of multi-tiered systems of support (MTSS) provides a framework for school leaders and teachers to utilise data to implement a system of scientifically based practices at class, group, and individual levels (Magyar & Pandolfi, 2012). The central principle of MTSS is that providing high-quality practices at the whole-of-class (Tier 1) level will support the needs of the majority of students in the school including those on the autism spectrum. This includes pro-actively planning and utilising instructional practices that align with the principles of Universal Design for Learning (UDL) and provide flexibility for students on the autism spectrum to build on their strengths by engaging in learning and performing in multiple ways. Tier 1 practice also necessitates the provision of instruction in areas underpinning learning such as social skills and positive behaviour support. These strategies need to be integrated with academic learning rather than implemented as additional learning. This has three benefits:

1. Feasibility within busy school programs.
2. Connecting students' learning in other areas with academic performance.
3. Providing all students with access to a range of strategies and support (Saggers et al., 2019).

Students who are not making progress when provided with Tier 1 strategies may need to access more systematic supports. Tier 2 strategies provide groups with short bursts of explicit and specialised instruction with the aim that this will address particular issues that are preventing students from progressing (Magyar & Pandolfi, 2012). Some students will require more intensive ongoing instruction at the individual (Tier 3) level. However, in MTSS, students who receive more individualised instruction would also be engaged in Tier 1 and possibly Tier 2 instruction. In other words, Tier 3 practices are used to supplement rather than as an alternative to Tier 1 instruction. This means that Tier 2 and 3 strategies are always addressing specific and measurable targets that will eliminate barriers preventing students from getting the full benefit of Tier 1 sup-ports. More importantly, the skills learned in these more intensive environments are always con-nected to the broader program so that students have many opportunities to practice and receive feedback and reinforcement for utilising these skills in class contexts. For example, students may lack a functional means of communicating and would spend some time receiving Tier 3 func-tional communication training. This would be provided in short bursts and would be followed with specific opportunities for the student to practice the skill in the classroom.

The use of data is critical to facilitating decision-making about the need for Tier 2 and 3 prac-tices. Teachers must establish clearly defined learning objectives for the class and individual stu-dents and must collect data to determine if the practices used are effectively supporting students to achieve these objectives. If more than 10–15% of students are not making adequate progress, then Tier 1 supports need to be adjusted (Magyar & Pandolfi, 2012; Roberts & Webster, 2020). Examples of practices that may comprise a multi-tiered system of supports for students on the autism spectrum are provided in Table 4.1.

Engaging in student-centred practice

Central to inclusive practice is a focus on student learning, rather than delivery of content (Carrington & Elkins, 2002). Teachers who utilise student-centred practices presume the com-petence of students on the autism spectrum and recognise the importance of allowing them to direct their own learning. This means clearly communicating learning objectives and expecta-tions, allowing students to utilise their interests and skills, and providing them with opportunities to exercise choice, goal setting, action planning, and reflection. In a student-centred class, teachers

> *Teachers who utilise student-centred practices presume the competence of students on the autism spectrum and recognise the importance of allowing them to direct their own learning.*

TABLE 4.1 MTSS for Students on the Autism Spectrum

Tier	Practices
Tier 1	Classroom instruction in social and communication skills using modelling, practice, and natural settings. Visual schedules and supports. Communicate clear learning objectives and expectations for behaviours. Students identify individual objectives. Enable students to build on interests and strengths by providing multiple ways to engage, learn, and demonstrate knowledge (UDL). Provide resources and instruction to promote self-regulation of sensory demands and self-management of tasks.
Tier 2	Targeted resources and instruction in academic and social emotional skills. Special interest groups. Targeted modelling and instruction on playground rules and behaviours.
Tier 3	Functional behaviour assessments and individualised behaviour plans. Functional communication training. Individual curriculum and learning plans. Explicit instruction of academic skills.

Source: Magyar and Pandolfi (2012); Roberts and Webster (2020)

recognise that supporting learning entails providing explicit instruction and learning opportunities to develop skills that support self-determination (Bennett, Webster, Goodall, & Rowland, 2018). For students on the autism spectrum, this also means providing instruction and activities that promote development of skills in need areas associated with autism (e.g., social communication, emotional regulation, executive functioning) and build on strengths of their learning.

Enacting inclusive practice

Mobilising and enacting inclusive practice is fundamental to successful inclusion of students with a number of needs. There are a number of chapters in this book that will support the mobilising and enacting of inclusive practices. For example, Chapter 3 describes practical examples about how to implement a whole-school approach to school connectedness; Chapter 5 reports on models of practice for teachers; Chapter 6 presents ways of using structured teaching strategies; and Chapter 7 provides practical ideas to improve the acoustics in classroom environments.

In the Autism CRC *Australian Autism Educational Needs Analysis*, educators, parents, and specialist staff identified a number of inclusive practices that were commonly implemented to support students on the autism spectrum at a school-wide, classroom, and individual level (Saggers et al., 2018). At a whole-school level, support was centred on building capacity of staff, students, and the school community to build an inclusive culture within the school. Provision of education and training revolved around two key areas:

- Education and training of staff and students.
- Increasing awareness, experience, and expertise across whole school communities.

In addition, whole-school practices were implemented to develop school policy, procedures, and programming to facilitate inclusive practice in classrooms and across the school (Saggers et al., 2018).

Participants also identified a range of classroom-based inclusive practices they utilised to support students on the autism spectrum. These practices focused on providing adjustments to classroom-based learning and the strategic use of classroom-based resources (Saggers et al., 2018). Classroom-based practices included provisions of adjustments to support:

- Academic learning (e.g., modified curriculum and assessment, small group learning).
- Organisation (e.g., extra time and instructions, scaffolding).
- Specific needs of students on the autism spectrum, including:
  o Social emotional adjustments (e.g., additional breaks, playground support).
  o Communication (additional receptive and expressive language support).
  o Sensory (e.g., environmental adjustments, sensory breaks, reduced exposure to stimuli).
  o Behavioural (e.g., rewards, positive behaviour support).

Classroom-based resources used to enact inclusive practices included:

- Human resources (e.g., parent involvement, allied health, teacher aide, or 1:1 support).
- Program resources (e.g., social programs, mental health, resilience, wellbeing).
- Material resources (e.g., visuals, social stories, individual learning plans, sensory tools, physical spaces).
- Technological resources (e.g., laptop, tablet, smartboard).

As mentioned earlier in this chapter, one approach that enables teachers to support a range of student needs is Universal Design for Learning (UDL). UDL is a framework which supports teachers to enact inclusive practice, proactively cater for students with a range of needs, and engage in student-centred practice. UDL is based on three principles: i) provide multiple means of engagement; ii) provide multiple means of representation; and iii) provide multiple means of action and expression (CAST, 2020; Rose, Gravel, & Gordon, 2014). As part of the Autism CRC *Australian Autism Educational Needs Analysis* (Saggers et al., 2018), interview data were also analysed to determine if teachers used strategies that aligned with the principles and guidelines of UDL (Carrington, Saggers, Webster, Harper-Hill, & Nickerson, 2020). Results indicated that teachers used pedagogies and practices that exemplified the principles of UDL to support engagement and learning of students on the autism spectrum. Table 4.2 provides information on the pedagogies used by teachers and provides examples of specific practices that illustrate these pedagogies.

Conclusion

A key element of any school program is the use of collaborative and data-based decision-making processes. These provide the foundation for determining how quality teaching and learning practices can be implemented across the school and how these can be used to support students on the autism spectrum. Rather than viewing support for students on the autism spectrum as an additional burden on their already overpacked schedule, schools should embrace this as an opportunity for improving practice for everyone. Researchers have also demonstrated clear alignment between inclusive practice and effective practice for students on the autism spectrum. Thus, implementing inclusive teaching for students on the autism spectrum is about improving practice and outcomes for all students. As a result, some key take-home messages are that inclusive pedagogy and practice is supported by:

- Leadership teams who play a critical role in establishing a culture and context to support inclusive practices.
- Three key pedagogies: i) utilising evidence-informed or evidence-based practice; ii) providing multi-tiered systems of support; and iii) engaging in student-centred practice, can support inclusive practices.

TABLE 4.2 Teaching Strategies Across Principles of UDL

Principles	Pedagogies	Specific practices
Provide multiple means of engagement	Appealing to students' interests/strengths	Provide opportunities to choose texts or write about special interests. Provide structured teaching activities to communicate expectations and enable to learn at own rate.
	Meeting sensory needs	Provide sensory breaks. Providing headphones to reduce noise.
	Promoting self-regulation	Look for early signs of distress and prompt to take a break/walk. Provide fidget toys. Allow to use different options for sitting/standing/moving during or between tasks.
Provide multiple means of representation	Visual systems	Establish workstations. Highlight salient information physically and verbally. Use visual schedules.
	Alternative approaches to teaching	Model, practice, and check use of skills in natural settings. Utilise explicit instruction at class and individual level. Use concrete materials. Engage in social and project tasks to promote experiential learning. Look for opportunities to explicitly teach social communication skills in regular routines/contexts.
	Scaffolding activities	Provide supplementary materials. Have information available prior to activity. Provide information about what to do, when to do it, and how to do it.
	Teacher behaviour and language	Be aware of use of language. Adjust language to communicate key points. Monitor amount of language. Selectively use words.
Provide multiple means of action and expression	Providing alternative approaches to assessment	Provide extra time to complete and/or prepare. Adjust and modify assessments to meet same learning criteria.
	Support for executive function	Break down or space task into smaller components. Provide visual checklist.
	Accepting and facilitating alternative means of communication	Give students cards to signal when distressed or need a break. Use of Picture Exchange Communication System (PECs). Use social stories. Use visual schedules.

Source: Adapted from Carrington et al. (2020)

- Teaching approaches that go beyond meeting academic needs, but also encompass instruction and practices that support a broader range of social and personal management skills.
- A focus on students' learning rather than delivery of content.

References

Anderson, J., & Boyle, C. (2015). Inclusive education in Australia: Rhetoric, reality and the road ahead. *Support for Learning*, 30(1), 4–22. doi:10.1111/1467-9604.12074.

Ashby, C. E., & Causton-Theoharis, J. N. (2009). Disqualified in the human race: A close reading of the autobiographies of individuals identified as autistic. *International Journal of Inclusive Education*, 13(5), 501–516. doi:10.1080/13603110801886673.

Bays, D. A., & Crockett, J. B. (2007). Investigating instructional leadership for special education. *Exceptionality: A Special Education Journal*, 15, 143–161. doi:10.1080/09362830701503495.

Bennett, M., Webster, A. A., Goodall, E., & Rowland, S. (2018). *Life on the autism spectrum: Translating myths and misconceptions into positive futures*. Singapore: Springer.

Biklen, D., & Burke, J. (2006). Presuming competence. *Excellence in Education*, 39, 166–175.

Buehl, M. M., & Beck, J. S. (2015). The relationship between teachers' beliefs and teachers' practices. In H. Fives & M. Gregoire Gill (Eds.), *International handbook of research on teachers' beliefs* (pp. 66–84). New York, NY: Routledge.

Carrington, S., Campbell, M., Saggers, B., Ashburner, J., Vicig, F., Dillon-Wallace, J., & Hwang, Y.-S. (2017). Recommendations of school students with autism spectrum disorder and their parents in regard to bullying and cyberbullying prevention and intervention. *International Journal of Inclusive Education*, 21(10), 1045–1064. doi:10.1080/13603116.2017.1331381.

Carrington, S., & Elkins, J. (2002). Comparison of a traditional and an inclusive secondary school culture. *International Journal of Inclusive Education*, 6(1), 1–16. doi:10.1080/13603110110061754.

Carrington, S., Saggers, B., Webster, A., Harper-Hill, K., & Nickerson, J. (2020). What Universal Design for Learning principles, guidelines, and checkpoints are evident in educators' descriptions of their practice when supporting students on the autism spectrum? *International Journal of Educational Research*. doi:10.1016/j.ijer.2020.101583.

CAST. (2020). *Universal design for learning*. Boston, MA: CAST. Retrieved from http://www.cast.org/.

Causton, J., & Theoharis, G. (2014). How do schools become effective and inclusive? In J. McLeskey, N. L. Waldron, F. Spooner, & B. Algozzine (Eds.), *Handbook of effective inclusive schools: Research and practice* (pp. 30–42). London: Routledge.

Child Australia. (2017). *What is pedagogy? How does it influence our practice?* Retrieved from https://childaustralia.org.au/wp-content/uploads/2017/02/CA-Statement-Pedagogy.pdf.

Costley, D., Clark, T., & Bruck, S. (2014). The Autism Spectrum Disorder Evaluative Education Model: A school-based method of assessing and selecting interventions for classroom use. *SAGE Open*, 4(4). doi:10.1177/2158244014556640.

Ehrich, L. C., & Carrington, S. (2018). Making sense of ethical leadership. In J. Harris, S. Carrington, M. Ainscow, B. Comber, L. C. Ehrich, V. Klenowski, J. Smeed, & N. Spina, *Promoting equity in schools: Collaboration, inquiry and ethical leadership* (pp. 121–141). Oxon: Routledge.

Hehir, T., Grindal, T., Freeman, B., Lamoreau, R., Borquaye, Y., & Burke, S. (2016). *A summary of the evidence on inclusive education*. Retrieved from https://alana.org.br/wp-content/uploads/2016/12/A_Summary_of_the_evidence_on_inclusive_education.pdf.

Horrocks, J. L., White, G., & Roberts, L. (2008). Principals' attitudes regarding inclusion of children with autism in Pennsylvania public schools. *Journal of Autism and Developmental Disorders*, 38, 1462–1473. doi:10.1007/s10803-007-0522-x.

Humphrey, N., & Lewis, S. (2008). "Make me normal": The views and experiences of pupils on the autistic spectrum in mainstream secondary schools. *Autism*, 12(1), 23–46. doi:10.1177/1362361307085267.

Humphrey, N., & Symes, W. (2010). Perceptions of social support and experience of bullying among pupils with autistic spectrum disorders in mainstream secondary schools. *European Journal of Special Needs Education*, 25(1), 77–91. doi:10.1080/08856250903450855.

Magyar, C. I., & Pandolfi, V. (2012). Considerations for establishing a multi-tiered problem-solving model for students with autism spectrum disorders and comorbid emotional-behavioral disorders. *Psychology in the Schools*, 49(10), 975–987. doi:10.1002/pits.21645.

Makoelle, T. M. (2014a). Inclusive education: Are we there? Some global challenges, contradictions and anomalies. *Journal of Sociology and Social Anthropology*, 5(3), 303–309.

Makoelle, T. M. (2014b). Pedagogy of inclusion: A quest for inclusive teaching and learning. *Mediterranean Journal of Social Sciences*, 5(20), 1259–1267. doi:10.5901/mjss.2014.v5n20p1259.

Mayton, M. R. (2005). The quality of life of a child with Asperger's disorder in a general education setting: A pilot case study. *International Journal of Special Education*, 20(2), 85–101.

McLeskey, J., Waldron, N. L., Spooner, F., & Algozzine, B. (2014). What are effective inclusive schools and why are they important? In J. McLeskey, N. L. Waldron, F. Spooner, & B. Algozzine (Eds.), *Handbook of effective inclusive schools: Research and practice* (pp. 3–16). London: Routledge.

Ravet, J. (2011). Inclusive/exclusive? Contradictory perspectives on autism and inclusion: The case for an integrative position. *International Journal of Inclusive Education*, 15(6), 667–682. doi:10.1080/13603110903294347.

Roberts, J., & Webster, A. (2020). Including students with autism in schools: A whole school approach to improve outcomes for students with autism. *International Journal of Inclusive Education*, 1–18. doi:10.1080/13603116.2020.1712622.

Rose, D. H., Gravel, J. W., & Gordon, D. (2014). Universal design for learning. In L. Florian (Ed.), *SAGE handbook of special education* (2nd ed., pp. 475–491). London: SAGE.

Rouse, M. (2010). Reforming initial teacher education: A necessary but not sufficient condition for developing inclusive practice. In C. Forlin (Ed.), *Teacher education for inclusion: Changing paradigms and innovative approaches* (pp. 47–55). London: Routledge.

Saggers, B. (2015). Student perceptions: Improving the educational experiences of high school students on the autism spectrum. *Improving Schools*, 18(1), 35–45. doi:10.1177/1365480214566213.

Saggers, B., Klug, D., Harper-Hill, K., Ashburner, J., Costley, D., Clark, T., … Carrington, S. (2018). *Australian autism educational needs analysis: What are the needs of schools, parents and students on the autism spectrum?* Brisbane: Cooperative Research Centre for Living with Autism (Autism CRC).

Saggers, B., Tones, M., Dunne, J., Trembath, D., Bruck, S., Webster, A., … Wang, S. (2019). Promoting a collective voice from parents, educators and allied health professionals on the educational needs of students on the autism spectrum. *Journal of Autism and Developmental Disorders*, 49(9), 3845–3865. doi:10.1007/s10803-019-04097-8.

Sciutto, M., Richwine, S., Mentrikoski, J., & Niedzwiecki, K. (2012). A qualitative analysis of the school experiences of students with Asperger syndrome. *Focus on Autism and Other Developmental Disabilities*, 27, 177–188. doi:10.1177/1088357612450511.

Segall, M. J., & Campbell, J. M. (2012). Factors relating to education professionals' classroom practices for the inclusion of students with autism spectrum disorders. *Research in Autism Spectrum Disorders*, 6(3), 1156–1167. doi:10.1016/j.rasd.2012.02.007.

Starratt, R. (2012). *Cultivating an ethical school*. New York, NY: Routledge.

Szumski, G., Smogorzewska, J., & Karwowski, M. (2017). Academic achievement of students without special educational needs in inclusive classrooms: A meta-analysis. *Educational Research Review*, 21, 33–54. doi:10.1016/j.edurev.2017.02.004.

Webster, A. A. (2016). Utilising a leadership blueprint to build capacity of schools to achieve outcomes for students with autism spectrum disorder. In G. Johnson & N. Dempster (Eds.), *Leadership for learning and effective change* (pp. 109–128). Melbourne: Springer.

Webster, A. A. (2018). Translating theory to practice for principals working within inclusive education policy. In K. Trimmer, R. Dixon, & Y. Findlay (Eds.), *The Palgrave handbook of education law for schools* (pp. 257–280). Melbourne: Palgrave Macmillan.

Webster, A. A., & Roberts, J. (2020). Implementing the school-wide autism competency model to improve outcomes for students on the autism spectrum: A multiple case study of three schools. *International Journal of Inclusive Education*, 1–19. doi:10.1080/13603116.2020.1735540.

5

MODELS OF PRACTICE FOR TEACHERS OF STUDENTS ON THE AUTISM SPECTRUM

Wendi Beamish, Trevor Clark, Susan Bruck, Annalise Taylor, Ainslie Robinson, Emma Gallagher, Vicki Gibbs and Keely Harper-Hill

A Model of Practice (MoP) is a universally designed, evidence-informed set of whole-class strategies. Recognising that Australian teachers in mainstream schools are required to meet the complex and diverse educational needs of all students, this chapter focuses on a collaborative design effort between researchers and teachers to develop two MoPs. The MoPs described in this chapter were developed to support teachers to choose the most appropriate practices for fostering the inclusion of students on the autism spectrum in the early years and the middle years of schooling. The cyclical nature of the design process resulted in a resource that was shaped by the continual input of Australian teachers. Involving teachers in such a pivotal way led to the MoPs being both respectful to teachers and valid for use in inclusive mainstream classrooms. Teachers indicated that the MoPs and the practices that they comprised had applicability across most of the students in their classrooms. The results also confirmed that professional learning opportunities which actively engage teachers in collaborative discussions with other educators about real-life complex classroom scenarios are more likely to change classroom practice. These MoPs will guide teacher decision-making and practice to develop autism-friendly classrooms, with curriculum and social emotional adjustments, and behavioural supports which are well suited and responsive to the inclusive classroom.

Previously, many Australian students on the autism spectrum were educated in mainstream primary and secondary schools (Keane, Aldridge, Costley, & Clark, 2012). However, a trend towards attendance in more segregated settings is emerging (Australian Institute of Health and Welfare, 2017; deBruin, 2019). In 2018, there were 101,900 students on the spectrum aged 5–20 years who were enrolled in schools or further education (Australian Bureau of Statistics [ABS], 2019), *all* of whom have the potential to contribute in ways which are distinctive, original, and positive. Nevertheless, many of these students encounter difficulties with learning (9.3%), communication (10.8%), fitting in socially (9.9%), and 9.4% require special access and tuition or other forms of support (22.9%) (ABS, 2019). It is critically important that these needs are addressed as the post-school outcomes for these students are frequently poor and include inadequate employment with low social and quality of life outcomes (Autism Spectrum Australia, 2013a; Baldwin, Costley, & Warren, 2014; Howlin, Goode, Hutton, & Rutter, 2004). Building the capacity of Australian teachers to meet the educational needs of students on the spectrum through appropriate autism pedagogy is an urgent priority.

Australian teachers in mainstream schools are required to meet the complex and diverse educational needs of all students, including those on the spectrum. Inclusive education aims to provide equitable opportunities through the introduction of supports and modifications to the design of lessons and classrooms (Australian Curriculum Assessment and Reporting Authority [ACARA], 2019). Successful participation in inclusive settings for some students requires appropriately tailored and frequently high levels of support for students on the autism spectrum (Pellicano, Dinsmore, & Charman, 2014). The implementation of appropriate autism pedagogy requires teachers to have high levels of efficacy, believing that they have the knowledge and the skills to both recognise and respond to student needs. However, research both in Australia and internationally suggests that teachers are unsure how to effectively support students on the spectrum (e.g., Simpson, Adams, Alston-Knox, Heussler, & Keen, 2019; Syriopoulou-Delli, Polychronopoulou, Kolaitis, & Antoniou, 2019).

> *Australian teachers in mainstream schools are required to meet the complex and diverse educational needs of all students, including those on the spectrum*

In part, the complexity of needs for students on the spectrum arises from varying and often extreme degrees of anxiety (Adams, Simpson, & Keen, 2020), pervasive difficulties with peer relationships (Autism Spectrum Australia, 2013a, 2013b; Campbell et al., 2017; Kloosterman, Kelley, Craig, Parker, & Javier, 2013), and different patterns of sensory processing (Howe & Stagg, 2016) these students may experience. Encouragingly, research indicates that appropriate classroom adjustments (e.g., sensory adjustments) can meet the needs of students and enable participation in a diverse range of activities (Charney et al., 2017) and that when adequate social and behaviour support are available, lower rates of bullying are reported (Campbell et al., 2017; Carrington et al., 2017).

Bullying, isolation, and being misunderstood can lead to breakdowns in home–school relationships and may prompt parents to educate their children at home. Many students and parents consider that educators are not sufficiently informed about autism and teaching students on the spectrum (Autism Spectrum Australia, 2013b; Saggers et al., 2018). Parents report that their children on the spectrum need additional support in the classroom (ABS, 2019; Autism Spectrum Australia, 2013b), and despite the information and documentation provided to the school (e.g., diagnostic reports), the majority of students surveyed believe their educational needs are not being met (Autism Spectrum Australia, 2013b). Despite this, more than a third of participating students report satisfaction with some aspects of learning and studying, such as having access to subject matter of interest (Autism Spectrum Australia, 2013b).

Consistent with student and parent perspectives, teachers and schools often feel underequipped and ill-prepared to successfully include and support the educational needs of their students on the autism spectrum (Busby, Ingram, Bowron, Oliver, & Lyons, 2012; Saggers et al., 2018; Soto-Chodiman, Pooley, Cohen, & Taylor, 2012). Many teachers describe receiving ad hoc, informal training about teaching students on the spectrum and describe accessing suitable training as problematic, citing a lack of time to attend training, inadequate funding by schools, and a lack of relevant programs to meet the needs of the teachers (Saggers et al., 2018). The nature of the reported training raises questions on the relevancy and sufficiency of adjustments made to meet the needs of the students on the spectrum (Clark, Adams, Roberts, & Westerveld, 2020). Importantly, teachers want autism-specific professional development that will alleviate a lack of relevant resources (Saggers et al., 2018).

Translation of research into the classroom

The challenges faced by students on the autism spectrum, their teachers, and families are compounded by the limited translation of autism research into evidence-informed educational programs into classrooms (Costley, Clark, & Bruck, 2014). These circumstances have left the education community with a shortage of rigourously assessed programs and practices, which is compounded by a time lag between research findings and translation into practice, estimated to be 17 years (Morris, Wooding, & Grant, 2011).

Successful translation is frequently elusive because changing teacher practice constitutes far more than imparting new knowledge (Rodriguez, 2012; Teras & Kartoglu, 2017). Professional learning opportunities are more likely to change classroom practice when teachers actively engage in collaborative discussions with other educators about real-life complex classroom scenarios (Teras & Kartoglu, 2017). Further, approaches must be flexible, sensitive, and responsive to teaching styles and the values underpinning these (Alexander, Ayres, & Smith, 2015; Guldberg, 2017; Parsons et al., 2013). Importantly within the Australian context, access to professional learning opportunities is frequently dependent on the geographical location of schools and teachers whereby costs and time associated with large distances can disadvantage remote and rural educators (Saggers et al., 2018). Ultimately, the decision to adopt a new classroom practice is multifactorial, influenced by individual, teacher-centric factors such as self-efficacy (Harper-Hill et al., 2020), school-centric factors such as opportunities to collaborate with colleagues, and resource-centric factors such as flexibility, availability, and evidence base (Alexander et al., 2015; Parsons et al., 2013).

> *Professional learning opportunities are more likely to change classroom practice when teachers actively engage in collaborative discussions with other educators about real-life complex classroom scenarios*

Co-producing a solution with teachers

In the project presented in this chapter, targeted online resources were developed to offer a feasible solution for building teacher capability in autism-specific pedagogy. To develop knowledge and skills for including and teaching students on the spectrum, teachers initially require resources that explain foundational instructional practices and provide clear instructions on how to implement individual practices. Using the analogy put forward in Chapter 1, these resources were to be designed so that they armed 'the carpenters of the education world' with 'actionable, workable, and sustainable practices that successfully address the diverse learning needs of the learners in their care' (p. 11). To this end, these resources aimed to deliver research-supported practices in the form of two Models of Practice (MoP), one for mainstream teachers in the early years (Early Years–MoP) and a corresponding model for middle years teachers (Middle Years–MoP).

To ensure actionable, workable, and sustainable practices, the MoPs would be underpinned by co-production. In its simplest terms, co-production is collaboration between stakeholders in order to solve an identified issue. Historically, the autistic community has rarely been provided with opportunities to contribute to the development and testing of evidence-supported educational practices. As a result, many of the evidence-supported practices may not be respectful of the autistic community. In the current project,

> *Involving stakeholders, particularly autistic people, leads to research outputs and content that is more relevant and respectful for all end-users.*

stakeholders included autistic people, parents/carers of students on the spectrum, classroom teachers, specialist educators, and allied health professionals in all stages of the research process. Involving stakeholders, particularly autistic people, leads to research outputs and content that is more relevant and respectful for all end-users.

Autistic researchers contributed to the MoP research project by identifying appropriate data collection tools, data collection, data analysis, reporting of results, dissemination of findings, and their translation to *inclusionED*,[1] the Autism CRC online information hub for teachers. As research team members, the autistic researchers ensured that consistent positive language about autism was used and they provided positive autistic role models to all participants and stakeholders.

Design and development of the Models of Practice for teachers

What is a Model of Practice?

An MoP provides a framework of research-supported, educational practices to assist teachers to make informed choices about the planning and delivery of high-quality learning experiences for students on the spectrum. Rather than more advanced interventions, each model included core teaching practices and foundational instructional supports in order to build specialised knowledge and understanding in autism education. Table 5.1 shows the Early Years–MoP organisational framework and details the finalised set of 23 practices, and Table 5.2 shows the Middle Years–MoP organisational framework and details the finalised set of 36 practices. All practices in these tables are presented in abbreviated form (this is discussed below).

Model of Practice design features

Prior to undertaking a series of design cycles which are described more fully below, desired design features for the MoPs were carefully considered by the project team. Practices within each MoP were organised into three areas within a matrix structure. For the Early Years–MoP (Table 5.1), *Belonging*, *Being*, and *Becoming*, the defining concepts themed throughout the *Australian Early Years Learning Framework* (EYLF; DEEWR, 2009), were used as organisers for the practices. *Belonging* practices focused on the creation and maintenance of an inclusive and structured

TABLE 5.1 Final Version of the Early Years Model of Practice with Abbreviated Practices

Belonging	*Being*	*Becoming*
Interact with every student	Engage with students	Assess student knowledge
Provide feedback on learning and behaviour	Teach friendship skills	Provide systematic instruction
Actively supervise class	Model emotional literacy	Monitor student progress
Provide an organised classroom	Teach self-regulation	Teach communication skills
Give clear directions	Teach social problem solving	Teach literacy skills
Reinforce classroom rules	Use peer-mediated instruction	Teach self-help skills
Consistently use routines	Conduct an ABC analysis*	
Consistently use schedules	Modify environment to reduce behaviour	
Prepare students for transitions		

* ABC analysis = antecedent–behaviour–consequence analysis

TABLE 5.2 Final Version of the Middle Years Model of Practice with Abbreviated Practices

Rigour	Relevance	Relationships
Instructional sequences	Teaching test preparation skills	Home–school communication
Active supervision	Modifications to intensity, methods, or curriculum	Parent communication – homework
Supporting receptive language	Test adjustments	Home base
Task analysis	Oral assessment adjustments and alternatives	Incidental social coaching and safety
Visual supports	Exemplars	Classroom rules
Organised classroom	Technology-aided instruction	Flexible grouping strategies
Student organisational supports	Adjustments for projects and assignments	Inclusive language and incidental social coaching
Prompting	Authentic assessment	School belonging
Supporting expressive language	Choice making	Reinforcing appropriate behaviour
Visual study guidelines, planners, and timelines	Special interests	Responding to inappropriate behaviour
Visual self-management tools	Self-monitoring	Peer interaction
Visual instructional supports	Sensory needs	
Routines and visual schedules		

classroom environment; *Being* practices focused on the development of student personal and social capabilities; and *Becoming* practices focused on the assessment and delivery of curriculum.

By comparison, the Middle Years–MoP framework (Table 5.2) was organised according to *Rigour, Relevance*, and *Relationships*, three elements of secondary curriculum for adolescents on the spectrum put forward by Test, Smith, and Carter (2014). *Rigour* practices focused on promoting student engagement in well-planned learning activities; *Relevance* practices focused on making the curriculum pertinent by employing teaching, learning, and assessment adjustments and building on students' individual strengths and interests; and *Relationships* practices focused on strengthening positive relations with peers, educators, family members, and the community through the provision of behavioural and social emotional supports.

In order to be readily understood, each practice within the MoPs was to be clearly defined in teacher-friendly language, with key elements of the practice included in the wording (Division for Early Childhood [DEC], 2015). Moreover, to provide consistency across the practices, each practice was written using a standardised format: *Teachers (1) – what (2) – how (3)*. For example, the *Being* practice of *Teach friendship skills* (abbreviated form) was written in its complete form as *Teachers (1) build friendship skills (2) by providing systematic instruction in play and social skills coupled with multiple opportunities for practice (3)*. Similarly, the *Relationships* practice *Inclusive language and incidental social coaching* (abbreviated form) was written as *Teachers (1) model and encourage tolerant and flexible attitudes towards all students (2), consistently using inclusive language and incidental social coaching (3)*.

Further, to increase the likelihood of teachers successfully implementing practices, each practice was accompanied by a practice brief. These two-page guides provided 'information about what the practice is, why it works, and whether there are any pitfalls in its implementation' (Falconer, Finlay, & Fincher, 2011, p. 114) together with a listing of three to five relevant and high-quality online sites and links to the *Australian Professional Standards for Teachers* (Australian Institute for Teaching and School Leadership [AITSL], 2012) that were related to practice use.

How were the Models of Practice developed?

Design-based research methodology (DBR; McKenney & Reeves, 2012), with its multiple cycles of *design–evaluate–redesign*, was used to generate, validate, and trial the two MoPs. Figure 5.1 shows the progressive refinement of each MoP across five cycles of research activity, which yielded the final versions of the Early Years–MoP with 23 practices (Table 5.1) and Middle Years–MoP with 36 practices (Table 5.2). Each of these cycles is described fully below.

- An *Initial Design Cycle* generated the first set of research-supported practices for inclusion in each MoP. The literature was searched to identify a large working set of relevant practices, which were subsequently scrutinised for alignment with the three organisers and for duplication. Practices that did not align with any of the organisers were discarded while the remaining and substantially reduced number of practices were sorted according to the three organisers, then reworded using the language and structure described above.
- The *Content Validation Cycle* evaluated and affirmed the content of every practice within each MoP. Two small groups of experts in autism education (eight in total) used online surveys to rate the relevance of each practice and comment on the importance, feasibility, and wording of that practice. High ratings established the content validity of practices across models except

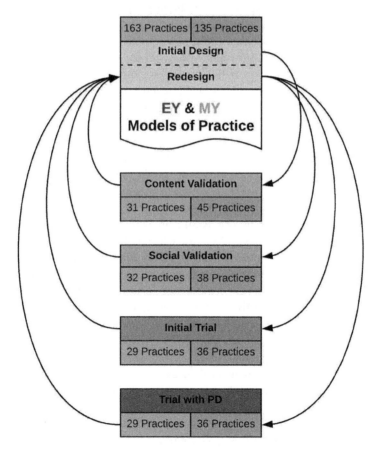

FIGURE 5.1 Iterative cycles of research activity taken to develop the Early Years (EY) and Middle Years (MY) Models of Practice.

for six practices in the Middle Years–MoP, which were discarded from that model. Comments from experts prompted the rewording of several practices in both models, while one multi-dimensional practice in the Early Years–MoP was divided into two distinct practices.

- The *Social Validation Cycle* evaluated and provided proof from teachers that practices within each MoP were valuable and important in educating students on the spectrum. A total of 230 early and middle years teachers from New South Wales, Queensland, and Victoria used online surveys to rate each practice and comment on that practice. High ratings of endorsement established the social validity of practices in both models. Teacher comments led to the rewording of some practices to improve their clarity. Three pairs of practices in the Early Years–MoP were combined and practice briefs amended accordingly. Two practices from the Middle Years–MoP were discarded. At the end of this validation cycle, the Early Years–MoP comprised 29 practices (10 = *Belonging*, 9 = *Being*, 10 = *Becoming*) while the Middle Years–MoP comprised 36 practices (13 = *Rigour*, 12 = *Relevance*, 11 = *Relationships*).

- The *Initial Trial Cycle* tested both models in 'real-world' conditions during the busy end-of-year school term. While schools and teachers were being recruited, two preparatory arrangements were made. First, a project website for the MoPs (including briefs) was constructed. Next, a procedure for providing differentiated levels of professional support from an autism specialist was devised to identify the level of support needed to facilitate future teacher uptake of the MoPs. Application of this procedure meant that recruited schools were assigned to one of three groups: i) teachers received two 2-hour face-to-face sessions with a specialist at their school to assist with practice implementation; ii) teachers received two 2-hour online sessions with a specialist to assist with practice implementation; and iii) teachers received information only from the website or a circulated hyperlinked MoP.

  Collectively, 69 practicing teachers at 32 mainstream primary and secondary schools in metropolitan, regional, and rural areas of New South Wales, Queensland, and Victoria collaborated with the research team to trial the MoP in classrooms with at least one student on the spectrum. These teachers completed a survey and interview, prior to and at the end of the eight-week trial period. The surveys gathered data predominately on: i) use of practices within each model; ii) frequency at which the model (framework and briefs) were accessed during the trial period; and iii) levels of teacher knowledge, confidence, and efficacy. By contrast, interviews were used to give teachers a voice and capture their impressions and experiences with the practice models. Results are reported in the subsections that follow.

- The final cycle, *Trial with PD*, tested MoP use when professional development (PD) activities were provided by an autism specialist, as many teachers in the initial trial indicated that they would have preferred more individualised support to better understand the practice model and to assist with practice implementation. Six teachers, none of whom participated in the previous trial, were recruited. Over a 10- to 15-week period, these teachers engaged in: i) an individualised webinar focused on using the MoPs and identifying three practices to implement in their classroom; ii) a 2-hour face-to-face on-site professional development session; and iii) two 1-hour online individualised professional development sessions. At the end of the trial, they were interviewed about their experience with this hybrid (face-to-face and online) mix of PD activities. Results are reported in the subsections that follow.

For more detailed reporting of i) the cyclical methodological procedures and practice refinement processes undertaken during the practice generation, content validation, and social validation cycles, see Taylor, Beamish, Tucker, Paynter, and Walker (2019); ii) the data collection procedures, measures, and data analysis used for initial trial cycle, see Beamish, Taylor, et al. (2020); and iii) the components and delivery of the hybrid model of professional development used in the final trial, see Bruck, Chandra, Cotter, Clark, and Gibbs (2020).

What did teachers have to say about the Models of Practice?

A series of themes arose from interview and survey data with teachers participating in the trials (see Table 5.3). In essence, these themes spoke to the benefits of teacher involvement in the design process leading to MoPs with practices which were well received and perceived as valuable.

Impressions of the Models of Practice

First impressions on seeing the MoPs spoke to the familiarity of the Early Years organisers and the usefulness of both MoPs to conceptualise what teachers regarded as effective teaching practices:

> I love that it's aligned with the Early Years Learning Framework and those areas of Belonging, Being and Becoming …
>
> (Early Years Teacher)

> I'm familiar with a lot of it. I'm just not quite in the structure, breaking down into rigour relevance and relationships. But a lot of it looks like they're things that I've read about with talking with colleagues and things like that.
>
> (Middle Years Teacher)

Some teachers reported that the MoPs positively reinforced their own practices as well as helped them to identify practices which they needed to develop further. Teachers also identified that the MoP enhanced their understanding of their own practice and provided them with the language to describe their practices that they currently used, knowingly and unknowingly:

> It also reminds me that there was terminology for practices that we do that we didn't know.
>
> (Middle Years Teacher)

TABLE 5.3 Themes Arising from Teacher Responses Prior to and During the Two Trials

	Prior to trial		*Initial trial*	*Final trial*
	First impressions of the MoPs	Experiences with the MoPs	Teacher knowledge, confidence, and efficacy (capability)	Experiences with the hybrid PD model

Themes	• Familiarity
	• Importance of the practices
		• Valuable resource:
		  – the MoP
		  – the practices
		• Beneficial to whole class
		• Usefulness for early career teachers
		• Lack of time
		• Professional support (pros and cons)
			• Feelings of knowledge, confidence, and capability (efficacy)	• Online and face-to-face
				• Need for sufficient time

> I think that I do these things, but I didn't knowingly know that I do these things. If that makes sense?
>
> (Early Years Teacher)

While some teachers valued the practices because they assisted them to personalise their practice in response to individual student needs, others recognised their applicability to many students:

> I thought it sort of comprises everything we want for, not just, I guess, ASD students, but also for any student in a class.
>
> (Early Years Teacher)

Confirming many teachers' initial impressions of the MoPs, the first theme to emerge during the initial trial was that of the MoP as a resource that was valuable to teachers as a tool to support students:

> That it was such a comprehensive collection of strategies that could be used to support students. It has been an excellent reference tool.
>
> (Middle Years Teacher)

Comments also indicated that the three organisers supported their work and professional learning:

> A fantastic toolbox of ideas to use when you need it most. A great professional development exercise that is scaffolded for your personal use through your own goal setting if you do it correctly. A wonderful reflection tool for your own practices.
>
> (Middle Years Teacher)

Teachers reported that they felt they had increased their knowledge, confidence, and capability during the initial trial:

> It's definitely strengthened my own practice, and it's boosted my confidence in catering for the needs of students on the spectrum.
>
> (Early Years Teacher)

For elaborations on key themes and additional examples of teacher viewpoints, see Beamish, Macdonald, et al. (2020), Bruck, Robinson, and Gallagher (2021), Clark et al. (2019), and Macdonald, Beamish, Taylor, Robinson, and Gallagher (2020).

Support for professional development

At the completion of the initial trial, teachers' comments on the different types of supports they received were clear and consistent. While teachers reported favourably on the MoPs as a practice framework, there was a strong wish for some opportunities for person-to-person explanation. Comments included:

> I think the model itself is fantastic but it would be good to have someone come out and explain it to us.
>
> (Early Years Teacher – no professional support; only had access to online material)

Felt a little at sea with some things especially in the beginning an expert would have been helpful to give a big picture or summary of the practices … and how they work together … hopefully we do develop it further next year.

(Middle Years Teacher – no professional support;
only had access to online material)

Those teachers who had received personal explanations during online or face-to-face professional support perceived that this was important for their understanding of the information contained in the practice briefs as well as with regards to the models themselves:

we just unpacked the briefs a lot more … we were quite lost before we had the coach … it was very valuable having her coming out.

(Early Years Teacher – face-to-face professional support)

The practical benefit expressed by those teachers who had received coaching was palpable:

I don't think I've ever had something that I've seen so much practical benefit from to my personal practice in my classroom.

(Early Years Teacher – face-to-face professional support)

While some teachers pointed to the need for more time from coaches:

Not enough expert support time to educate me properly … Time is our shortest commodity but the most valuable foundation for effective practice … as a teacher of a high needs autistic student in an integrated mainstream classroom in rural remote NSW.

(Middle Years Teacher – face-to-face professional support)

At the completion of the final trial which included a hybrid model of professional support, participating teachers in regional and rural locations reported practical advantages to the model adopted:

I think it helps to bridge the distance really. You know being in a regional town we don't have access to that.

(Teacher – hybrid model of professional support)

… she also got a feel for what I was like as a teacher and to guide me. And if that had been done online I just don't think it would have been maybe as clear or helpful.

(Teacher – hybrid model of professional support)

However, not every teacher reported the face-to-face support as being an absolute necessity:

I enjoyed the face-to-face session. It was nice to actually have that human contact, I guess. But in saying that, I think as long as you had someone that is enthusiastic, like engaged, I think an online session.

(Teacher – hybrid model of professional support)

Technology via Zoom is the way to go with support from an expert actively working with high needs students for: problem solving, spring boarding ideas and getting practical advice that works from a compassionate advisor.

(Teacher – hybrid model of professional support)

Feelings of knowledge, confidence, and capability (efficacy)

Teachers who used the Early Years–MoP in the initial trial provided data on their usage patterns. The 15 teachers who engaged with the MoP framework and practice briefs on at least two occasions and used one or more of the practices in the classroom were viewed to be 'active users'. On the other hand, the four teachers who used the MoP framework to reflect on their practice were viewed to be 'superficial users'. Of these 19 users, approximately 80% reported at the end of the trial that their level of knowledge together with feelings of confidence and capability had increased. For example:

> accessing the model and the practice briefs has maintained what I already knew, but it's also deepened my knowledge … and the hyperlinks [from the practice briefs] to outside sources extends that even further.
>
> (Early Years Teacher, Initial Trial, active user)

> I think, cause we've had so much success, I do feel a lot more confident now.
>
> (Early Years Teacher, Initial Trial, active user)

This qualitative evidence of perceived increases in knowledge, confidence, and capability (efficacy) from interviews and surveys was replicated through analysis of quantitative measures where increased ratings of knowledge, confidence, and capability by teachers who used the Early Years–MoP were statistically significant.

Similarly, at the end of the initial trial, increased levels of knowledge were reported by nine of the 15 (60%) middle years teachers, and 'good' or 'very good' levels of confidence by 12 of the 15 (80%) of participating teachers. The comment below explicitly illustrates a middle years teacher's acknowledgment of how the experience of trialling the Middle Years–MoP increased her confidence and capability arising from the opportunity for reflection:

> … helped me be more prepared with my lessons, helped me realise what I could expect and also helped encourage me to be more organised with my differentiation. Also gave me some confidence when I saw the things I'm already doing that I didn't even realise would help me out.
>
> (Middle Years Teacher, Initial Trial, survey)

Key findings and take-home messages

Analysis of teacher responses during interviews and survey questions across two cycles of trialling enabled the identification of important findings about the MoPs, the influence of professional support on teachers' use of the MoPs, and the effect of MoP use on teachers' knowledge, confidence, and efficacy. Findings and implications have been integrated and clustered into three areas: i) viability of the MoPs; ii) role of professional development and support; and iii) impact on teacher knowledge, confidence, and efficacy.

Viability of the Models of Practice

Findings indicate that both MoPs are viewed as valuable resources for building specialised knowledge and skills in the teaching of students on the spectrum. Overall, teachers endorsed the MoPs; they commented on the logical structure of the models, the importance of the foundational

> *The evidence suggests that in adopting the MoPs, teachers can feel confident that the practices are valid for use in inclusive mainstream classrooms.*

practices, the usefulness of the teacher-friendly briefs, and the overall practical worth of the models. For some teachers, the models supported their everyday planning, while for others, they were used as reflective tools. Many teachers considered the practices to be applicable to the whole class. Further, several teachers suggested that the MoPs have additional value for early career teachers. In summary, the level of teacher endorsement of the MoPs, combined their varied applications and benefits, points to the MoPs being viable resources within Australian schools.

The first of three implications is immediately apparent: the MoPs can be recommended for adoption by Australian teachers. The evidence suggests that in adopting the MoPs, teachers can feel confident that the practices are valid for use in inclusive mainstream classrooms. Further, teachers can be assured that the practices were initially identified according to an 'evidence-informed' criterion.

A second implication is that design-based research (DBR) methodology provided a rigourous and highly effective process through which participating teachers provided critical information on social validity, content validity, and utility of the MoPs within classroom practice. The cyclical nature of the design enabled the design of a resource from the ground up, shaped by the continual input of Australian teachers. The success of the process, evidenced by the viability of the MoPs, strongly positions DBR as a method for translating knowledge into Australian classrooms.

Information on the MoP research project itself and each of the 65 practices is housed on *inclusionED*: a freely accessible, online community of practice which supports teachers to implement recommendations from the Autism CRC research. In addition to the practice briefs developed during the project, *inclusionED* includes video modelling of each practice and links to external online information that is recommended by the research team.

> *The cyclical nature of the design enabled the design of a resource from the ground up, shaped by the continual input of Australian teachers.*

The *inclusionED* platform supports teachers to adopt MoP teaching practices using a process of professional learning consistent with the *Australian Charter for the Professional Learning of Teachers and School Leaders* (Education Services Australia, 2018). Given the potential reach of *inclusionED*, placing the MoPs on the platform will further facilitate teachers' access, increasing benefits to students.

A final implication from the findings is the appropriateness of these practice models to support pre-service and early career teachers and directly speaks to the value of choosing to showcase foundational practices. As both MoPs are research-informed, contextually relevant, and user-friendly, Australian teacher educators at universities and within schooling sectors should find the resources extremely usable in courses and professional learning opportunities related to inclusive education and teaching students on the autism spectrum.

Role of professional development and support

Findings from the initial trial indicate that professional support (face-to-face or online) was beneficial and facilitated teacher uptake and use of the MoPs. Without any additional support, many teachers found it difficult to engage with the resource material and expressed the desire to receive some level of support when being introduced to the models. Subsequently, findings from the final trial of the MoPs showed that the hybrid model of professional development and support (a combination of face-to-face and online) bridged the distance between the autism specialist and individual teachers, motivated teachers to use the MoPs, and enabled practices to be customised for classroom use. In summary, professional development accompanied by professional support was found to play a key role in teacher uptake and use of the MoPs. Findings from the final trial strongly support the provision of a hybrid model of professional support for teachers developing their classroom practice. The recommendations for coaching of an appropriate duration has direct implications for planning and adequate funding of professional development opportunities with the serious intention to facilitate change to teachers' classroom practices.

Impact on teacher knowledge, confidence, and efficacy

Findings indicate that teachers' use of the MoPs resulted in increased perceptions of knowledge, confidence, and efficacy. Many users of the MoPs indicated that their knowledge regarding the education of students on the spectrum had increased and, in some cases, became deeper or more extensive. They also reported feeling more confident when it came to the implementation of selected practices in response to individual student need. Finally, teachers' sense of efficacy increased with perceived capability following MoP use. In summary, MoP use positively impacted teachers' overall perceptions of knowledge, confidence, and efficacy, with statistically significant increases in these three teacher attributes being reported by users during the initial trial.

The significant improvement measured in levels of teacher efficacy with the early years teachers is particularly noteworthy. As an important indicator of whether teachers are likely to try new practices, that these teachers had reported improved efficacy speaks not only to the value to their immediate classroom practice but also potentially to their ongoing engagement with professional learning. For elaborations on these findings and implications, see Clark et al. (2019).

Conclusion

This chapter provides an overview of how the research team worked in partnership with mainstream teachers in schools across New South Wales, Queensland, and Victoria to develop, trial, and evaluate two viable MoPs to support the inclusion and education of students on the autism spectrum in early and middle year classrooms. To date, classroom teachers engaging with the practice models have endorsed not only their foundational and flexible nature but also their usefulness in the planning and teaching process when combined with some level of professional support.

The research-informed and teacher-friendly resources can now be freely accessed through *inclusionED*. As the online platform to disseminate the research findings of the School Years Program of the Autism CRC, *inclusionED* presents each of the practices from the MoPs using a range of audiovisual and written resources. These resources demonstrate the practice in action and support teachers to implement the practices within a cycle of professional learning that is consistent with the best-practice model adopted by the Australian Institute of Teaching and School Leadership (AITSL, 2017). Importantly, the *inclusionED* community of practice provides the opportunity for teachers to share their experiences of using the MoP practices in their classrooms.

By positioning the practices included in each of the MoPs on *inclusionED*, their wider application throughout Australia will support teachers in their day-to-day work with diverse learners and the ongoing challenge to provide a quality education to all students.

Note

1 www.inclusioned.edu.au

References

Adams, D., Simpson, K., & Keen, D. (2020). Exploring anxiety at home, school, and in the community through self-report from children on the autism spectrum. *Autism Research,* 13, 603–614.

Alexander, J. L., Ayres, K. M., & Smith, K. A. (2015). Training teachers in evidence-based practice for individuals with autism spectrum disorder: A review of the literature. *Teacher Education and Special Education*, 38, 13–27.

Australian Bureau of Statistics (ABS). (2019). *4430.0 – Disability, ageing and carers, Australia: Summary of findings, 2018: Autism in Australia.* Retrieved from https://www.abs.gov.au/AUSSTATS/abs@.nsf/Lookup /4430.0Main+Features102018.

Australian Curriculum Assessment and Reporting Authority (ACARA). (2019). *Planning for student diversity.* Retrieved from https://www.australiancurriculum.edu.au/resources/student-diversity/ planning-for-student-diversity/.

Australian Institute for Teaching and School Leadership (AITSL). (2012). *Australian professional standards for teachers.* Retrieved from https://www.aitsl.edu.au/teach/standards.

Australian Institute for Teaching and School Leadership (AITSL). (2017). *Improving teacher professional learning.* Retrieved from https://www.aitsl.edu.au/teach/improve-practice/improving-teacher-professional-learning.

Australian Institute of Health and Welfare. (2017). *Disability in Australia: Changes over time in inclusion and participation in education.* Retrieved from https://www.aihw.gov.au/getmedia/34f09557-0acf-4adf-837d-eada7b74d466/Education-20905.pdf.aspx.

Autism Spectrum Australia. (2013a). *We belong: Investigating the experiences, aspirations and needs of adults with Asperger's disorder and high functioning autism.* Retrieved from http://www.autismspectrum.org.au/ content/we-belong-key-findings.

Autism Spectrum Australia. (2013b). *We belong too: The experiences, needs and service requirements of adolescents with autism spectrum disorder.* Retrieved from https://www.autismspectrum.org.au/content/summary-findings-we-belong-too.

Baldwin, S., Costley, D., & Warren, A. (2014). Employment activities and experiences of adults with high-functioning autism and Asperger's disorder. *Journal of Autism and Developmental Disorders*, 44, 2440–2449.

Beamish, W., Macdonald, L., Hay, S., Taylor, A., Paynter, J., & Tucker, M. (2020). Trialling a Model of Practice for Australian teachers of young school-aged children on the autism spectrum. *International Journal of Disability, Development and Education.* doi:10.1080/1034912X.2020.1774046.

Beamish, W., Taylor, A., Macdonald, L., Hay, S., Tucker, M., & Paynter, J. (2020). *Field-testing a Model of Practice for teaching of young school-aged students on the autism spectrum* [Manuscript submitted for publication]. School of Education and Professional Studies, Griffith University.

Bruck, S., Chandra, S., Cotter, J., Clark, T., & Gibbs, V. (2020). *Addressing the professional development needs of regional and remote teachers of students on the autism spectrum using the Models of Practice (Final Report).* Retrieved from https://www.autismcrc.com.au/our-programs/school-years/.

Bruck, S., Robinson, A., & Gallagher, E. (2021). A Model of Practice for improving autism knowledge in teachers of mainstream students on the autism spectrum in Australia. *Australasian Journal of Special and Inclusive Education.*

Busby, R., Ingram, R., Bowron, R., Oliver, J., & Lyons, B. (2012). Teaching elementary children with autism: Addressing teacher challenges and preparation needs. *Rural Educator*, 33(2), 27–35.

Campbell, M., Hwang, Y.-S., Whiteford, C., Dillon-Wallace, J., Ashburner, J., Saggers, B., & Carrington, S. (2017). Bullying prevalence in students with autism spectrum disorder. *Australasian Journal of Special Education*, 41(2), 101–122.

Carrington, S., Campbell, M., Saggers, B., Ashburner, J., Vicig, F., Dillon-Wallace, J., & Hwang, Y.-S. (2017). Recommendations of school students with autism spectrum disorder and their parents in regard to bullying and cyberbullying prevention and intervention. *International Journal of Inclusive Education*, 21, 1045–1064.

Charney, L., Bartello, F., Soulsby, E., Waltman, D., McLaughlin, E., Salak, A., & Jorda, J. (2017). Effectiveness of sensory and social group interventions to improve the participation of children with autism spectrum disorder via goal attainment scaling. *American Journal of Occupational Therapy*, 71(4). doi:10.5014/ ajot.2017.71S1-PO5018.

Clark, M., Adams, D., Roberts, J., & Westerveld, M. (2020). How do teachers support their students on the autism spectrum in Australian primary schools? *Journal of Research in Special Educational Needs*, 20, 38–50.

Clark, T., Beamish, W., Bruck, S., Robinson, A., Gallagher, E., Taylor, A., & Macdonald, L. (2019). *Models of Practice to support the transition of students on the autism spectrum into and between early and middle years classrooms (Final Report)*. Retrieved from https://www.autismcrc.com.au/our-programs/school-years/transition-models-practice-teachers.

Costley, D., Clark, T., & Bruck, S. (2014). The Autism Spectrum Disorder Evaluative Education Model: A school-based method of assessing and selecting interventions for classroom use. *SAGE Open*, 4(4). doi:10.1177/2158244014556640.

deBruin, K. (2019). The impact of inclusive education reforms on students with disability: An international comparison. *International Journal of Inclusive Education*, doi:10.1080/13603116.2019.1623327.

Department of Education Employment and Workplace Relations for the Council of Australian Governments (DEEWR). (2009). *Belonging, being & becoming – The Early Years Learning Framework for Australia*. Canberra: Commonwealth of Australia.

Division for Early Childhood (DEC). (2015). *DEC recommended practices interactive glossary*. Retrieved from http://www.dec-sped.org/dec-recommended-practices.

Education Services Australia. (2018). *The Australian charter for the professional learning of teachers and school leaders*. Retrieved from https://www.aitsl.edu.au/tools-resources/resource/australian-charter-for-the-professional-learning-of-teachers-and-school-leaders.

Falconer, I., Finlay, J., & Fincher, S. (2011). Representing practice: Practice models, patterns, bundles. *Learning, Media and Technology*, 36, 101–127.

Guldberg, K. (2017). Evidence-based practice in autism educational research: Can we bridge the research and practice gap? *Oxford Review of Education*, 43, 149–161.

Harper-Hill, K., Beamish, W., Hay, S., Whelan, M., Kerr, J., & Villalba, C. (2020). Teacher engagement in professional learning: What makes the difference to teacher practice? *Studies in Continuing Education*. doi: 10.1080/0158037X.2020.1781611.

Howe, F. E., & Stagg, S. D. (2016). How sensory experiences affect adolescents with an autistic spectrum condition within the classroom. *Journal of Autism and Developmental Disorders*, 46, 1656–1668. doi:10.1007/s10803-015-2693-1.

Howlin, P., Goode, S., Hutton, J., & Rutter, M. (2004). Adult outcome for children with autism. *Journal of Child Psychology & Psychiatry*, 45(2), 212–229. doi:10.1111/j.1469-7610.2004.00215.x.

Keane, E., Aldridge, F. J., Costley, D., & Clark, T. (2012). Students with autism in regular classes: A long-term follow-up study of a satellite class transition model. *International Journal of Inclusive Education*, 16(10), 1001–1017. doi:10.1080/13603116.2010.538865.

Kloosterman, P. H., Kelley, E. A., Craig, W. M., Parker, J. D., & Javier, C. (2013). Types and experiences of bullying in adolescents with an autism spectrum disorder. *Research in Autism Spectrum Disorders*, 7(7), 824–832. doi:10.1016/j.rasd.2013.02.013.

Macdonald, L., Beamish, W., Taylor, A., Robinson, A., & Gallagher, E. (2020). *Regional and rural teachers' experiences with two models of practice supporting the education of students on the autism spectrum* [Manuscript submitted for publication]. School of Education and Professional Studies, Griffith University.

McKenney, S., & Reeves, T. C. (2012). *Conducting educational design research*. New York, NY: Routledge.

Morris, Z. S., Wooding, S., & Grant, J. (2011). The answer is 17 years, what is the question: Understanding time lags in translational research. *Journal of the Royal Society of Medicine*, 104, 510–520. doi:10.1258/jrsm.2011.110180.

Parsons, S., Charman, T., Faulkner, R., Ragan, J., Wallace, S., & Wittemeyer, K. (2013). Commentary – Bridging the research and practice gap in autism: The importance of creating research partnerships with schools. *Autism*, 17, 268–280.

Pellicano, L., Dinsmore, A., & Charman, T. (2014). What should autism research focus upon? Community views and priorities from the United Kingdom. *Autism*, 18, 756–770.

Rodriguez, V. (2012). The teaching brain and the end of the empty vessel. *Mind, Brain, and Education*, 6(4), 177–185. doi:10.1111/j.1751-228X.2012.01155.x.

Saggers, B., Klug, D., Harper-Hill, K., Ashburner, J., Costley, D., Clark, T., … Carrington, S. (2018). *Australian autism educational needs analysis: What are the needs of schools, parents and students on the autism spectrum?* Brisbane: Cooperative Research Centre for Living with Autism (Autism CRC).

Simpson, K., Adams, D., Alston-Knox, C., Heussler, H., & Keen, D. (2019). Exploring the sensory profiles of children on the autism spectrum using the short sensory profile-2 (SSP-2). *Journal of Autism and Developmental Disorders*, 49, 2069–2079.

Soto-Chodiman, R., Pooley, J. A., Cohen, L., & Taylor, M. F. (2012). Students with ASD in mainstream primary education settings: Teachers' experiences in Western Australian classrooms. *Australasian Journal of Special Education*, 36, 97–111.

Syriopoulou-Delli, C. K., Polychronopoulou, S. A., Kolaitis, G. A., & Antoniou, A. S. G. (2019). Views of teachers on anxiety symptoms in students with autism spectrum disorder. *Journal of Autism and Developmental Disorders*, 49, 704–720.

Taylor, A., Beamish, W., Tucker, M., Paynter, J., & Walker, S. (2019). Designing a model of practice for Australian teachers of young school-age children on the autism spectrum. *Journal of International Special Needs Education*. doi:10.9782/18-00017.

Teras, H., & Kartoglu, U. (2017). A grounded theory of professional learning in an authentic online professional development program. *International Review of Research in Open and Distributed Learning*, 18(7), 191–212.

Test, D., Smith, L., & Carter, E. (2014). Equipping youth with autism spectrum disorders for adulthood: Promoting rigor, relevance, and relationships. *Remedial and Special Education*, 35, 80–90.

6

USING STRUCTURED TEACHING STRATEGIES IN MAINSTREAM CLASSROOMS

Research to practice

Libby Macdonald, Jill Ashburner and Keely Harper-Hill

Visual schedules and work systems are two of the practices included in structured teaching, both of which have commonalities with some of the practices included in the MoPs described in Chapter 5. These practices support students by making visual, structured adjustments to classroom environments and tasks. They were initially developed specifically in response to the needs of students on the autism spectrum in largely segregated settings. In this chapter, we report on research into the use of visual schedules and work systems in inclusive classroom settings because most students who are learning in inclusive settings usually benefit from structure and predictability. The trial of these strategies and engagement with teachers in the first of two projects resulted in the development of a written guide for teachers. Informed by teacher perspectives reported in the first project, a second project developed a series of online resources to support the application of visual schedules and work systems in inclusive settings. Despite teacher reports that visual schedules and work systems were valuable additions to their classroom practice, teachers working individually to implement these cite time as a barrier to their use. It is proposed that this can be addressed by a whole-of-school solution-focused response to the creation, production, and implementation of these resources.

Most students benefit from structure and the predictability that it provides (Hulac & Briesch, 2017). Harlacher (2015) defines structure as 'the amount of predictability in the classroom, including established procedures for specific activities' which comprise 'a series of steps students take in order to manage a task on their own, with little to no teacher guidance' (p. 42). Several teaching practices have the potential to provide predictability for all students and make expectations clear and accessible. Such practices are frequently indicated at those times during the school day when opportunities arise for students to become 'off-task' (Harlacher, 2015), for example during transitions which are inherently less structured, during times when students are expected to work independently, or when expectations of student behaviour are not necessarily understood by students and need to be explicitly taught (e.g., Hulac & Briesch, 2017; Marzano, Marzano, & Pickering, 2003). Providing predictability for students through classroom procedures, routines, and schedules is an aim of many strategies embedded within the broad literature on effective classroom and behaviour management (e.g., Harlacher, 2015; Hulac & Briesch, 2017; Marzano et al., 2003). In contrast, 'visual schedules' and 'work systems' are practices which, while remarkably similar in intention to those found in the general literature, are specifically positioned within the autism literature and researched particularly with students on the autism spectrum.

Work systems and visual schedules are two components of 'structured teaching' which has its foundations in the comprehensive intervention program Treatment and Education of Autistic and related Communication handicapped CHildren (TEACCH; Mesibov, Shea, & Schopler, 2005; Schopler, Mesibov, & Hearsey,1995). The development of the TEACCH program responded, in part, to a need to ensure understanding by students on the spectrum. Students on the spectrum present with a strong need for predictability and sameness (Flannery & Horner, 1994; Goris et al., 2019) exceeding that of most of the students in 'general' classrooms. The degree of student anxiety caused by not knowing which events or activities to anticipate made it critical for adjustments to ensure that all students could understand the upcoming sequence of activities (Mesibov, Howley, & Naftel, 2016). In combination with this, processing of spoken language by students on the spectrum may not be commensurate with their age peers (Kim, Paul, Tager-Flusberg, & Lord, 2014). Students may

> *Work systems and visual schedules are two components of 'structured teaching'*

also require more support to switch their attention towards the teacher and to maintain attention to adults, peers, and/or activities (Ashburner, Ziviani, & Rodger, 2010). Working memory capacity, sequencing, and organisational capacities can further impact on classroom performance (Hume & Reynolds, 2010) and the way in which students on the spectrum access and use these supports.

Schedules, commonly used in the form of timetables in the Australian educational context, inform or communicate the order of upcoming events and/or activities to students (Harlacher, 2015; Mesibov et al., 2016) and provide greater predictability and an associated sense of security (Harlacher, 2015). 'Visual schedules' provide this information visually, using pictures, photos, symbols, or text depending on the needs and abilities of the student (see Figures 6.1 and 6.2). Research has shown that using visual schedules with students on the spectrum is associated with

Asked the occupational therapist – student can visually process left-to-right as well as top-to-bottom.

Student has a digital watch.

Time	Monday	Tuesday	Wednesday	Thursday	Friday
9:00 – 10:00	Maths	Handwriting / English	Maths	Maths	CHANGE ! Mr. Dawson out of class.
10:00 – 11:00	Reading & spelling	Reading & spelling	Reading & spelling	Reading & spelling	Mrs Robinson teaching in class.
1st break					
11:50 – 12:50	Handwriting / English	Library	Handwriting / English	Music	Handwriting / English
12:50 – 1:20	Science	P.E.	Technologies	Handwriting / English	
2nd break					
1:40 – 2:40	Reading / History	Reading / Science	Reading / Art (1:50 – 2:25)	Reading / Science	Reading / History
2:40 – 3:00		Technologies	Assembly (2:25 – 2:55)	Health & P.E.	Health & P.E.

Teacher has this timetable on the whiteboard – changes can be shown by an electronic Post-it.

Subjects are colour-coded as agreed with student.

FIGURE 6.1 Visual timetables – Whole-of-class or individual.

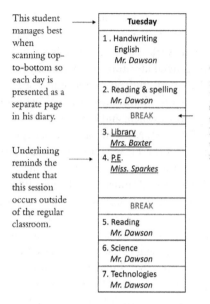

FIGURE 6.2 Visual timetables – Personalised.

lower levels of anxiety (Mesibov & Shea, 2010), higher levels of student engagement and time spent on-task, as well as reduced behavioural challenges (Knight, Sartini, & Spriggs, 2015).

Specific step-by-step actions expected of students to complete familiar classroom activities may be referred to in the mainstream classroom as routines (Hulac & Briesch, 2017) or procedures (Harlacher, 2015; Marzano et al., 2003). Routines and procedures promote efficient classroom operation by structuring tasks such that materials, furniture, and students are in the appropriate place at the appropriate time, and that students are engaged in expected activities using appropriate methods (Hulac & Briesch, 2017). Similarly, and despite being specifically developed in response to the needs of students on the spectrum, 'work systems' also structure tasks by providing information for students on how to perform an activity or a sequence of steps. Work systems specifically include details on what to do, how much there is to do, how to tell the task is finished, and what to do next. As with visual schedules, this information is provided through a sequence of steps which might be ordered from left to right, top to bottom, and/or numbered. Work systems can also present: i) more detailed, task-specific information including any necessary materials; ii) the means for students to easily see, or monitor, what there is left to do; and iii) the procedure for completing the task. While in some settings work systems are built around, or incorporate, individual work stations, this information can be delivered in a variety of ways. An example of a work system is shown in Figures 6.3 and 6.4.

While visual supports such as visual schedules and work systems have previously been shown to be effective in assisting students on the spectrum with staying on-task and moving independently between tasks (Howley, 2015; Hume, Plavnick, & Odom, 2012; Hume & Reynolds, 2010; Mesibov et al., 2016), most studies have involved implementation and evaluation of these strategies outside inclusive classrooms. As with much research in the field of education and autism, student participants are frequently either in segregated environments or taken away from their

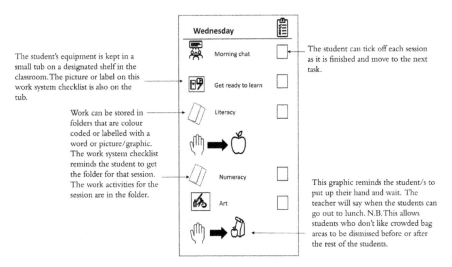

The student's equipment is kept in a small tub on a designated shelf in the classroom. The picture or label on this work system checklist is also on the tub.

The student can tick off each session as it is finished and move to the next task.

Work can be stored in folders that are colour coded or labelled with a word or picture/graphic. The work system checklist reminds the student to get the folder for that session. The work activities for the session are in the folder.

This graphic reminds the student/s to put up their hand and wait. The teacher will say when the students can go out to lunch. N.B. This allows students who don't like crowded bag areas to be dismissed before or after the rest of the students.

FIGURE 6.3 An example of a hybrid work system and visual schedule.

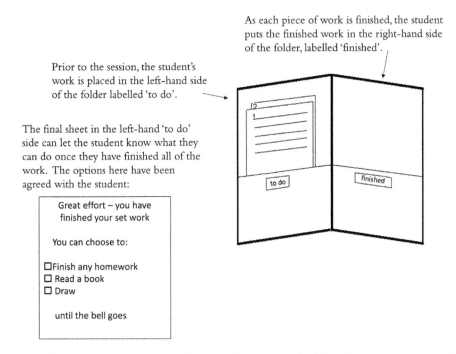

As each piece of work is finished, the student puts the finished work in the right-hand side of the folder, labelled 'finished'.

Prior to the session, the student's work is placed in the left-hand side of the folder labelled 'to do'.

The final sheet in the left-hand 'to do' side can let the student know what they can do once they have finished all of the work. The options here have been agreed with the student:

Great effort – you have finished your set work

You can choose to:

☐ Finish any homework
☐ Read a book
☐ Draw

until the bell goes

FIGURE 6.4 Work system to organise activities to be completed within 'literacy' or 'numeracy' from Figure 6.3.

mainstream class to a separate location to use intervention materials or learn associated skills (Kasari & Smith, 2013). Researchers, allied health professionals, or teacher aides often take an active role in the implementation process while classroom teachers continue their work with the rest of the class (Martinez, Werch, & Conroy, 2016). Research conducted in this way may successfully demonstrate the effectiveness of an intervention in a controlled environment and may also include measures to establish the generalisation of skills to mainstream classroom settings.

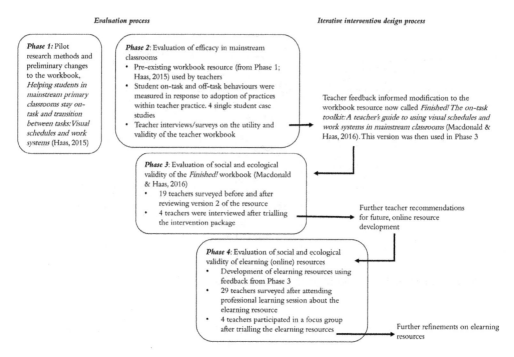

Evaluation process   *Iterative intervention design process*

FIGURE 6.5 Two Autism CRC projects across four phases of design and trial.

However, this approach doesn't necessarily address the practicalities of sustainable implementation in a mainstream school setting. For teachers to be able to use these strategies in their classrooms, they are likely to need a package that provides appropriate information, can be delivered with current, limited resources and staff numbers, and that is not overly demanding of their time (Dykstra Steinbrenner et al., 2015).

Visual schedules and work systems in inclusive settings

This chapter describes two Autism CRC projects which aimed to address this need. The first of these projects, Helping Students Stay on Task and Move between Tasks, investigated the effectiveness of visual schedules and work systems as part of inclusive mainstream teaching practice. This project was conceived with the ultimate aim of producing a practical, low tech information package and resource that could be put into practice in real classrooms and involved designing a research process which i) addressed the priorities of teachers and ii) evaluated visual schedules and work systems within inclusive classroom settings. The second project (The Development of an eLearning Package for Teachers to Help Students Stay on Task and Move between Tasks) developed online resources specifically in response to teacher feedback collected at the conclusion of the first project. How the findings from each project informed the final version of the elearning resources is discussed more fully below.

Supporting teachers to help students stay on-task and transition between tasks in inclusive school settings

Four distinct phases across the two Autism CRC projects (see Figure 6.5) aimed to

1. Establish the effectiveness and social validity of visual schedules and work systems in inclusive school settings using a combination of quantitative data (time-sampling of student behaviour, teacher surveys) and qualitative data (interviews and focus groups).
2. Design and produce resources that support educators to implement visual schedules and work systems in inclusive settings.

The first phase piloted the research methods with a single student on the spectrum (Macdonald et al., 2017) in order to identify behaviours that teachers consider relevant and to finalise adequate observation methods to record changes in behaviour in the sometimes unpredictable classroom setting. In other words, the research process was intended to provide information about how visual schedules and work systems could help teachers to support students on the spectrum as part of their everyday classroom teaching practice. This phase included initial modifications to a teacher resource workbook called *Helping Students in Mainstream Primary Classrooms Stay On-Task and Transition between Tasks: Visual Schedules and Work Systems* (Haas, 2015).

The second phase evaluated the introduction of visual schedules and work systems with four students on the autism spectrum in four Australian classrooms (using a multiple-baseline study design; Macdonald, Trembath, Ashburner, Costley, & Keen, 2018). By separately measuring each student's behaviour on several occasions before introducing the visual schedules and work systems (i.e., at baseline), and then introducing these at staggered starting times, researchers can be more confident that observed changes are in response to the introduction of the visual schedules and work systems rather than simple improvement over time. Teachers were consulted on two important aspects of the second phase method:

1. The selection of a regular activity during which each student would be observed.
2. Any 'off-task' behaviours particular to each participating student and in addition to those defined in Phase 1.

Three of the four students were observed during creative writing and the fourth during independent work within regular, whole-class lessons with a visiting teacher.

The benefits experienced by students in Phases 1 and 2 are presented below.

Benefits of visual schedules and work systems for students in mainstream classrooms

In Phase 2, observations of each student showed that three of the four students spent significantly more time on-task after the introduction of both visual schedules and work systems suggesting potential for these strategies to be effectively employed by teachers to support students on the spectrum to engage in classwork with the rest of their peers. Off-task behaviour decreased for three students, but the decrease was not statistically significant.

As a measure of student independence, the rate of teacher prompting was also recorded wherein greater student independence would result in fewer teacher prompts. During Phase 2, the rate of teacher prompting did not change in direct response to the introduction of visual schedules and work systems. However, teachers interviewed in later phases reported broader benefits from the strategies than those measured in the multiple-baseline study including greater student independence. While these final phases were primarily interested in how valid the teachers perceived the final version of the workbook (*Finished! The On-Task Toolkit*; Macdonald & Haas, 2016) and the elearning resources to be, both of these later phases elicited further information on the benefits experienced by those students in classrooms where visual strategies and work systems were used. The following quotes, for example, discuss the potential benefit for student independence that these two practices offer:

> If you have a system like this in place, it does mean that you don't have to spend so much time directing these students. You can have them learning, you can have them doing work, and you don't have to be babysitting them all the time
>
> (Special education teacher, Phase 3, in Macdonald et al., 2019, p. 9)

> I felt like with having something like that in place, it allows me to step back. It helps him to feel some success … he's wanting to be independent … He was able to stay on track … without me needing to be there all the time
>
> (Teacher, Phase 4, in Winter, Ashburner, Callaghan, & Bobir, 2018, p. 18)

One teacher reported that the strategies also increased independence across different class activities during the day:

> I think because the structure in the toolkit too and the things we've done with him in here, are very simple and clear, and he knows exactly what's going on and where he's supposed to be
>
> (Teacher, Phase 3, in Macdonald et al., 2019, p. 7)

Increasing independence in this way may be a key element in successful inclusion of students on the spectrum as they grow older (Carnahan, Hume, Clarke, & Borders, 2009) and may also alter the way teachers interact with these students by reducing some of the need for individual support.

There were, however, concerns that the use of visual schedules and work systems could single out students and potentially lead to instances of social exclusion, as shown in the following teacher quote:

> I was doing an individual schedule on the right [of his desk] … but he just didn't want that … and looking back I think it's because it actually showed him as being different to others.
>
> (Teacher, Phase 4, in Winter et al., 2018, p. 17)

In response, adjustments to the resources included discretely placed Post-it notes which still served to provide the student with visual information. Other teachers noted the potential of the practices to help many of the students in the class, and not just those on the spectrum:

> The visual schedules … I couldn't imagine not using it. In terms of work schedules … I would be looking for ways in which I could use that, not just for children with a diagnosis
>
> (Teacher, Phase 4, in Winter et al., 2018, p. 16)

> If they don't know what they're doing or what they need it's up there, and that's all of them, not just [the student on the spectrum] because a lot of them don't know and they're sitting there. You think they know but they don't.
>
> (Teacher, Phase 3, in Macdonald et al., 2019, p. 7)

In addition to the qualitative information on the benefits of visual schedules and work systems, the third and fourth phases explored the experiences of teachers when using the written and elearning resources.

Utility of visual schedules and work systems for teacher practice

The content and format of resources for teachers were developed and refined using an iterative design process (Dykstra Steinbrenner et al., 2015; Parsons et al., 2013). During this process, teachers provided feedback on both the utility and social validity of the resources presented and/or trialled. Three written versions of the teacher workbook, or toolkit (Haas, 2015; Macdonald & Haas, 2016), were created during Phases 1, 2, and 3.

In Phase 3, a total of 19 Australian teachers were surveyed before and after downloading the final iteration of the teacher workbook, *Finished! The On-Task Toolkit* (Macdonald & Haas, 2016). Responses indicated that teachers found the written information about both strategies, checklists, printable resources, and links to further information easy to use and useful (Macdonald et al., 2019).

At the completion of Phase 3, survey responses and interviews with teachers confirmed that the information provided was useful in strengthening implementation of these practices. The interviewed teachers recommended additional ways to augment the method for delivering the content to teachers including:

- Demonstration of the practices via face-to-face support and video modelling.
- Provision of visual examples (i.e., more resources).
- Online forums for sharing ideas for implementation with other teachers.

In response, online resources which were more accessible to time-poor teachers and more engaging for students were developed. To this end, a series of short animated videos, video-models, PowerPoint presentations, and quick reference guides were designed to provide teachers with information on structured teaching, visual schedules, and work systems.

The resources were presented via face-to-face professional development sessions with 29 teachers. A post professional development survey was conducted immediately after the session and four teachers trialled the visual schedules and work systems in their classrooms and participated in a focus group. Feedback collected via both surveys and focus groups informed the final iteration of the resources.

Teachers perceived that both the toolkit and elearning resources supported them to refine and strengthen the effectiveness of existing practices through nuanced adaptations. One teacher reflected that previous implementation of visual schedules had been too complex for her student on the spectrum. 'We threw too much at him,' she said (in Macdonald et al., 2019, p. 6). Similarly,

> I've done the visual scheduling for quite a few years but having listened to you, I've definitely changed a little bit to putting numbers … I definitely noticed a big difference with newer ASD students responding to that very well. I can just say we are up to number two on the board … that definitely helps
>
> (Teacher, Phase 4, in Winter et al., 2018, p. 15)

The toolkit and elearning materials emphasised the need for consistency in implementing the strategies, and this too helped some teachers to adapt their existing practice:

> What I took out of your presentation was making sure it [the work system] was just daily … and the feedback that I got from my ASD child is that he really enjoyed having that there.
>
> (Teacher, Phase 4, in Winter et al., 2018, p. 18)

Barriers to practice

Teachers cited a lack of time as a major difficulty in both preparing resources for their students to use and in accessing paper-based or online professional learning materials. Some examples of remarks about creating resources were:

> When I use that [visual schedules] next year … [with] the number of different subjects we have, finding the cards and putting them up is too time consuming.
>
> (Teacher, Phase 4, in Winter et al., 2018, p. 16)

> I would like it if you did all the work for me … and then all I had to do was print things out and laminate it [said with humour].
>
> (Teacher, Phase 3, in Macdonald et al., 2019, p. 9)

Teacher self-efficacy

Confidence, or self-efficacy, has been identified as an important factor in the implementation of evidence-based practices (Damschroder et al., 2009; Fixsen, Naoom, Blase, & Friedman, 2005), and teachers were asked to rate their knowledge of, and confidence using, visual schedules and work systems before and after looking at the information provided in the 'toolkit' (Macdonald & Haas, 2016). While the clear increase in teachers' reported levels of knowledge between the surveys was not statistically significant, an increase in teachers' reported confidence levels was significant. Increased feelings of confidence were also noted by teachers who attended professional learning sessions provided during Phase 4:

> I found it [professional development] really helpful … I felt like after having the PD, and looking through the resources and making a plan for what I want to do with [student's name], I felt like I gained a little bit of control.
>
> (Teacher, Phase 4, Winter et al., 2018)

Given the role played by self-efficacy in determining teachers' decisions to implement evidence-based practices (Damschroder et al., 2009; Fixsen et al., 2005), this finding has promising implications for the successful utilisation of these strategies. Teachers across both projects reported that they would consider using the strategies with future classes.

Development of resources that meet the needs of teachers

The original workbook developed for the first project was refined through an iterative design process to become a paper-based toolkit. Teachers' concerns with lack of time to develop resources and the need for greater accessibility were further addressed through the development of elearning materials and many of these resources are now available on the *inclusionED* website[1]. Across both projects, teachers mentioned a preference for online learning to be paired with some face-to-face professional learning. One teacher remarked, 'Definitely good to access it online … we are just constantly on the computer' (in Winter et al., 2018, p. 16).

Implications for inclusive practice approaches

Although the research above promoted whole-class implementation within inclusive classrooms, some teachers highlighted the potential for visual schedules and work systems to set apart students as 'different', akin to 'microexclusion' as described by Cologon (2019). Given the risk this poses to a student's 'sense of belonging and being valued' (Petriwskyj, 2010), further consideration is required. It was evident that some teachers did not consider whole-of-class implementation and instead focused on one student on the spectrum. A whole-of-class approach may have decreased or circumvented the stigmatisation that can result when interventions focus solely on students on the spectrum.

Only a small number of teachers trialled the practices in Phases 2–4 but they were willing participants, presumably motivated to support the needs of their students on the autism spectrum by investing time to develop their teaching practice. Many of these teachers reported that the time taken to prepare resources was an additional pressure. As components of effective classroom practices in 'general' classrooms, many mainstream teachers readily implement schedules, routines, and procedures to provide

> To counteract the perception that visual schedules and work systems are an 'additional' demand, a whole-of-class practice approach can be implemented, and students provided with options to personalise their resource.

structure and predictability. Indeed, Carter and Hughes (2006) found that, along with rules, 'procedures', or routines, were rated by all educators as the most important practice to be used in mainstream classrooms – for both students with disabilities and without. It would seem important that in order for teachers to use visual schedules and work systems in general settings, a necessary prerequisite is that they first conceptualise these as belonging in their repertoire of teaching practices that provide structure and predictability. We propose that one of the primary impediments to this absorption of visual schedules and work systems into a teacher's expected repertoire of practices stems from how efficiently teachers differentiate work in response to the needs of the student on the spectrum. Students who are having trouble transitioning between activities and completing work independently may be experiencing difficulty comprehending the current classroom structure. To support these students, teachers may need to adjust their practice to communicate classroom routines and structure in accessible ways.

It is likely that some students will need explicit structure to support their participation in most classroom activities, that this structure will need to be presented in a highly visual format, positioned physically close to the student, and that their attention will need to be drawn to it. As described in Chapter 4, teachers often require support from in-school support teachers and external specialists to develop visual schedules and work systems which can meet the needs of many students in any classroom. In the transition to truly inclusive classrooms and school practices, a range of visual schedules and work systems would be positioned as practices that address the diversity within the school, for use by all members of school staff.

To counteract the perception that visual schedules and work systems are an 'additional' demand, a whole-of-class practice approach can be implemented, and students provided with options to personalise their resource. An active dialogue with individual students regarding the utility and acceptability of their personalised adaptations is consistent with a pedagogy of listening

(Macartney, 2012) and enables teachers to maintain an 'awareness of the lived effect of our ... practices' in order to promote student participation (Macartney & Morton, 2013, p. 787). While a visual schedule may be on the wall, students can choose to have one on their desk. If all items on the schedule are numbered, then teachers are able to redirect all students by saying 'We're doing number 2'. Those students who may be slower in processing the verbal redirection 'you should be well into your maths exercises by now' are able to find the 'number 2'. In this case, the diversity of student understanding within an inclusive classroom is anticipated, recognised, and accepted, and teaching practice is designed accordingly.

In order to be inclusive, it is important that educators and teachers work together to ensure that practices meet not only diversity of *learning* needs but are balanced with the student need to *belong*. Activities and practices that are designed to present information visually and verbally must also position the child within their cohort. It is interesting to note that in the initial phases of this research (Phases 1 and 2), teachers working with students in Years 3–5 were targeted because visual supports are more commonly employed in early years classrooms, whereas the same level of use is not always maintained into later years. The discontinuation of some visual supports in secondary schooling is no doubt multifactorial. However, the need for these will not necessarily decrease as students get older. Hampshire, Butera, and Bellini (2016) found that self-management strategies involving a homework checklist (similar to a work system) coupled with self-selected rewards were effective in enabling adolescent middle year students on the spectrum to complete homework tasks independently, with reduced prompting from parents. Teachers in this study observed improvements in the student's organisational skills, attitudes, and academic achievements. This finding suggests that structured teaching approaches have potential for older students. Replacing childish graphics with photographs or text are likely to meet a student's need to learn *and* belong into the secondary years of schooling and beyond. Continuing to use inappropriately childish graphics not only facilitates microexclusion but potentially furthers perceptions that such needs are outside of those expected for students in the class and underscore that such adjustments are created in 'addition', rather than simply in response to existing diversity.

> In order to be inclusive, it is important that educators and teachers work together to ensure that practices meet not only diversity of learning *needs but are* balanced with the student need to belong.

Of course, developing new resources each school year to support the use of visual schedules and work systems demands resources. Reducing the demands on individual teachers can be achieved through the adoption of co-ordinated whole-of-school approaches where visuals for schedules and systems are designed for use by many teachers with many students and efficiently produced centrally. Such collaborative problem-solving approaches are critical to effective inclusion (Carter & Hughes, 2006). This again reinforces that the resources are meeting the diversity of need inherent in the school community rather than an additional requirement of resources and time for specific students.

Historically, all of the practices referred to above were developed by educators in response to the needs of students in separate education settings, thus laying the foundation that these practices were either 'general' or 'special'. Accordingly, research has primarily investigated the needs of these 'general' and 'special' students according to diagnosis, further reinforcing that the need for structure and predictability when experienced by students on the spectrum is inherently different from the need of 'other' students as per Cologon (2019). In this chapter, we have maintained that the need is the same; while the means and representation of these practices may differ, they share a common purpose. That these practices meet a common need is borne out through teacher reports that they considered the practices to be valid with a range of students in the classroom.

The social validity for using practices within inclusive classrooms is a common theme throughout many of the Autism CRC school-based projects. Beyond the diagnosis of students who participated in Phase 2, the behaviours which visual schedules and work systems were to support were determined in partnership with classroom teachers. By doing so, the practices were implemented in response to the real-world needs of students and teachers. Future research could further promote perceptions that such practices are not in response to a diagnosis but in response to need. Including many students who present with off-task behaviours, become confused or distracted, and don't complete tasks provides further evidence that such practices have utility for teachers meeting the needs of all students.

Conclusion

The impetus for this research was to develop a professional learning resource which would support teachers in inclusive classrooms to use visual schedules and work systems. These practices have an evidence base when used with students on the spectrum in 'specialist' settings. The results described from Phases 2–4 contribute to emerging evidence that visual schedules and work systems can be used to support students to remain on-task in mainstream settings. Students were observed to engage in off-task behaviours less often, although this was not statistically significant. Teachers also reported how these practices supported students to move between tasks with greater independence within the 'mainstream' classrooms.

However, successful implementation in inclusive settings requires whole-school and whole-class approaches where adjustments made to timetables or classroom procedures are recognised to potentially meet the needs of all students in the classroom; not simply those with a diagnosis of autism. Schools who strive for inclusivity need to develop systems which enable teachers to readily include these in their everyday whole-of-class practice.

Note

1 www.inclusioned.edu.au

References

Ashburner, J., Ziviani, J., & Rodger, S. (2010). Surviving in the mainstream: Capacity of children with autism spectrum disorders to perform academically and regulate their emotions and behavior at school. *Research in Autism Spectrum Disorders*, 4(1), 18–27. doi:10.1016/j.rasd.2009.07.002.

Carnahan, C. R., Hume, K., Clarke, L., & Borders, C. (2009). Using structured work systems to promote independence and engagement for students with autism spectrum disorders. *Teaching Exceptional Children*, 41, 6–14. doi:10.1177/004005990904100401.

Carter, E., & Hughes, C. (2006). Including high school students with severe disabilities in general education classes: Perspectives of general and special educators, paraprofessionals, and administrators. *Research and Practice for Persons with Severe Disabilities*, 31(2), 174–185. doi:10.1177/154079690603100209.

Cologon, K. (2019). *Towards inclusive education: A necessary process of transformation*. Melbourne: Children and Young People with Disability Australia.

Damschroder, L., Aron, D. C., Keith, R. E., Kirsh, S., Alexander, J. A., & Lowery, J. C. (2009). Fostering implementation of health services research findings into practice: A consolidated framework for advancing implementation science. *Implementation Science*, 4(1). doi:10.1186/1748-5908-4-50.

Dykstra Steinbrenner, J. R., Watson, L. R., Boyd, B. A., Wilson, K. P., Crais, E. R., Baranek, G. T., … Flagler, S. (2015). Developing feasible and effective school-based interventions for children with ASD: A case study of the iterative development process. *Journal of Early Intervention*, 37(1), 23–43. doi:10.1177/1053815115588827.

Fixsen, D. L., Naoom, S. F., Blase, K. A., & Friedman, R. M. (2005). *Implementation research: A synthesis of the literature* (FMHI publication No. 231). Tampa, FL: University of South Florida, Louis de la Parte Florida Mental Health Institute, National Implementation Research Network.

Flannery, K. B., & Horner, R. H. (1994). The relationship between predictability and problem behavior for students with severe disabilities. *Journal of Behavioral Education*, 4, 157–176.

Goris, J., Brass, M., Cambier, C., Delplanque, J., Wiersema, J. R., & Braem, S. (2019). The relation between preference for predictability and autistic traits. *Autism Research*. doi:10.1002/aur.2244.

Haas, K. (2015). *Helping students in mainstream primary classrooms stay on-task and transition between tasks: Visual schedules and work systems* [A workbook for teachers]. Sydney: Autism Spectrum Australia (Aspect).

Hampshire, P., Butera, G., & Bellini, S. (2016). Self-management and parents as interventionists to improve homework independence in students with autism spectrum disorders. *Preventing School Failure: Alternative Education for Children and Youth*, 60(1), 22–34. doi:10.1080/1045988X.2014.954515.

Harlacher, J. (2015). *Designing effective classroom management*. Bloomington, IN: Marzano Research.

Howley, M. (2015). Outcomes of structured teaching for children on the autism spectrum: Does the research evidence neglect the bigger picture? *Journal of Research in Special Educational Needs*, 15(2), 106–119. doi:10.1111/1471-3802.12040.

Hulac, D., & Briesch, A. (2017). *Evidence-based strategies for effective classroom management*. New York, NY: The Guilford Press.

Hume, K., Plavnick, J., & Odom, S. (2012). Promoting task accuracy and independence in students with autism across educational setting through the use of individual work systems. *Journal of Autism and Developmental Disorders*, 42(10), 2084–2099. doi:10.1007/s10803-012-1457-4.

Hume, K., & Reynolds, B. (2010). Implementing work systems across the school day: Increasing engagement in students with autism spectrum disorders. *Preventing School Failure: Alternative Education for Children and Youth*, 54(4), 228–237. doi:10.1080/10459881003744701.

Kasari, C., & Smith, T. (2013). Interventions in schools for children with autism spectrum disorder: Methods and recommendations. *Autism*, 17(3), 254–267. doi:10.1177/1362361312470496.

Kim, S. H., Paul, R., Tager-Flusberg, H., & Lord, C. (2014). Language and communication in autism. In F. R. Volkmar, S. J. Rogers, R. Paul, & K. A. Pelphrey (Eds.), *Handbook of autism and pervasive developmental disorders* (4th ed., pp. 230–262). Hoboken, NJ: John Wiley & Sons, Inc.

Knight, V., Sartini, E., & Spriggs, A. (2015). Evaluating visual activity schedules as evidence-based practice for individuals with autism spectrum disorders. *Journal of Autism and Developmental Disorders*, 45(1), 157–178. doi:10.1007/s10803-014-2201-z.

Macartney, B. (2012). Teaching through an ethics of belonging, care and obligation as a critical approach to transforming education. *International Journal of Inclusive Education*, 16(2), 171–183. doi:10.1080/13603111003686218.

Macartney, B., & Morton, M. (2013). Kinds of participation: Teacher and special education perceptions and practices of 'inclusion' in early childhood and primary school settings. *International Journal of Inclusive Education*, 17(8), 776–792. doi:10.1080/13603116.2011.602529.

Macdonald, L., & Haas, K. (2016). *Finished! The on-task toolkit: A teacher's guide to using visual schedules and work systems in mainstream classrooms* [Intervention package]. Brisbane: Cooperative Research Centre for Living with Autism (Autism CRC).

Macdonald, L., Keen, D., Ashburner, J., Costley, D., Haas, K., & Trembath, D. (2017). Piloting autism intervention research with teachers in mainstream classrooms. *International Journal of Inclusive Education*, 21(12), 1228–1244. doi:10.1080/13603116.2017.1335355.

Macdonald, L., Trembath, D., Ashburner, J., Costley, D., Haas, K., & Keen, D. (2019). Utilisation of an intervention to support students on the autism spectrum: Examining teachers' responses to Finished! The On-task Toolkit. *Journal of International Special Needs Education*. doi:10.9782/17-00019.

Macdonald, L., Trembath, D., Ashburner, J., Costley, D., & Keen, D. (2018). The use of visual schedules and work systems to increase the on-task behaviour of students on the autism spectrum in mainstream classrooms. *Journal of Research in Special Educational Needs*, 18(4). doi:10.1111/1471-3802.12409.

Martinez, J. R., Werch, B. L., & Conroy, M. A. (2016). School-based interventions targeting challenging behaviors exhibited by young children with autism spectrum disorder: A systematic literature review. *Education and Training in Autism and Developmental Disabilities*, 51(3), 265–280.

Marzano, R., Marzano, J., & Pickering, D. (2003). *Classroom management that works: Research-based strategies for every teacher*. Alexandria, VA: Association for Supervision and Curriculum Development.

Mesibov, G., Howley, M., & Naftel, S. (2016). *Accessing the curriculum for learners with autism spectrum disorders using the TEACCH programme to help inclusion* (2nd ed.). Abingdon: Routledge.

Mesibov, G., & Shea, V. (2010). Evidence-based practices and autism. *Autism*, 15(1), 114–133. doi:10.1177/1362361309348070.

Mesibov, G., Shea, V., & Schopler, E. (2005). *The TEACCH approach to autism spectrum disorders*. New York, NY: Kluwer Academic/Plenum Publishers.

Parsons, S., Charman, T., Faulkner, R., Ragan, J., Wallace, S., & Wittemeyer, K. (2013). Commentary– Bridging the research and practice gap in autism: The importance of creating research partnerships with schools. *Autism*, 17(3), 268–280. doi:10.1177/1362361312472068.

Petriwskyj, A. (2010). Who has rights to what? Inclusion in Australian early childhood programs. *Contemporary Issues in Early Childhood*, 11(4), 342–352. doi: 10.2304/ciec.2010.11.4.342.

Schopler, E., Mesibov, G., & Hearsey, K. (1995) Structured teaching in the TEACCH system. In E. Schopler & G. Mesibov (Eds.), *Learning and cognition in autism* (pp. 243–268). New York, NY: Plenum.

Winter, S., Ashburner, J., Callaghan, S., & Bobir, N. (2018). *The development of an eLearning package for teachers to help students stay on task and transition between tasks: Full report, executive summary and visual snapshot*. Brisbane: Cooperative Research Centre for Living with Autism (Autism CRC).

7

SOUND AMPLIFICATION IN SCHOOL CONTEXTS

Implications for inclusive practice

Keely Harper-Hill, Wayne Wilson, Rebecca Armstrong,
Kelsey Perrykkad, Cerys Downing and Jill Ashburner

The research described in the previous chapter highlighted the benefits of a structured, visual classroom environment. This type of approach was developed in response to the needs of students on the spectrum but evidence suggests that such an approach also supports the needs of many students. The research reported in this chapter investigates a universal environmental adjustment to improve classroom *listening* environments: sound field amplification (SFA). Increased demands on listening caused by poor classroom acoustics affect everyone in the classroom and can be particularly challenging for some students. As such, the authors present classroom acoustics as a risk factor that, if appropriately managed, can put all students in a better position to learn while recognising that their learning still has to take place over time. A series of environmental adjustments which can safely make the teacher's voice louder (increase the signal) while designing the classroom to be quieter (decrease the noise) are discussed. These adjustments can support educators to make the classroom more accessible for all students while also responding to the needs of diverse learners in inclusive ways. We have stressed the importance of a shared understanding of inclusion between allied health professionals and educators when working in inclusive schools. The chapter further contributes to our understanding of the many interactive and dynamic factors that pave the way for successful student participation and learning.

Put simply, classroom acoustics describes how sound 'behaves' in the classroom. The behaviour of the sound contributes positively or negatively to the listening conditions for students and the speaking conditions for the teacher. In part, the acoustics of a classroom is influenced by the materials used and the size and shape of the space. Elements that can contribute to the quality of the acoustics in a room are described in Figure 7.1 and include the level (volume) of the sound in a room when it is both occupied and unoccupied, reverberation times, signal-to-noise ratio (SNR), and measures of speech intelligibility such as the speech transmission index. The Joint Australia/New Zealand Standard – AS/NZS 2107:2016 – recommends preferred values for many of these aspects which, when met, can help create better listening conditions for all students

(Standards Australia, 2016). However, many Australian classrooms do not meet the recommended standards and tend to be too noisy and/or reverberant, making it difficult for learners in those classrooms to listen (Wilson et al., 2019).

Listening in the classroom – A hierarchy of listening skills

The ability to accurately hear and recognise what is said can be referred to as 'speech perception'. Adequate speech perception is thought to require a hierarchy of listening skills that progress from earlier events such as hearing (being able to detect sound) and auditory processing (being able to process the frequency, intensity, timing, and location of sound) to later events such as auditory attention (being able to attend to sound) and language processing (being able to process words and sentences) (Crandell & Smaldino, 2000; Johnson, 2000; Moore, Cowan, Riley, Edmondson-Jones, & Ferguson, 2011).

Listening in a classroom with poor acoustics

Listening in poor acoustic environments can be challenging for students and adults alike. Consider how difficult it can be to hear someone across the table in a canteen with uncovered hard surfaces and floors, loud talking, and the clatter of cutlery. Many students experience similar listening challenges in their classrooms as they contend with noise sources both internal (e.g., background chatter, chairs scraping) and external (e.g., lawnmowers, traffic noise) in classrooms with high reverberation. This can make it sound like the teacher is talking in a stair well (Wilson et al., 2019).

A concerning feature of poor classroom acoustics is its potential to place high demands on students at every level of the listening hierarchy (Dockrell & Shield, 2004). In the earlier stages of the hierarchy, these demands can include making it difficult for students to simply hear the

> **Unoccupied sound level:** The sound present in the classroom when students and teachers are absent.
>
> **Reverberation time (RT):** The time it takes for sound to decrease in the classroom; how long the sound 'bounces around' the room.
>
> **Occupied sound levels:** The sound present in the classroom when the students and teachers are present.
>
> **Signal-to-noise ratio (SNR):** The ratio of the level of the signal (e.g., the teacher's voice) to the noise (e.g., the background noise of the classroom).
>
> **Speech transmission index (STI):** An estimate of how easy it is to hear speech sounds in a classroom.

FIGURE 7.1 Elements that contribute to a classroom's acoustics.

> *Increased demands on listening caused by poor classroom acoustics is concerning for all students, but can be particularly concerning for certain student populations.*

teacher's voice and increasing the load on auditory processing skills to process the basic features of the sound. In the later stages of the hierarchy, these demands can include increasing the load on auditory attention and language processing as students need to use more of their attention and language skills, as well as their prior experience and other contextual cues, to 'fill in the gaps' and make informed predictions about what was said. This can see students expending greater cognitive effort than would be needed otherwise when listening to the teacher (Baldwin, 2008). These demands can be made worse by maturation with many of these auditory processing, attention, and language skills not expected to fully mature until as late as the teenage years (Baldwin, 2008; Johnson, 2000; Moore et al., 2011).

Increased demands on listening caused by poor classroom acoustics is concerning for all students, but can be particularly concerning for certain student populations. This could include students who rely more on listening as their major means of learning in the classroom and students whose listening abilities could be compromised by other factors. Such populations could include younger students (e.g., Rosenberg et al., 1999) as well as students who attend schools in poorer socio-economic areas (e.g., Kazmierczak-Murray & Downes, 2015), have English as a second language (e.g., Massie & Dillon, 2006), have fluctuating conductive hearing impairment (e.g., Heeney, 2004), and/or have neurodevelopmental disorders such as attention deficit hyperactivity disorder, specific learning difficulties, auditory processing disorders, or are on the autism spectrum (e.g., O'Connor, 2012; Reynolds, Kuhaneck, & Pfeiffer, 2016; van der Kruk et al., 2017).

The potential benefit underpinning our call to improve classroom acoustics

The potential for students to benefit from improved classroom is represented in Figure 7.2. In this analogy, the higher steps represent increasing improvements in classroom acoustics. A high-quality signal can be heard more clearly; this makes for easier listening conditions for learning and demands less of cognitive processing. While an oversimplification, Figure 7.2 captures the premise of our research into classroom acoustics. The legibility of the writing on each student's t-shirt shows the extent to which their personal learning needs could be affected. On the top step, both students have legible t-shirts, which means they are each in a better position to learn from what they have heard.

While the means by which improved classroom acoustics could benefit students can be described in many ways (Figure 7.1), perhaps the simplest is to consider SNR. The SNR is the ratio of the level of a desired signal (e.g., the teacher's voice) to the level of the noise (e.g., the general background noise). When represented in decibels, the SNR can be conveniently calculated as the difference between the signal and noise levels (Crandell & Smaldino, 2000; Siebein, Gold, Siebein, & Ermann, 2000). The potential for an improved classroom SNR to help students at all levels of the listening hierarchy is represented in Figure 7.3. In this analogy, improving the classroom's SNR by increasing the level of the teacher's voice and/or decreasing the level of classroom noise (preferably both) can be seen as one way to help students to better hear the teacher's voice and lessen the auditory and cognitive demands on their ability to listen in the classroom.

How to improve classroom acoustics – The basics

The basics of improving the acoustics of a classroom might best be approached from the perspective of the SNR. Using this approach, improving the acoustics of a classroom proceeds as a

THIS IS STUDENT A.

HIS LANGUAGE SKILLS
AND HEARING ARE BOTH
PRETTY GOOD.

THIS IS STUDENT B.

HE HAS TROUBLE
WITH LANGUAGE
PROCESSING & HE
HAS AN UNDIAGNOSED
EAR INFECTION.

FIGURE 7.2 Ideal classroom acoustics position for students to learn.

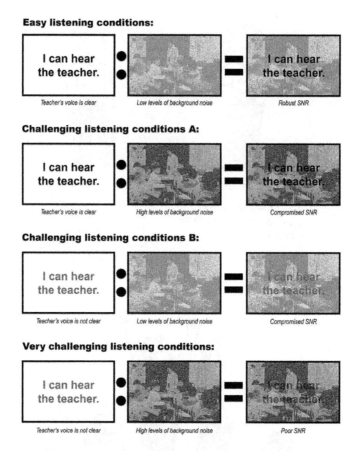

FIGURE 7.3 Influence of the teacher's voice and background noise levels on classroom listening conditions. Moving from left-to-right along each row, the quality of the teacher's voice (the 'signal') in relation to the levels of background noise (the 'noise') is presented as ratios, the Signal:Noise Ratios. The SNRs are presented in the boxes on the very right of each row.

series of actions to make the teacher's voice louder (increase the signal) and the classroom quieter (decrease the noise).

> ... *improving the acoustics of a classroom proceeds as a series of actions to make the teacher's voice louder (increase the signal) and the classroom quieter (decrease the noise).*

Methods for making the teacher's voice louder can range from the simple to the complex. Simpler options can include: i) re-arranging classroom furniture or seating positions (but should avoid identifying individual students as the 'other' who always sits at the front of the class as this can be a form of microexclusion); and ii) the teacher actively monitoring classroom activities to reposition herself as the listening needs of students change during the course of a lesson. The all too common method of simply having the teacher raise her voice should be avoided due to it increasing the risk of vocal strain and teacher fatigue (e.g., Cutiva, Vogel, & Burdorf, 2013).

More complex options for making the teacher's voice louder include using devices such as remote microphone hearing aids (RMHAs) or sound field amplification (SFA). RMHAs see the teacher wear a microphone and transmitter to transmit her voice directly to an individual student wearing a receiver and ear piece. SFA sees the teacher wear the same microphone and transmitter to transit her voice to a speaker that then projects her voice evenly across the classroom (Keith & Purdy, 2014).

Making the classroom quieter is all about identifying the sources of noise both inside (e.g., air vents, fans, chair legs scraping on the floor) and outside (neighbouring classroom noise, school maintenance work, road traffic) and doing something to reduce those noises. Methods for doing this can also range from the simple to the complex. Simpler options can include: i) opening windows to allow the noise to escape out of the room (where feasible, with this action being counter-productive if a loud noise source is present outside the classroom; e.g., traffic noise from a main road); ii) reducing the noise at its source (e.g., sticking half-tennis balls on the ends of chair legs to reduce the scraping noise); iii) repositioning, removing, or replacing noisy devices; and iv) covering acoustically hard surfaces with acoustically soft surfaces to reduce reverberation (e.g., covering hard windows with soft curtains, covering hard floors with soft carpet, etc.) (Acoustical Society of America, 2003a, 2003b; National Acoustic Laboratories, 2018; Siebein et al., 2000; The HEARing Cooperative Research Centre, 2018).

More complex options for making the classroom quieter can include installing acoustic barriers to separate dual classrooms, installing (and maintaining) central air conditioning systems with long duct lengths, and reducing classroom volume by adding a lay-in ceiling. It can also include avoiding poor acoustic builds such as those often used in open plan and demountable classrooms (Acoustical Society of America, 2003a, 2003b; National Acoustic Laboratories, 2018; Siebein et al., 2000; The HEARing Cooperative Research Centre, 2018).

How to improve classroom acoustics – Where to get help

Many educators will understandably be daunted by the prospect of taking a 'do-it-yourself' approach to improving the acoustics of their classroom. Luckily, help is at hand from a range of sources, including those referenced in the section above.

Taking your first steps to improving the acoustics in your classroom can come from online resources such as the 'Improve your Classroom's Acoustics' practice module[1] on the Autism CRC's *inclusionED* web-based platform. This module details a range of information, tools, strategies, and a community of practice to help teachers to both assess and manage the acoustics in their classrooms. Included in this module is information about the SoundOut Room Acoustics Analyzer app for iPads created by the National Acoustic Laboratories in Australia. This app provides step-by-step instructions to guide users through the measurements outlined in Figure 7.1 in this chapter, their interpretation, and what can be done to improve the classroom acoustics for classrooms that don't meet Australian standards on these measures.

Finally, educators can also seek professional help from acoustic engineers and some audiologists who can measure the 'acoustic health' of existing classrooms. The Australian Acoustical Society website has information on acoustic engineers according to specialty and locality in Australia[2].

Improving classroom acoustics – A hierarchy of potential benefit

With regards to the functional benefits to individual students, research suggests that some student behaviours could be expected to change sooner and others later following improvements in classroom acoustics (e.g., Good & Gillon, 2014; Grube, Kumar, Cooper, Turton, & Griffiths, 2012; Reynolds et al., 2016). This hierarchy of potential benefit could follow the hierarchy of listening skills. If the immediate benefit of improving classroom acoustics is that the teacher's voice is easier to hear, then its potential benefits could flow from proximate to distant on the listening hierarchy. In this argument, proximate benefits would be expected first in student hearing and auditory processing as these areas would benefit more immediately from improved classroom acoustics alone.

Distant benefits would be expected later in student phonological processing, auditory attention, memory, and language as these areas would benefit less immediately from improved classroom acoustics alone. Instead, benefits in these areas would need *sustained* improvements in classroom acoustics (providing students with consistently clear, less effortful access to the teacher's voice in the classroom) plus the presence of other factors for improvements to be realised. This argument of proximate versus distant benefits is consistent with our proposition that improving classroom acoustics could put students in a better position to learn, but their learning still has to take place over time.

Improving classroom acoustics as a universal adjustment within inclusive classrooms

Improving classroom acoustics could be implemented universally as part of a commitment to the *Disability Standards for Education* (Commonwealth of Australia, 2006) which mandate for the right of all students to have equitable access to choices and opportunities within their learning environment. As discussed in Chapter 4, the second principle of Universal Design for Learning (UDL) is to 'Provide multiple means of representation of information' (CAST, 2020a). Within this principle, UDL recognised that learning is compromised 'when information is presented in formats that require extraordinary effort' (CAST, 2020b) and advocates for different options in the presentation of visual or auditory information in the classroom. Further, it recommends that information should be customised in response to the perceptual needs of students (Checkpoint 1.1) by improving perceptual clarity including the volume of speech. Improving classroom acoustics could serve as a universal adjustment that puts all students in a better position to learn.

In the above context, improving a classroom's acoustics is particularly appealing because some of its methods can potentially benefit all students with no one student appearing to be 'different'. This potential can be seen in the example of using RMHAs that require individual students to wear a receiver and ear piece versus SFA that requires a speaker to be placed in the classroom to assist students on the spectrum. While reporting students on the spectrum benefited from RMHA use, Rance, Saunders, Carew, Johansson and Tan (2014) reported some students on the spectrum refused to wear ear pieces as it set them apart from their peers. This was thought to relate to Polgar's (2010) argument that acceptance of particular technologies is mediated not only by the functional advantage they provide the user but the degree to which they are perceived as 'stigmatising' by the user. Rance et al. (2014) and Schafer et al. (2013) have also reported some students on the spectrum having difficulty tolerating RMHAs due to tactile sensitivities. Countering these suggestions that SFA more than RMHAs could serve as a universal adjustment within inclusive classrooms is the risk that students who are hyper-sensitive to noise may not tolerate amplification systems of any sort, be it from SFA or RMHA technologies.

> *… improving a classroom's acoustics is particularly appealing because some of its methods can potentially benefit all students with no one student appearing to be 'different'.*

Research method

The Autism CRC classroom acoustics research described in this chapter sought to contribute to the many interactive and dynamic factors that pave the way for successful student participation and learning as described in this volume. The premise of the research presented here is *not* that low-quality acoustics is *the direct* or primary cause of poor classroom performance or learning outcomes for all students. Rather, the premise is that classroom acoustics have the *potential* to support or impede subsequent processing of what the teacher says. This identifies classroom acoustics as an important risk factor (after Bishop, 2006; Halliday, Tuomainen, & Rosen, 2017) which we assert needs to be managed appropriately in the inclusive classroom.

Research aim

Our overall aim was to determine if a diverse group of students benefitted from the use of SFA in their classrooms.

Research design

Our research design was a two-group, randomised controlled trial (RCT) with crossover. The two groups were as follows: i) students on the autism spectrum; and ii) classroom peers who were not on the autism spectrum (referred to as 'classroom peers'). The RCT meant that classrooms in which the students were located were randomly allocated an SFA system for the first or the second semester of an academic year. The crossover meant that classrooms allocated an SFA system in Semester 1 'crossed over' to not be allocated an SFA system in Semester 2, and vice versa, helping us to separate any effects of the SFA from effects of the time of year in which we completed the assessments.

Participants

Table 7.1 details participants from 12 schools in the greater Brisbane area, Australia who took part in the study.

Seventeen students had an SFA system in their classrooms in Semester 1 and 13 in Semester 2 of the same school year. Students classified as being on the autism spectrum had previously received a clinical diagnosis and had been verified through the stringent process administered by the Queensland Department of Education. The allocation of students to each group was supported by parental ratings of their child on the Social Responsiveness Scale, 2nd edition (SRS-2; Constantino, 2012), the Short Sensory Profile (SSP; Dunn, 2014), and the Social Communication Questionnaire-Lifetime (SCQ-L; Rutter, Bailey, & Lord, 2003). While both groups of students performed similarly on a measure of non-verbal intelligence (the non-verbal component of Kaufman Brief Intelligence Test, 2nd edition [KBIT-2; Kaufman & Kaufman, 2004]), the groups performed differently on a measure of verbal intelligence (the verbal component of Kaufman Brief Intelligence Test, 2nd edition [KBIT-2, Kaufman & Kaufman, 2004]) and a measure of receptive language (the concepts and following directions sub-test of the Clinical Evaluation of Language Fundamentals, 4th edition [CELF-4; Semel, Wiig, & Secord, 2003]).

Measures

We were interested in measuring potential proximate and distant benefits from SFA. Our measures of potential proximate benefits were a questionnaire for the teachers to appraise student

TABLE 7.1 Research Participants

	Students on the autism spectrum	Classroom peers
Number of Year 3 students	13	17
Male:Female ratio	9M:4F	7M:10F
Age range (years, months)	7yrs, 6mo to 8yrs, 4mo	7yrs, 6mo to 9yrs, 3mo

TABLE 7.2 Assessments and Sub-Tests Administered and Domains Measured

Measures for potential proximate benefits of SFA administered at the end of each semester (twice in total)

Assessment	Sub-test	Domain
The Listening Inventory For Education-Revised, Teacher Appraisal of Listening Difficulty (LIFE-R TALD)[a]	-	Level of challenge when listening and learning in different situations in the classroom
Video recordings of students' listening behaviours during normal classroom activities		Student response time to teacher question or directive

Measures of potential distant benefits of SFA administered at the beginning of Semester 1, between semesters, and at the end of Semester 2 (three times in total)

Assessment	Sub-test	Domain
Comprehensive Test of Phonological Processing, 2nd edition (CTOPP-2)[b]	Nonword repetition in quiet	Phonological processing
	Nonword repetition in noise: Presented with four-speaker babble noise[c]	Phonological processing in the presence of background noise
	Blending nonwords in quiet	Phonological processing
	Blending nonwords in noise: Presented with four-speaker babble noise	Phonological processing in the presence of background noise
Test of Variables of Attention (TOVA™)[d]	Auditory attention	Attention
Test of Auditory Processing Skills, 3rd edition (TAPS-3)[e]	Number memory forward Number memory backward	Memory
Kaufmann Test of Educational Achievement, 3rd edition (KTEA-3)[f]	Literacy Numeracy	Literacy and numeracy

[a] Anderson, Smaldino, & Spangler, 2011
[b] Wagner, Torgesen, Rashotte, & Pearson, 2013
[c] the nonword repetition sub-test of the CTOPP-2 was adapted to present half of the stimuli in noise
[d] Greenberg, Kindschi, Dupuy, & Hughes, 2008
[e] Martin & Brownell, 2005
[f] Kaufman & Kaufman, 2014.

listening difficulty in the classroom and a video analysis of student response times to teacher questions and directives. Our measures of potential distant benefits were standardised measures of phonological processing, auditory attention, memory, and educational achievement. These measures are shown in Table 7.2 and in further detail below.

Questionnaires

At the end of each semester, teachers used the Listening Inventory For Education–Revised Teacher Appraisal of Listening Difficulty (LIFE-R TALD; Anderson, Smaldino, & Spangler, 2011) to reflect on the listening behaviour of the participating students. This questionnaire asked teachers to reflect on participation behaviours recognised to be sensitive to acoustic changes to the environment; for example, 'Attending to and following directions and class activities'. The teachers completed this questionnaire once for the semester in which their classroom had SFA and once for the semester in which their classroom did not have SFA.

Video observation

On a morning towards the end of each semester, approximately three hours of regular classroom activity was captured by two cameras positioned at the front and rear of each classroom, providing one recording with SFA and one recording without SFA. These videos were analysed for occasions of teacher instructions or questions that required a response from the students. Responses were timestamped to identify the average time taken by each student in each recording to respond to teacher instructions and questions. These analyses were completed in each classroom once with SFA (in the semester where the classroom had SFA), and once without SFA (in the semester where the classroom did not have SFA).

Standardised measures

Before, between, and after the two semesters in the year of our study, we assessed the participating students using a range of standardised measures (see Table 7.2). These measures included:

1. A modified version of the Nonword Repetition (NWR) and Blending Nonwords (BNW) sub-tests from the Children's Test of Phonological Processing, version 2 (CTOPP-2; Wagner, Torgesen, Rashotte, & Pearson, 2013) to assess phonological processing in quiet and in noise.
2. The auditory component of the Test of Variables of Attention (TOVA; Greenberg, Kindschi, Dupuy, & Hughes, 2008) to assess auditory sustained attention.
3. The Number Memory Forward (NMF) and Number Memory Backwards (NMB) sub-tests of the Test of Auditory Processing Skills, 3rd edition (TAPS-3; Martin & Brownell, 2005) to assess auditory short-term memory and auditory working memory.
4. The Kaufman Test of Educational Achievement, 3rd edition (KTEA-3 Brief; Kaufman & Kaufman, 2014) to assess academic achievement in the areas of spelling, reading, and mathematics. These assessments were conducted on each participating student before Semester 1 (as a baseline assessment) and at the end of the semester in which their classroom had SFA and at the end of the semester in which their classroom did not have SFA.

Results

The results of our study are shown in Figure 7.4. Our main findings showed that following one semester of SFA, teachers reported improved listening behaviour (LIFE-R TALD) for all participating students, and improvements were seen in one aspect of phonological processing (BNW) in students on the spectrum but not their classroom peers. We found no changes following SFA in student response times to teacher questions or directives (video analysis), auditory attention (TOVA), memory (TAPS-3 NMF and NMR), or academic achievement (KTEA-3). Finally, we received no reports of SFA aggravating hypo- or hyper-sensitivity to sounds, phonophobia, or over-interest in sounds in any of the participating students.

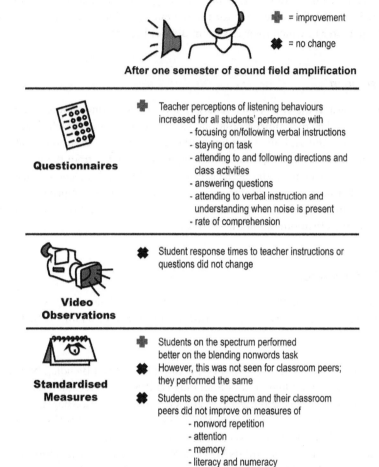

FIGURE 7.4 Summary of the findings following analysis of student performance on questionnaire responses, classroom observations, and standardised measures.

Conclusions and take-home messages for teachers

Our results were consistent with our proposition that any benefits from improved classroom acoustics could proceed along the hierarchy of listening skills. In this regard, the teacher reports of improved listening behaviour for all participating students could be seen as a proximate benefit of SFA resulting more directly from students being in a better position to hear the teacher's voice. The improvements in one aspect of phonological processing in students on the spectrum following SFA could be seen as a more distal benefit of SFA resulting from those students being in a *sustained* better position to hear the teacher's voice and benefitting from that position by going on to improve one aspect of their phonological processing.

The absence of improvements in our other measures of student performance adds further support to our proposition that any benefits from improved classroom acoustics could proceed along the hierarchy of listening skills. In this regard, the absence of benefit in response times reminds us that improving classroom acoustics will not automatically realise all potential proximate listening benefits. Similarly, the absence of benefits in other aspects of student phonological processing as well as auditory attention, memory, and educational outcomes reminds us that improving classroom acoustics may not be enough on its own to realise potential distant benefits, particularly in the short term such as the single semester of SFA used in our study.

Finally, the benefits realised in the absence of any reports of SFA aggravating hypo- or hypersensitivity to sounds, phonophobia, or over-interest in sounds in any of the participating students supports the consideration of SFA as a universal adjustment for a potentially wide range of students in the classroom.

Limitations

Our study had several limitations including the low number of participating students, the need for these students to complete long batteries of standardised tests, the duration of SFA being limited to one semester only, and the study being limited to one academic year only. Taken together, these limitations suggest that while the results of this research were promising, caution is needed before applying the study's results to individual students on the spectrum, to the use of SFA for periods longer than one semester, to student outcomes beyond those measured in the study, and to student outcomes measured beyond a single academic year.

Take-home messages

Take-home message 1: Classrooms can be noisy

Many Australian classrooms do not meet the recommended standards and tend to be too noisy and/or reverberant, making the listening environment difficult for learners in those classrooms.

Take-home message 2: Listening in the classroom requires a hierarchy of skills

Listening in the classroom requires a hierarchy of skills starting with hearing (being able to detect sound) and progressing to other skills such as auditory processing (being able to process the frequency, intensity, timing, and location of sound), auditory attention (being able to attend to sound), and language processing (being able to process words and sentences).

Take-home message 3: Poor classroom acoustics challenges the hierarchy of listening skills

Poor classroom acoustics places high demands on students at every level of the listening hierarchy. This can be worse for students who are younger, from poorer socio-economic areas, are attending school in a language other than their first language, have hearing loss, and/or have neurodevelopmental disorders.

Take-home message 4: Improving classroom acoustics could benefit students on a hierarchy from proximate to distant

Improving classroom acoustics could lead to more immediate, proximate benefits to listening skills more dependent on simply being able to hear, as well as later, distant benefits to listening and other skills dependent on more than simply being able to hear.

Take-home message 5: Improving classroom acoustics could put students in a better position to learn, but they still have to go on to learn

Improving classroom acoustics will not lead to improved listening and other skills in all students. Instead, improving classroom acoustics can put students in a better position to learn, but students still have to go on to learn.

Take-home message 6: Improving classroom acoustics can be a universal adjustment within inclusive classrooms

By potentially benefitting all students within the classroom without stigmatising individuals, improving classroom acoustics could be implemented as a universal adjustment within inclusive classrooms. In Australia, this could form part of a commitment to the *Disability Standards for Education* (Commonwealth of Australia, 2006) which mandate for the right of all students to have equitable access to choices and opportunities within their learning environment.

Take-home message 7: Help is available

Educators can get help for managing the acoustics in their classroom from a range of sources including the Autism CRC's *inclusionED* teacher practice titled 'Improve your Classroom's Acoustics', apps such as the SoundOut Room Acoustics Analyzer app for iPads created by the National Acoustic Laboratories in Australia, and professional groups such as the Australian Acoustical Society[3].

Creating a genuinely inclusive educational setting: Closing thoughts for the health professional

It is readily apparent that allied health professionals such as audiologists, speech pathologists, and occupational therapists have a role to play in supporting students who could benefit from improved classroom acoustics. Historically, health services were positioned to be allied to medicine, situated within clinical settings and defined by the 'disorder' for which they provided treatment. In this regard, audiology assessments may include, but are not necessarily restricted to, evaluation of hearing and auditory processing; speech pathology assessments include evaluation of speech and language skills; and occupational therapy assessments include evaluation of classroom functioning; all with the purpose of remediating any deviations from the expected norm. This identifies students who fall 'outside the normal range' as being 'others' who are in need of service provision.

It is clear that the translation of allied health services into a genuinely inclusive education setting, as described by Cologon (2019), cannot be a cut and paste of regular clinical service. The ableism which is inherent within such services is an uncomfortable fact for many clinicians who are deeply dedicated to improving student outcomes and driven to ensure that all students, in all of their diversity, have equitable opportunities to participate in school.

> *There is a need to ensure the acoustics of all classrooms meets the relevant Australian standards in order to provide equitable learning opportunities for all students in all classrooms.*

Cologon (2019) suggests that one of the social outcomes from a conflict between ableist attitudes within inclusive school environments is perpetuation of exclusion. This is clearly inconsistent with beneficence, a primary principle underpinning the work of allied health professionals and provides an impetus to interrogate the role of allied health professionals, and the service delivery models adopted in inclusive settings. Prolonged, confronting discussion and debate is required if educators are to be supported in the provision of education opportunities which are inclusive of all students. As allied health professionals, the authors of this chapter have interrogated their own potential for bias and attempted to present and discuss the implications of this research through the lens of genuine inclusion. There is a need to ensure the acoustics of all classrooms meets the relevant Australian standards in order to provide equitable learning opportunities for all students in all classrooms.

Notes

1 https://www.inclusioned.edu.au/node/2400
2 https://www.acoustics.asn.au/joomla/index.php
3 https://www.acoustics.asn.au/joomla/index.php

References

Acoustical Society of America. (2003a). *Classroom acoustics I: A resource for creating learning environments with desirable listening conditions.* Retrieved from http://acousticalsociety.org/classroom-acoustics/.

Acoustical Society of America. (2003b). *Classroom acoustics II: Acoustical barriers to learning.* Retrieved from http://acousticalsociety.org/classroom-acoustics/.

Anderson, K. L., Smaldino, J. J., & Spangler, C. (2011). *Listening Inventory For Education – Revised (LIFE-R). Teacher checklist: Self-advocacy and instructional access.* Retrieved from https://successforkidswithhearingloss.com/.

Baldwin, C. (2008). *Auditory cognition and human performance: Research and applications.* Boca Raton, FL: Taylor & Francis Group.

Bishop, D. (2006). Developmental cognitive genetics: How psychology can inform genetics and vice versa. *The Quarterly Journal of Experimental Psychology,* 59(7), 1153–1168. doi:10.1080/17470210500489372.

CAST. (2020a). *Provide multiple means of representation.* Retrieved from http://udlguidelines.cast.org/representation.

CAST. (2020b). *Provide options for perception.* Retrieved from http://udlguidelines.cast.org/representation/perception.

Cologon, K. (2019). *Towards inclusive education: A necessary process of transformation.* Melbourne: Children and Young People with Disability Australia.

Commonwealth of Australia. (2006). *Disability standards for education 2005 plus guidance notes.* Canberra: Australian Government Publishing Service. Retrieved from https://docs.education.gov.au/system/files/doc/other/disability_standards_for_education_2005_plus_guidance_notes.pdf.

Constantino, J. N. (2012). *Social Responsiveness Scale* (2nd ed.). Torrance, CA: WPS.

Crandell, C. C., & Smaldino, J. J. (2000). Classroom acoustics for children with normal hearing and with hearing impairment. *Language, Speech & Hearing Services in Schools,* 31(4), 362–370. doi:10.1044/0161-1461.3104.362.

Cutiva, L. C. C., Vogel, I., & Burdorf, A. (2013). Voice disorders in teachers and their associations with work-related factors: A systematic review. *Journal of Communication Disorders,* 46(2), 143–155. doi:10.1016/j.jcomdis.2013.01.001.

Dockrell, J. E., & Shield, B. M. (2004). Noise in schools: Children's perception of their acoustic environment at home and at school. *Journal of Acoustical Society of America,* 115, 2964–2973.

Dunn, W. (2014). *Sensory Profile 2.* Sydney: Pearson.

Good, P. V., & Gillon, G. (2014). Exploring the benefits of integrating sound-field amplification and phonological awareness intervention for young school-aged children. *Speech, Language and Hearing,* 17(1), 2–14. doi:10.1179/2050572813Y.0000000022.

Greenberg, L. M., Kindschi, C. L., Dupuy, T. R., & Hughes, S. J. (2008). *TOVA clinical manual*. Los Alamitos, CA: TOVA Company.

Grube, M., Kumar, S., Cooper, F., Turton, S., & Griffiths, T. (2012). Auditory sequence analysis and phonological skill. *Proceedings of the Royal Society B: Biological Sciences*, 279(1746), 4496–4504. doi:10.1098/rspb.2012.1817.

Halliday, L. F., Tuomainen, O., & Rosen, S. (2017). Auditory processing deficits are sometimes necessary and sometimes sufficient for language difficulties in children: Evidence from mild to moderate sensorineural hearing loss. *Cognition*, 166, 139–151.

Heeney, M. (2004). *Creating enhanced learning environments: The benefits of sound-field amplification systems*. Wellington: Oticon Foundation.

Johnson, C. (2000). Children's phoneme identification in reverberation and noise. *Journal of Speech Language and Hearing Research*, 43(1), 144–157. doi:10.1044/jslhr.4301.144.

Kaufman, A. S., & Kaufman, N. L. (2004). *Kaufman Brief Intelligence Test* (2nd ed.). Bloomington, MN: Pearson.

Kaufman, A. S., & Kaufman, N. L. (2014). *Kaufman Test of Educational Achievement* (3rd ed.). Bloomington, MN: Pearson.

Kazmierczak-Murray, S., & Downes, P. (2015). Classroom sound field amplification systems for language development during early school years in contexts of socio-economic exclusion: The neglected role of classroom contextual dimensions. *International Journal of Early Childhood Special Education*, 7(1), 24–50. doi:10.20489/intjecse.31608.

Keith, W. J., & Purdy, S. C. (2014). Assistive and therapeutic effects of amplification for auditory processing disorder. *Seminars in Hearing*, 55(1), 27–38.

Martin, N. A., & Brownell, R. (2005). *Test of Auditory Processing Skills* (3rd ed.). Novato, CA: Academic Therapy Publications.

Massie, R., & Dillon, H. (2006). The impact of sound-field amplification in mainstream cross-cultural classrooms: Part 1 educational outcomes. *Australian Journal of Education*, 50(1), 62–77.

Moore, D. R., Cowan, J. A., Riley, A., Edmondson-Jones, A. M., & Ferguson, M. A. (2011). Development of auditory processing in 6- to 11-yr-old children. *Ear and Hearing*, 32(3), 269–285. doi:10.1097/AUD.0b013e318201c468.

National Acoustic Laboratories. (2018). *Improving listening in classrooms*. Retrieved from https://www.nal.gov.au/improving-listening-in-classrooms/.

O'Connor, K. (2012). Auditory processing in autism spectrum disorder: A review. *Neuroscience and Biobehavioral Reviews*, 36, 836–854.

Polgar, J. (2010). The myth of neutral technology. In M. M. K. Oishi, I. M. Mitchell & H. F. M. Van der Loos (Eds.), *Design and use of assistive technology: Social, technical, ethical, and economic challenges* (pp. 17–23). New York, NY: Springer. doi:10.1007/978-1-4419-7031-2_2.

Rance, G., Saunders, K., Carew, P., Johansson, M., & Tan, J. (2014). The use of listening devices to ameliorate auditory deficit in children with autism. *Journal of Pediatrics*, 164(2), 352–357. doi:10.1016/j.jpeds.2013.09.041.

Reynolds, S., Kuhaneck, H. M., & Pfeiffer, B. (2016). Systematic review of the effectiveness of frequency modulation devices in improving academic outcomes in children with auditory processing difficulties. *American Journal of Occupational Therapy*, 70(1). doi:10.5014/ajot.2016.016832.

Rosenberg, G. G., Blake-Rahter, P., Heavner, J., Allen, L., Redmond, B. M., Phillips, J., & Stigers, K. (1999). Improving classroom acoustics (ICA): A three-year FM sound field classroom amplification study. *Journal of Educational Audiology*, 7, 8–28.

Rutter, M., Bailey, A., & Lord, C. (2003). *The Social Communication Questionnaire (SCQ) [Manual]*. Torrance, CA: Western Psychological Services.

Schafer, E. C., Mathews, L., Mehta, S., Hill, M., Munoz, A., Bishop, R., & Moloney, M. (2013). Personal FM systems for children with autism spectrum disorders (ASD) and/or attention-deficit hyperactivity disorder (ADHD): An initial investigation. *Journal of Communication Disorders*, 46(1), 30–52. doi:10.1016/j.jcomdis.2012.09.002.

Semel, E., Wiig, E. H., & Secord, W. A. (2003). *The clinical evaluation of language fundamentals* (4th ed.). San Antonio, TX: The Psychological Corporation.

Siebein, G. W., Gold, M. A., Siebein, G. W., & Ermann, M. G. (2000). Ten ways to provide a high-quality acoustical environment in schools. *Language, Speech and Hearing Services in Schools*, 31(4), 376–384. doi:10.1044/0161-1461.3104.376.

Standards Australia. (2016). *Acoustics – Recommended design sound levels and reverberation times for building interiors (AS 2107-2016)*. Sydney: Standards Australia.

The HEARing Cooperative Research Centre. (2018). *HEARnet learning module: The listening environment*. Retrieved from https://hearnetlearning.org.au/mod/page/view.php?id=185.

van der Kruk, Y., Wilson, W., Palghat, K., Downing, C., Harper-Hill, K., & Ashburner, J. (2017). Improved signal-to-noise ratio and classroom performance in children with autism spectrum disorder: A systematic review. *Review Journal of Autism and Developmental Disorders*, 4(3), 243–253. doi:10.1007/s40489-017-0111-7.

Wagner, R. K., Torgesen, J. K., Rashotte, C. A., & Pearson, N. A. (2013). *Comprehensive Test of Phonological Processing* (2nd ed.). Austin, TX: Pro-Ed.

Wilson, W., Downing, C., Perrykkad, K., Armstrong, R., Arnott, W., Ashburner, J., & Harper-Hill, K. (2019). The "acoustic health" of primary school classrooms in Brisbane, Australia. *Speech, Language and Hearing*. doi:10.1080/2050571X.2019.1637042

PART 4

Transition to life after school

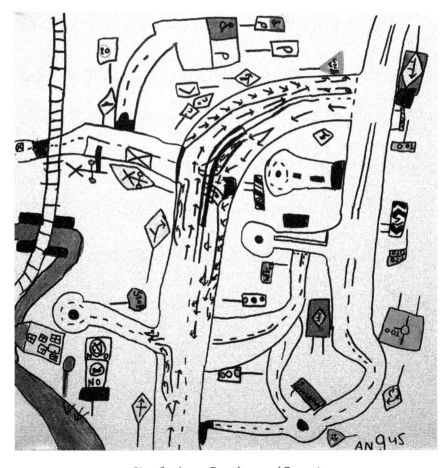

Signs (by Angus Reardon, aged 7 years)

'I love drawing signs and maps. It's my favourite thing to do. I hope you like it too.'

8

POST-SCHOOL TRANSITIONS

Supportive strategies informed by real-life experiences

Rachel Aberdein and Beth Saggers

> This first chapter of Part 4 gives an insider account of one of the authors' experiences transitioning from school to her adult life. As an undiagnosed person on the autism spectrum at school, she was often perceived as 'disorganised' and found the post-school transition to the workplace particularly challenging. The chapter discusses how school experiences can influence post-school outcomes, with the author reflecting on what supports and adjustments may have helped prepare her for adult life, providing practical suggestions for educators wishing to implement inclusive school and learning experiences for students on the autism spectrum and to help prepare them for the transition to post-school adult life.

In the 2018 summary of findings from the Australian Bureau of Statistics' Survey of Disability, Ageing and Carers, a confronting 92.3% of students on the autism spectrum reported experiencing some form of education restriction (Australian Bureau of Statistics [ABS], 2018). When attending a school setting, 77.7% of students reported a range of issues they experienced that influenced their learning participation and engagement, with 59.8% reporting this related to the social elements of school, 55.3% reporting learning difficulties, and 51.5% relating to the communication elements of school. Almost half reported receiving additional support and almost half (45.9%) reported needing more support than they currently received. It has also been well documented in research that students on the spectrum are underperforming in school in comparison to their learning potential and are experiencing poorer post-school outcomes (Ashburner, Ziviani, & Rodger, 2010; Estes, Rivera, Bryan, Cali, & Dawson, 2011; Jones et al., 2009; Keen, Webster, & Ridley, 2015).

Post-school outcomes for students on the spectrum

Given ABS data on the less than satisfactory school experiences of students on the spectrum, it is not surprising that post-school outcomes for this population are also poorer than outcomes achieved by other students (ABS, 2018). For example, results of the 2018 Australian Bureau of Statistics' Survey of Disability, Ageing and Carers suggest that people on the autism spectrum are less likely than others to complete a post-school qualification. The results of the survey suggested that people on the spectrum were less likely to achieve Advanced Diploma, Diploma, or Certificate III or IV qualifications than people with no diagnosed disability or diagnosed disabilities. Furthermore, people on the spectrum were found to experience greater challenges entering the workforce. For example, the unemployment rate for people on the autism spectrum was 34.1%, more than three times the rate for people with disability generally (10.3%) and almost eight times the rate of people without disability (4.6%) (ABS, 2018).

These challenging statistics highlight the importance of improving the school experiences of students on the spectrum in inclusive settings, effectively supporting their post-school transition, and ensuring that the skills learned in school can help to do this.

> Research has highlighted that a key challenge to successful post-school outcomes for this group of students is a lack of transition planning that is responsive to their unique needs

The difficulties adolescents on the spectrum experience transitioning to post-school activities of work, life, leisure, and education are now well documented (Hatfield, Ciccarelli, Falkmer, & Falkmer, 2017; Howlin, Moss, Savage, & Rutter, 2013; Taylor & Seltzer, 2011). Research has highlighted that a key challenge to successful post-school outcomes for this group of students is a lack of transition planning that is responsive to their unique needs (Morningstar & Clark, 2003).

Transition planning and students on the spectrum

Transition planning has been described as involving 'a set of coordinated activities that support adolescents in secondary school to successfully negotiate the move from school into adult life' (Hatfield, Ciccarelli, et al., 2017, p. 3). This type of planning involves helping students to prepare for three key post-school activities, including i) employment; ii) post-school education; and iii) vocational training (Hatfield, Ciccarelli, et al., 2017; Roberts, 2010). Research has found there are a number of benefits of this type of planning, including improvements in:

- Self-determination.
- Rates of employment.
- Success in post-secondary settings.
- Happiness.
- Community participation.
  (Hatfield, Ciccarelli, et al., 2017; King, Baldwin, Currie, & Evans, 2005)

While research has highlighted the importance of supporting social emotional competence as an educational need, it is often overlooked as a focus in schools and planning for students on the spectrum (Lee & Carter, 2012; Saggers et al., 2018). Social emotional support is a particularly important consideration in transition planning as many elements of post-school transition rely heavily on social emotional competence for success. The importance of supporting autism-specific needs such as social emotional competence and autism-specific transition planning therefore need further consideration in schools (Saggers et al., 2018). Additionally, it is important to consider the role of the student in their own transition planning with support and planning for their equitable, active participation, and self-advocacy important elements to be considered as part of the transition planning process.

Research suggests that in only 23% of cases are students on the spectrum involved in their own transition planning and, when they are, their role is less active than their non-disabled peers or other students with disabilities (Hatfield, Ciccarelli, et al., 2017; Shogren & Plotner, 2012). There is a need, therefore, for more to be done to determine what the transition planning needs of this specific group of students are in order to ensure the process is meaningful and effective (Hatfield, Ciccarelli, et al., 2017; Lee & Carter, 2012). In addition, transition planning for students on the spectrum requires further exploration because even when transition planning does occur, the outcomes can still be less positive than those of their peers (Newman et al., 2011).

Important factors in transition planning with students on the spectrum

A recent study by Hatfield, Ciccarelli et al. (2017) highlighted some important factors in transition planning with this group of students. Some of these factors support previous findings in research (Test et al., 2009; Test, Smith, & Carter, 2014) and include:

- Having a coordinated plan for transition planning.
- Having a strengths-focused approach for transition planning.
- Having support from a team in transition planning.
- Encouraging skill development in transition planning.

Other more novel findings of Hatfield, Ciccarelli et al. (2017) included the influence of the adolescents':

- Motivation.
- Insights.
- Levels of anxiety regarding the transition process.

Parents and educators involved in the research identified a lack of motivation, insight, and heightened levels of anxiety of the student on the spectrum as key challenges. These are particularly relevant to transition planning. Key factors that were identified that help overcome these issues included:

- Preparing and planning for post-school transition is critical and the planning needs to start as early as possible. This planning needs to have a clear process for the transition period and involve the setting of appropriate goals (Hatfield, Falkmer, Falkmer, & Ciccarelli, 2017).
- Having guidance from a team whose makeup is tailored to needs of the student (Hatfield, Ciccarelli, et al., 2017; Hatfield, Falkmer, et al., 2017).
- Supporting the student to develop skills needed for post-school activities and engagement in real-life experiences (Hatfield, Ciccarelli, et al., 2017). This involved making sure the student on the spectrum had grasped the big picture by helping them to see how things they were currently doing may help with future plans post-school. Real-life experiences have been identified as the best way to do this and were considered one of the most important elements of transition planning. Activities that helped them explore different career options as part of the process were also identified as helpful in giving them a bigger picture view (Hatfield, Falkmer, et al., 2017).
- Developing a clear transition plan and a coordinated response (Hatfield, Ciccarelli, et al., 2017). This included having the student be part of the transition planning. This was considered essential and helped give them a sense of control over the process which in turn

helped reduce anxiety and increase motivation. Encouraging the student to have high aspirations and expectations was also important but these expectations also needed to be flexible (Hatfield, Falkmer, et al., 2017).

The next section of this chapter highlights one of the authors' post-school experiences and provides her reflections on some key issues in her transition to post-school life. It also highlights some of the strategies she learned to put in place to help. Retrospective reflections can help inform schools' inclusive approaches to the development and implementation of transition planning with students on the spectrum and promote more successful post-school transitions. It is important to remember that this chapter is only providing one person's views of their personal post-school experiences, but it does highlight a number of things that are important to consider when collaboratively planning for post-school transitions with learners on the spectrum to maximise their post-school success.

A real-life experience of post-school transition

In this section, I will discuss from my perspective the challenges I experienced transitioning to post-school life. These challenges relate to gaining employment and dealing with a workplace environment. I will also discuss the strategies I used to address the challenges I experienced in looking for work, preparing for job interviews, participating in job interviews, gaining and maintaining employment, and managing the workplace itself. I would like to make it clear that these are based on my own experiences and views and that I'm not trying to speak for anyone else.

Until early adulthood, I spent my life as an undiagnosed person on the autism spectrum. Throughout my school years, my autistic traits were far from invisible but were generally perceived as character flaws or emotional issues, or not even really noticed because I was academically bright and well-behaved, and teachers had more pressing things to worry about than an 'anxious', 'messy', 'disorganised' student. This pattern of misinterpretation continued into my adult life and impacted on my ability to search for and obtain employment. In addition to this, once I left school, with its structure and its clear expectations, I had much greater difficulty in being successful because I didn't know what was expected of me, and I didn't have a clear plan for how to transition into work. The skills that were needed to succeed in school were also very different from the skills that were needed to succeed in the working world. At school, I didn't need social skills to succeed. In the working world, I needed to be adept socially to even have the chance to prove myself as a worker.

Looking for work

When looking for work, I experienced two key challenges that related to: i) difficulties I experienced with executive functioning; and ii) knowing what recruiters were really asking for.

Executive function

When looking for a job, challenges I experienced with my executive function skills related to:

- *Having to do things outside of my routine.*
- *Difficulty starting the task of job searching.*

- *Difficulty focusing once I began job searching.*
- *Trouble coming up with new approaches when my current approach was unsuccessful.*
- *Losing the materials that I needed to search for and apply for jobs.*
- *Becoming overwhelmed by all the different steps involved in the process of job searching and applying for jobs which would often result in me getting 'stuck' because I had no idea what to do next.*

I worked on a few strategies to overcome the executive function challenges I experienced. To start with, I built job searching into my routine, because I knew that if something was in my routine, it would get done, and that the only way for something to get done was if it was in my routine.

To begin job searching, I used alarms. I found it useful to use two alarms: a warning alarm to allow me to disengage from my current activity, because I found abrupt transitioning especially challenging, and a second alarm to begin job searching. To help me to focus on the task of job searching, strategies I used included forcing myself to work for a short amount of time, which usually gave me some momentum and meant I would work for much longer, and taking a task-based rather than time-based approach. This is because if you say 'I'm going to work for an hour' it's easy to waste 20 minutes of that hour on Facebook, but if you say 'I'm going to do 10 job applications and I don't care if it takes 10 hours', that is amazingly motivating.

> *To avoid getting overwhelmed, I broke things down into steps and forced myself to focus on only a single step at a time.*

To avoid losing essential materials, I kept them in one place in a format I knew I wouldn't lose, such as a computer or a single notebook. To avoid getting overwhelmed, I broke things down into steps and forced myself to focus on only a single step at a time. When I was stuck and couldn't think of new approaches, I went online and asked people for help. This was helpful for two reasons:

1. *I find written communication easier than spoken.*
2. *There's much more information available on the Internet than from the small set of people I speak to in person.*

Knowing what job descriptions really mean

In terms of knowing what recruiters were asking for, the issue was that the language in job advertisements ranged from vague statements in the job description such as 'good customer service skills' to statements in the job description that were open to interpretation such as 'flexible hours' (meaning you need to be available 24/7). I was also confused by the inclusion of things that should go without saying such as 'must be reliable, punctual, and polite'. If I had taken most job advertisements as being literally true, I would have thought that the standard employee was lazy, dishevelled, unreliable, made constant careless mistakes, and always fought with their co-workers and that employers were desperately trying to find someone better.

To help me understand the real meaning behind job descriptions, I used the approach I use for most non-literal communication: I treated the language used in job advertisements as a code. For example, if a job posting listed 'flexible hours', I would at least heavily imply that I was available every second of every day. I would also look up concrete examples of things that the advertisements used vague language for, using searches such as, 'what exactly are the actual, concrete actions that people with good customer service skills do?' and I would make it clear in my job applications that I was skilled in performing those actions.

Preparing for the interview

When preparing for an interview, key challenges I experienced related to:

- *The speech processing issues I experienced while listening to people on the phone intensified.*
- *Knowing what to wear to a job interview.*
- *The possibility of public transport going wrong.*
- *The possibility of getting lost on the way to the interview, because I was capable of getting lost while walking down the street.*

Strategies I implemented to deal with speech processing issues involved trying to make sure I was some-where quiet when I had to take a phone call. Sometimes when on the phone to prospective employers I also had to ask them to repeat themselves. When this happened, I would apologise and say that I was in a noisy environment, even if I wasn't. The reason I did this was that if I blamed the environment rather than the clarity of the interviewer's speech, I felt it would mitigate the possibility of the interviewer feeling bad, because if you make people feel bad, they are less inclined to help you.

To decide what to wear, I looked up ideas online or, if I had been to the workplace, I tried to dress similarly to employees who were working in the role that I would be interviewed for. To deal with the possibility of public transport going wrong, I assumed that everything that could go wrong would, and left a lot of buffer space at all stages of the journey. Google Maps was helpful because it gave information on everything: where you are on the bus route, where to go once you get off the bus, and it can be used to print hard copies of the route in case of lost Internet access.

At the interview

The job interview was the most challenging stage of the process for me. Many of the challenges I experienced related to body language, including eye contact. The biggest issue I had with body language was that my natural body language came across as unenthusiastic, underconfident, and uninterested, which was apparently not what employers are looking for.

Regarding eye contact, 90% of my issue was that I forgot to do it; the other 10% was that it felt either predatory or uncomfortably intimate, and that I had difficulty simultaneously listening and making eye contact. However, reminding myself to maintain eye contact was simple. To ease the discomfort, I pretended I was an actor playing the role of a job interviewee, which gave me some distance. If I had trouble focusing on what the interviewer was saying, I looked slightly away from their eyes, and showed through my body language; that is, orienting my body towards them, leaning slightly forward, nodding and giving short replies where relevant, mirroring the interviewer's body language, showing that I was paying attention to them.

> I prepared short speeches about my strengths and their relevance to the workplace …

I also experienced challenges with verbal communication as I don't think in words, so any language is a translation of my actual thoughts. I also had trouble putting words together on the spot, and my ability to speak was worse when I was under stress. To deal with verbal communication challenges, I researched what employers were looking for; for example, what made candidates stand out, and what were good questions to ask. I prepared short speeches about my strengths and their relevance to the workplace, and I looked up good answers to common interview questions and practised them until they didn't sound scripted.

I also had trouble with open-ended and vague questions like 'Tell me about yourself' and 'Why should we hire you?', and I had trouble promoting myself to potential employers; for example, knowing what made me better than the other candidates when I knew nothing about the other candidates.

To help with body language, I found it useful to draw on what I'd learned in my childhood acting lessons. I also researched how to read body language, and I looked up what 'confident', 'enthusiastic', and 'engaged' looked like and practised them until they looked natural.

I have spoken to people about the work I've done to be more successful in job interviews, particularly the work I've done in learning more appropriate body language. Some of the people I have spoken to expressed concern that this meant I wasn't being my true self. I didn't see it that way. The seemingly unengaged, underconfident, uninterested body language that I exhibited prior to working on my job interview skills wasn't something I made the conscious choice to do, it was just how I acted automatically. In reality, I was often highly engaged in things, I didn't have a confidence problem, and if I was at a job interview, I was always interested in the job. Working on my body language allowed me to communicate to people in such a way that what they saw me as feeling was congruent with what I was actually feeling. It didn't mean I wasn't being my true self; it meant I was expressing my true self in a way that other people would understand.

Challenges once I had a job and was in the workplace

Challenges once I had a job and I was in the workplace came under three categories: i) the work itself and the official hierarchy in the workplace; ii) social issues; and iii) sensory issues. Regarding the work itself and the official hierarchy in the workplace, I had trouble accepting authority for its own sake, I had trouble with criticism, I was a perfectionist because I couldn't gauge which seemingly tiny mistakes would be fatal, and I got wildly confused by the slightest ambiguity. As a result, I developed a number of strategies for dealing with the work itself and the actual hierarchy. If I was having issues accepting authority, I would ask questions that were ostensibly to show interest but also helped me understand why things had to happen in a particular way. For my trouble with ambiguity, I asked clarifying questions. This was actually a huge asset in jobs that required a lot of attention to detail. If I knew that my question would seem stupid, I acknowledged it using humour.

My strategies for perfectionism and having difficulty dealing with criticism included regularly seeking feedback so that I could monitor how well I was doing and fixed small problems before they turned into big problems; asking what was most important to work on so that I could prioritise; trying to interpret criticism as being about the job, rather than about me as a person; and watching my co-workers to try and gauge what imperfections might be acceptable, since these things were never spelled out explicitly.

Regarding social issues in the workplace, I chose less socially demanding jobs where possible, and I used my work as an excuse to stop socialising. I also learned basic social scripts, and I would mention my own interests to find common ground with people. To show social reciprocity, my biggest strategy was to reflect people's questions back at them; for example 'I did x, y, and z over the weekend; how about you?'

Generally, I observed the most socially successful people, and emulated them. A good example of this was when I worked in the retail sector and was often told how good I was at answering the phones. All I did was copy the phrasing and intonation of the store manager. In terms of social issues, the biggest challenge was that I had a very low social tolerance. I also didn't find most socialising very interesting. I had trouble with group work, difficulty with social reciprocity, and trouble with unspoken rules and unofficial hierarchies.

Regarding sensory issues, I had trouble concentrating with noise, as I didn't experience foreground and background noise; I had sounds that I was trying to focus on and sounds that were working to distract me from what I was focusing on, and I found too much noise painful. To mitigate the sensory issues, I tried to work in quiet environments, and I used headphones and listened to music to shut out distractions. I also went for short walks, for example to fill my water bottle, if I found that it was too noisy, or if I was getting distracted and needed to reset my focus.

Conclusion and reflection

In this section, I will suggest strategies that could be considered to support post-school transition planning for students on the spectrum. These are based on my experiences and that I have identified would have been useful to me to transition from education to work. I will also outline some important issues regarding autism and the workplace and outline some things I do that aren't directly work related but that help generally with my ability to work and find work.

What things could have been done in school to help with the transition to work?

Looking for work

When I was in school, people knew I was disorganised. Sadly, there was no executive function support; the only help I was given was being told 'You're so disorganised'. It would have been more helpful to have been taught basic planning and organisational skills such as goal-setting, implementing strategies, organising my physical possessions, and adapting when things went wrong. It would also have been useful to have had training on breaking down and sequencing complex tasks; that is, how to determine what steps are needed for a project, and how to break down and prioritise those steps.

More specifically to job searching, it would have been useful to have training and practice on effective job searching, and activities where I practised interpreting and responding to job advertisements, interpreting the language used rather than the usual 'This is how to format your resume, and here are the basics of English grammar'.

Preparing for the interview

Things that would have helped me at this stage include practice with phone conversations, and activities where I could practise navigating from one place to another.

At the interview

When I was in school, the biggest thing that would have helped me at this stage would have been the opportunity to practise mock interviews with clear instruction on what non-verbal language would be useful in interviews: not just 'look interested' but actually model what 'interested' looks like.

Important issues and helpful tips

In this section, I will discuss important issues regarding autism and the workplace and share things that I do that help generally with my ability to gain and maintain employment. The first issue is that we need to teach autistic people how to advocate for their needs. In many jobs, it's not unreasonable to use headphones or go for the occasional walk, but many workplaces treat these harmless strategies almost as crimes. A lot of social skills training seems to be based on compliance and how to be nice. There needs to be more emphasis on self-advocacy and standing up for your rights. The second issue, which autistic people can be especially vulnerable to, is the danger of falling prey to job scams, being taken advantage of in the workplace, and getting stuck in bad job environments. It's important to teach young people how to see when these things are happening, how to know when a job offer is too good to be true, and how they can get out of a bad job situation.

> *... I think it's important to give children and young people the opportunity to practise their social skills in a fun, supportive environment.*

Regarding the social issues, I think it's important to give children and young people the opportunity to practise their social skills in a fun, supportive environment. I've been in musical ensembles since I was very young, and I participated in team sports in primary school, and I think that those types of structured social environments can be very useful to autistic children. They would be particularly useful in conjunction with clear feedback on what the children are doing right, how they can improve, and how they can generalise the social skills used to less structured environments. It is my opinion that no matter how much someone with autism practises socialising, it will always be hard. Many entry-level jobs are highly social, and it's important to make autistic students aware that there are less socially oriented jobs out there. Everyone does best in jobs that play to their strengths.

Finally, I will discuss things I do that help generally with my ability to work and find work. The biggest thing I do is to stay healthy. I exercise a few times a week, I eat a balanced diet, and I get plenty of sleep. I also do the work I find the hardest when I'm at my best: for example, I don't want to think too hard first thing in the morning. I find that I can get a lot of work done in tiny chunks; for example, between weightlifting sets. It adds up. I build small relaxation activities into everything to reset my focus; for example, I have a lot of games on my phone that take less than 30 seconds to play. I also give myself small rewards for getting things done. More generally, I train my thinking to be flexible by doing things like lateral thinking puzzles and cryptic crosswords.

The advantages of how I was treated

Throughout this reflection, I have focused more on the disadvantages of how I was treated during my school days and what my schools could have done differently. There were, however, distinct advantages to how I was treated. The first is that I was judged almost entirely based on my strengths. While recognising many of the barriers autistic people face, I think that people live up to the expectations you set for them. If you constantly tell someone 'you are smart, talented, and capable', they will act as someone who is smart, talented, and capable. This has certainly been the case for me. The second big advantage is that the way I was treated left me with a very strong sense of personal agency. I think that if a person is given constant close guidance throughout their life, they will grow up expecting that guidance to continue, and not develop the ability to cope with problems themselves. My experience of constantly being told 'you're smart, figure out for yourself how to deal with your problems' acted as protection against this.

It is hoped that listening to the experiences of people on the spectrum and their accounts can help inform our approaches to learning and support a more informed approach to transition planning that will in turn lead to improved outcomes for people on the autism spectrum as they transition to life after school. While this chapter focuses solely on the experiences of one autistic person and provides their personal perspective of the transition from school to a post-school context, it does highlight a number of key things that may be important to consider as part of the transition process, including:

- Planning that identifies and helps to minimise things that may be barriers to success.
- Supporting social understanding, executive function skills, and time management.
- Taking a strengths-based approach.
- Teaching skills that will support seeking and gaining employment (e.g., writing a resume, understanding job advertisements, preparing for and taking a job interview, developing the skills required for specific job contexts, choosing jobs that play to your strengths).

For post-school outcomes to improve, transition planning needs to play a far more active school role for this group of students. The planning needs to be responsive to the unique needs of the individual and supportive in preparing the students for post-school life (Hatfield, Ciccarelli, et al., 2017; Morningstar & Clark, 2003; Roberts, 2010). Transition planning that involves a coordinated team approach and a strength and skill development focus is crucial (Test et al., 2009; Test et al., 2014). Most importantly, the transition planning needs to support the student on the spectrum to have an active and equitable voice in their transition needs and goals and the strategies identified to support their post-school dreams.

References

Ashburner, J., Ziviani, J., & Rodger, S. (2010). Surviving in the mainstream: Capacity of children with autism spectrum disorders to perform academically and regulate their emotions and behavior at school. *Research in Autism Spectrum Disorders*, 4(1), 18–27. doi:10.1016/j.rasd.2009.07.002.

Australian Bureau of Statistics (ABS). (2018). *Disability, ageing and carers Australia: Autism in Australia* (cat. no. 4430.0). Canberra: Australia. Retrieved from https://www.abs.gov.au/AUSSTATS/abs@.nsf/Lookup/4430.0Main+Features102018?OpenDocument.

Estes, A., Rivera, V., Bryan, M., Cali, P., & Dawson G. (2011). Discrepancies between academic achievement and intellectual ability in higher-functioning school-aged children with Autism Spectrum Disorder. *Journal of Autism and Developmental Disorders*, 41(8), 1044–1052. doi:10.1007/s10803-010-1127-3.

Hatfield, M., Ciccarelli, M., Falkmer, T., & Falkmer, M. (2017). Factors related to successful transition planning for adolescents on the autism spectrum. *Journal of Research in Special Educational Needs*, 18(1), 3–14. doi:10.1111/1471-3802.12388.

Hatfield, M., Falkmer, M., Falkmer, T., & Ciccarelli, M. (2017). "Leaps of faith": Parents' and professionals' viewpoints on preparing adolescents on the autism spectrum for leaving school. *Journal of Research in Special Educational Needs*, 17(3), 187–197. doi:10.1111/1471-3802.12377.

Howlin, P., Moss, P., Savage, S., & Rutter, M. (2013). Social outcomes in mid- to later adulthood among individuals diagnosed with autism and average nonverbal IQ as children. *Journal of the American Academy of Child & Adolescent Psychiatry*, 52(6), 572–581. doi:10.1016/j.jaac.2013.02.017.

Jones, C. R., Happe, F., Golden, H., Marsden, A. J., Tregay, J., Simonoff, E., ... Charman, T. (2009). Reading and arithmetic in adolescents with autism spectrum disorders: Peaks and dips in attainment. *Neuropsychology*, 23(6), 718–728. doi:10.1037/a0016360.

Keen, D., Webster, A., & Ridley, G. (2015). How well are children with autism spectrum disorder doing academically at school? An overview of the literature. *Autism*, 20(3), 276–294. doi:10.1177/1362361315580962.

King, G., Baldwin, P., Currie, M., & Evans, J. (2005). Planning successful transitions from school to adult roles for youth with disabilities. *Children's Health Care*, 34, 195–216.

Lee, G., & Carter, E. (2012). Preparing transition-age students with high-functioning autism spectrum disorders for meaningful work. *Psychology in the Schools*, 49, 988–1000.

Morningstar, M., & Clark, G. (2003). The status of personnel preparation for transition education and services: What is the critical content? How can it be offered? *Career Development and Transition for Exceptional Individuals*, 26, 227–237.

Newman, L., Wagner, M., Knokey, A., Marder, C., Nagle, K., Shaver, D., ... Schwarting, M. (2011). *The post-high school outcomes of young adults with disabilities up to 8 years after high school: A report from the National Longitudinal Transition Study–2 (NLTS2)*. Menlo Park, CA: SRI International. Retrieved from www.nlts2.org/reports/.

Roberts, K. D. (2010). Topic areas to consider when planning transition from high school to postsecondary education for students with autism spectrum disorders. *Focus on Autism and Other Developmental Disabilities*, 25(3), 158–162.

Saggers, B., Klug, D., Harper-Hill, K., Ashburner, J., Costley, D., Clark, T., ... Carrington, S. (2018). *Australian autism educational needs analysis: What are the needs of schools, parents and students on the autism spectrum?* Brisbane: Cooperative Research Centre for Living with Autism (Autism CRC).

Shogren, K., & Plotner, A. (2012). Transition planning for students with intellectual disability, autism, or other disabilities: Data from the National Longitudinal Transition Study–2. *Intellectual and Developmental Disabilities*, 50, 16–30.

Taylor, J., & Seltzer, M. (2011). Employment and postsecondary educational activities for young adults with autism spectrum disorders during the transition to adulthood. *Journal of Autism & Developmental Disorders*, 41, 566–574.

Test, D., Fowler, C., Richter, S., White, J., Mazzotti, V., Walker, … Kortering, L. (2009). Evidence-based practices in secondary transition. *Career Development for Exceptional Individuals*, 32(2), 115–128.

Test, D., Smith, L., & Carter, E. (2014). Equipping youth with autism spectrum disorders for adulthood: Promoting rigor, relevance, and relationships. *Remedial and Special Education*, 35(3), 80–90.

9

BOOSTING POST-SCHOOL OUTCOMES

Supporting adolescents on the autism spectrum to feel ready for life after school

Megan Hatfield, Marina Ciccarelli, Cheryl Mangan and Michael Whelan

The journey to adulthood for all young people commences in adolescence and continues on through the final years of school. For neurotypical travellers, the transition from school to employment, study, or training is supported by a range of systems and processes, typically commencing in the final year of school. For young people on the autism spectrum, the journey can be more complex and challenging, and evidence suggests that programs of post-school transition support can commence much sooner. This chapter provides evidence-based 'Employability Principles' to guide transition planning for adolescents on the spectrum to enhance their success in finding employment after leaving school. Despite their numerous strengths, many adolescents on the autism spectrum have difficulty transitioning from high school to employment or further education and training. To remediate these barriers and enhance success post-school, adolescents can engage in formal transition planning, ideally beginning in Year 9. This chapter outlines a set of practical strategies and resources developed as part of a transition planning program which supports teachers and students to put the Employability Principles into action in the classroom setting. In addition to the evidence-based research that underpins this post-school transition program, this chapter includes transcripts of interviews with program participants, their families, and teachers which highlight the rich lived experiences of the program.

The transition out of high school into post–school employment or study is one of the biggest and most pivotal challenges in life. Transition from school is a critical developmental period, in which adolescents form their identity and develop a sense of autonomy to find their place in society. Many young Australians are unemployed (8.7–15.1%) or underemployed (12%) (Australian Bureau of Statistics [ABS], 2014) and the 2018 study by the Foundation for Young Australians that followed the employment trajectories of 14,000 young people over a decade found significant barriers to full-time employment. Some of these barriers included limited job availability and opportunities for work experience, insufficient education and training, and a lack of career planning and management skills (Foundation for Young Australians, 2018).

> *The most recent ABS data reported the unemployment rate for autistic individuals of working age (15–64 years) was 34.1%, over three times the rate for people with disability (10.3%) and almost eight times the rate of people without disability (4.6%)*

Autistic young people may experience a range of additional challenges that impact their ability to secure and maintain employment. These can include difficulty with social communication, differences in sensory processing (related to sounds, bright lights, smells, touch, and movement), and they may also require structure, routine, or predictability in work tasks and instructions (Lee & Carter, 2012). Other challenges encountered by this cohort may include managing anxiety about life after school, difficulty imagining life after high school, and limited access to opportunities to engage in real-life experiences that help them develop crucial skills for work and independent living (Stewart, 2013).

The most recent ABS data reported the unemployment rate for autistic individuals of working age (15–64 years) was 34.1%, over three times the rate for people with disability (10.3%) and almost eight times the rate of people without disability (4.6%) (ABS, 2018). Educational attainment is one of the strongest predictors of future employment, health, income, and welfare (Lamb, Jackson, Walstab, & Huo, 2015), yet only 26% of autistic people aged 15 years and over attain post-secondary qualifications of a diploma, advanced diploma, certificate III/IV, or Bachelor degree or higher; considerably less than those with other disabilities (ABS, 2018). In addition, only 8.1% of autistic individuals hold a Bachelor degree or higher, compared with 16.1% of those with a disability (ABS, 2018).

This significant disparity in employment based on diagnosis reveals that a majority of adults on the autism spectrum of working age are not given opportunities to use their diverse strengths and interests, and too many are not reaching their potential. Autistic people have many strengths and attributes that are unique and can make them sought-after employees. Some have in-depth knowledge and skills related to topics of interest, excellent memory, creativity, and superior skills in pattern recognition (Mottron, 2011; Patten Koenig & Hough Williams, 2017). Many have other characteristics that make them excellent employees such as the exceptional ability to focus on tasks and attention to detail, reliability, punctuality, and integrity (Hagner et al., 2012; Westbrook et al., 2015). However, unemployment figures suggest that further work needs to be done to support young people on the autism spectrum to transition to employment, where they can become valued members of the workforce.

Young people on the autism spectrum often experience challenges in transitioning from high school to further education, training, and employment (King, Baldwin, Currie, & Evans, 2005). Those who do not make a successful transition are at a significantly higher risk of long-term exclusion from the labour force, as well as social isolation, and physical and mental health issues (Cederlund, Hagberg, Billstedt, Gillberg, & Gillberg, 2008; Hagner et al., 2012; Hendricks, 2010). Conversely, a successful transition from school to adult life leads to earlier potential for employment, higher job satisfaction and productivity in the

> *Autistic people have many strengths and attributes that are unique and can make them sought-after employees.*

workplace, and greater capacity for independent living. The economic benefit of increased productivity among autistic adults is significant and is estimated to be between $1.86B and $3.22B per annum (Synergies Economic Consulting, 2011). Having a clear and coordinated approach to transition planning increases the likelihood of an adolescent on the spectrum getting a job after leaving school or getting into post-secondary education (Hatfield, Ciccarelli, Falkmer, & Falkmer, 2018).

Transition planning aims to prepare the adolescent for leaving high school and the transition into post-school activities, which may include further training, post-secondary education, and employment (Cobb & Alwell, 2009; Roberts, 2010). Transition planning results in improved self-determination, success in post-school employment and education, higher levels of happiness, and greater community participation (Wei, Wagner, Hudson, Yu, & Javitz, 2016). However, many adolescents on the spectrum are not actively engaging in the transition planning process (Chandroo, Strnadová, & Cumming, 2018). A tailored career planning program that provides autistic adolescents with early transition support will increase their engagement in the transition planning process, and set them up for future success with employment and its associated benefits.

The BOOST-A

The Better OutcOmes and Successful Transition for Autism (BOOST-A) was developed to address the unique needs of adolescents on the spectrum in transition planning (Hatfield, Falkmer, Falkmer, & Ciccarelli, 2017a). The BOOST-A program aims to literally 'boost' the opportunity, enthusiasm, and engagement of autistic adolescents as they take those first tentative steps on the path to life after school. BOOST-A is autism-specific and web-based, and supports the development of future job pathways and employment-readiness skills through the application of five 'Employability Principles'. A nation-wide trial of BOOST-A determined that the program increased career exploration and self-determined behaviour related to transition planning among adolescents on the spectrum (Hatfield et al., 2017a). This finding and the other findings of the BOOST-A research by Hatfield and colleagues provided the evidence base for this successful transition planning tool.

myWAY Employability

It was important that knowledge and recommendations for successful transition planning from the BOOST-A research became available for use by the autism community via a widely accessible platform and, with this in mind, *myWAY Employability* was developed.[1] *myWAY Employability* translates the findings from the BOOST-A research and incorporates the BOOST-A program, in an accessible interactive community resource. *myWAY Employability* is co-designed with and for young people on the spectrum to assist them to plan and prepare for life after high school, including further education, vocational training, and employment. This online resource provides a holistic approach to transition planning and can also be used by people who support young people in transition planning, including parents, allied health professionals, employment specialists, and teachers.

Because the transition from high school is a different experience for every person, *myWAY Employability* asks users to create a personalised profile for their transition plan. A guided systematic process places the young person at the centre of decision-making and supports them to participate at a level that is just right for them. Based on a strengths-based approach and Employability Principles of the BOOST-A, *myWAY Employability* guides users to identify their personal strengths, interests, and preferences for types of work environments. This information is matched to information about potential relevant careers and pathways to employment, including higher education, vocational training, or on-the-job training. The young person is prompted to create a team, including a 'champion', to support them in their transition plan, and they have the option of sharing with other members of their team their transition plan and progress updates. Goals are written and actions assigned to team members with anticipated timeframes for completion. Reflection of progress towards goals uses a growth mindset approach (Blackwell, Trzesniewski, & Dweck, 2007), where difficult tasks are viewed as opportunities to develop skills, and modifications to goals can be made at any time as necessary to reinforce flexibility in thinking and approach.

myWAY Employability also contains useful information articles and videos co-produced with the autistic community. Topic areas include finding and preparing for a work experience; self-advocacy and communication in the workplace; using public transport; and applying for jobs.

LIAM'S STORY

Before using the BOOST-A, Liam had already started thinking about what he wanted to do after leaving school. He knew computing was his passion, but he wasn't sure what area of computing he wanted to work in, or how to get there. Liam says that he was initially a little reluctant to use the BOOST-A, but as he worked through the program, he started to see the benefits. His mum, Tanya, says, 'It helped to open up the conversation whilst he was still at school'.

The BOOST-A helped Liam confirm that he was on the right track, and helped him work out that he wanted to get into coding. The career exploration and goals he set in the BOOST-A led Liam to complete work experience in software testing. Tanya reported that he absolutely loved this experience and just 'blossomed'. They then looked at what study or training courses would enable a career in software testing, and then went to university open days. 'It just all started to fall into place', Tanya says.

When reflecting on using the BOOST-A, Liam says that it 'was pretty easy to use and it explained things well. The experience was absolutely amazing'. Liam's advice to other adolescents on the autism spectrum around transition planning is, 'Even if you don't feel like you are going to get anything out of it, you probably will, even if it's just some small minute detail'. Liam urges other adolescents to 'give it a go. If life gives you an opportunity, take it. You never know where it might take you. Because of where BOOST-A led me in cementing my idea of what I wanted to do, it led me to a computing major in coding at university'. Liam is now studying a Bachelor of Science majoring in computing at university and is also working part-time as a software tester.

Source: Produced with permission from Tanya and Liam

Employability Principles

To provide guidance on how to implement high-quality transition planning for adolescents on the spectrum, five evidence-based Employability Principles were developed (Figure 9.1). The principles are inter-related and should be used together to ensure success in transition planning. They are not listed in order of priority, nor should they necessarily be used sequentially. They provide an overarching philosophy and mindset for working in the transition planning space. The aim of these employability principles is to provide a positive environment in which the adolescent can develop resilience, self-esteem, and a growth mindset in relation to planning for their working life.

Development of the Employability Principles

The Employability Principles were developed through several research studies. A needs assessment was conducted to identify factors that enhance and improve the transition planning for adolescents on the spectrum (Green & Kreuter, 1999). Quantitative and qualitative data were gathered from a variety of sources, as recommended in needs assessment guidelines (Bartholomew, Parcel, Kok, Gottlieb, & Fernandez, 2011). Two phases were completed: i) a survey of adolescents on the spectrum, parents, and professionals who support transition planning (Hatfield, Ciccarelli, et al., 2018); and ii) interviews with parents and professionals (Hatfield, Falkmer, Falkmer, & Ciccarelli, 2017b). In addition, a literature review was completed that identified current best-practice in transition planning for adolescents with disability. A systematic review was also completed to evaluate existing career planning tools that could be used for people on the spectrum (Murray, Hatfield, Falkmer, & Falkmer, 2016). This information was used to develop the BOOST-A transition planning program, which involved two pilot studies, a randomised-controlled trial, and a process evaluation. All of these studies provided an iterative process for gathering information and insights about the most important aspects of transition planning for adolescents on the spectrum.

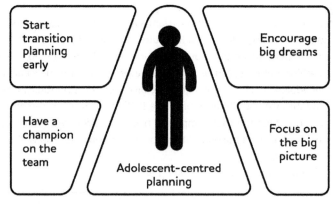

Employability Principles

Start transition planning early

Encourage big dreams

Have a champion on the team

Adolescent-centred planning

Focus on the big picture

Employability Principles

1. **Encourage the adolescent to dream big:** Have high expectations and always be strengths-based.

2. **Start transition planning early:** In Year 9 or as soon as possible.

3. **Promote adolescent-centred planning:** The adolescent should be an active participant, and work towards becoming the transition planning team leader.

4. **Focus on the 'big picture':** Support the adolescent to understand what life after school will be like through real life experiences; e.g., work experience, mentoring, volunteering, and part-time work.

5. **Have a champion on the team:** A champion is someone who is passionate and enthusiastic, and provides new opportunities and information to support transition planning.

FIGURE 9.1 Employability Principles for adolescents on the autism spectrum.

Overview of the Employability Principles

Encourage the adolescent to dream big

A major goal of transition planning is to enhance self-determination, the sense of control and autonomy one feels over their life (Mithaug, Mithaug, Agran, Martin, & Wehmeyer, 2003). Self-determination is an important prerequisite to becoming a self-governing adult. When parents and teachers have high expectations for adolescents, they have greater self-determination, and are more likely to have post-school success (Test, Smith, & Carter, 2014). In addition, adolescents' sense of control and confidence grows when they consistently receive positive messages about their potential to achieve after school (Duffy & Murray, 2013). Therefore, it is important that parents, teachers, and other professionals support adolescents to 'dream big' and have high expectations for their future. It is also important to support adolescents to feel that their goals are flexible and that they can change their minds about their future plans as they experience the inevitable ups and downs that come with this stage of life (Hatfield et al., 2017b).

A crucial method in enhancing self-determination and high expectations is to focus on the adolescent's strengths (Test, Mazzotti, et al., 2009b). Having a strengths-based approach with adolescents on the spectrum has been linked to successful transition planning (Hatfield, Ciccarelli, et al., 2018). Families who are strengths-focused improve their child's resilience and overall family connectedness (Bayat, 2007) and using a strengths-based assessment supports adolescents to identify personal interests that can be leveraged into career pathways (Lee & Carter, 2012). Transition planning that is focused on the aspirations of the adolescent enhances their engagement in the process (Hatfield et al., 2017b), and having the adolescent take an active role in the transition planning process is essential for success.

> *A crucial method in enhancing self-determination and high expectations is to focus on the adolescent's strengths*

Start transition planning early

Formal planning for leaving school should ideally start when the adolescent is 14 years old, or Year 9 (Martin & Williams-Diehm, 2013; Weidenthal & Kochhar-Bryant, 2007). Adolescents on the spectrum generally start transition planning later than recommended, with many starting in Year 10 or later (Hatfield, Ciccarelli, et al., 2018). Formal transition planning often doesn't begin until the final year of school, when 'actual decisions [are] made in a mad scramble in the summer when school was already at an end' (Duffy & Murray, 2013, p. 308). Transition planning needs to start earlier in high school to give adolescents time to develop their career aspirations, develop confidence in life skills, and engage in work experiences that will support the development of self-determination.

Promote adolescent-centred planning

The adolescents should be actively involved in *every* step of the transition planning process. The aim is for the adolescent to eventually lead the transition planning team through running meetings and following up on goals. This active participation further enhances self-determination and ensures they will have the skills to independently continue their career planning post-school. Not only is it considered best practice to ensure adolescents with disability are active participants in their transition planning (Kohler, 1996; Lee & Carter, 2012; Martin & Williams-Diehm, 2013; Test, Fowler, et al., 2009a), but it has been linked to increased self-determination, improved post-school outcomes, and higher expectations by professionals and parents (Ankeny & Lehmann, 2010). As mentioned earlier in this chapter, when compared to their peers with other disabilities, adolescents on the spectrum are not as likely to be closely involved in their transition planning (Cameto, Levine, & Wagner, 2004; Shogren & Plotner, 2012). Barriers to active participation range from managing anxiety, challenges with social communication, and low motivation to participate because they might have difficulty with understanding the 'big picture' (Hatfield, Ciccarelli, et al., 2018; Hatfield et al., 2017b). It is important therefore to address these barriers to support the active involvement of adolescents on the spectrum in their transition planning.

Focus on the 'big picture'

The 'big picture' in this context refers to imagining what life might be like after school, and understanding how current actions may influence this future. For adolescents on the spectrum, this connection can be particularly important if they have difficulties with conceptualising events they have not experienced directly, or with abstract thinking (Fullerton, Stratton, Coyne, & Gray, 1996). Difficulty understanding the big picture can lower motivation to engage in transition planning (Hatfield et al., 2017b). Having a job provides more than a pay cheque – it provides opportunities for independent living; autonomy in what and when purchases are made; a network of social connections; and a sense of having a place in, and contribution to, society. Without an understanding of these other benefits of employment, adolescents on the spectrum may not be motivated to plan for the steps to achieve employment. Therefore, promoting the big picture in transition planning is important to enhance an adolescent's engagement.

To support an adolescent to understand the big picture, it is important for them to engage in real-life experiences (for example, work experience, mentoring, volunteering, and part-time work). Self-determination is developed by *doing*; through engaging in challenging activities that provide a sense of competence and autonomy (Ryan & Deci, 2000; Wehmeyer & Schalock, 2001). Real-life experiences allow the development of skills in a community context and have been linked to greater post-school success (Mazzotti, Test, & Mustian, 2014; Test, Fowler, et al., 2009a). From a practical perspective, real-life experiences are essential additions to a resume for future job applications. Adolescents who engaged in real-life experiences through transition planning reported feeling like their future was clearer and felt less abstract (Hatfield, Falkmer, Falkmer, & Ciccarelli, 2018). It is very important when engaging in these real-life experiences that parents and adolescents are supported with any challenges that may arise, in order to be prepared for the transition out of school (Kirby, Diener, Adkins, & Wright, 2020).

> To support an adolescent to understand the big picture, it is important for them to engage in real-life experiences

Have a champion on the team

Having a strong transition planning team that includes family and professionals is an essential feature of post-school success for adolescents with disability (Lee & Carter, 2012; Test et al., 2014). In addition to having a team, it is important for the adolescent to have a 'champion' on the transition planning team. A champion is someone who is passionate and enthusiastic, and provides new opportunities and information (Hatfield, Falkmer, et al., 2018). The champion could be a family member, a teacher or other professional, or a friend. The champion is proactive in supporting transition planning activities to be timely and in line with the adolescent's goals. Without a champion on the team, there is a risk that the process could become stagnant, with team members waiting for someone else to take charge and give direction. A champion will provide opportunities with an optimal level of challenge to support adolescents to learn how to self-regulate and adjust their feelings and actions in particular situations, therefore enhancing self-determination (Shogren et al., 2008). Having a champion with knowledge, enthusiasm, and resources to guide the transition planning process is essential to the success of the transition planning process (Hatfield, Falkmer, et al., 2018).

ETHAN'S STORY

Ethan started using the BOOST-A when he was in Year 9 and his mum, Rhona, reflects that this was an ideal time to start transition planning because 'you really need that time to plan, and also to get you and your child used to the enormity of what is out there. It's something that is very foreign to what you have been doing up until then. All of a sudden you have to start thinking about what they are going to do when they leave school. Starting to think about a part-time job, volunteering, and work experience. All the kind of things that they are going to need to get their skillset up, build their confidence, to give them an idea of what is involved in leaving school. That the security and safety of school, wonderful as it is, will cease at the end of Year 12, and what you don't want is for them is to all of a sudden be feeling enormous worry and stress because they haven't been prepared for it'.

Ethan says that at first he didn't really understand why he needed to use the BOOST-A, but that it made more sense as they went through the process. The BOOST-A helped Ethan to identify his strengths; he is creative, and likes helping people. It prompted Ethan to engage in work experience in a library, and start volunteering at the Lego club at school, which helped him to gain confidence and develop skills in working with younger children. The BOOST-A helped Ethan to identify the many different job pathways he could take after school, ranging from nursing through to health promotion. This supported Ethan to feel prepared to select his Year 10 subjects. He also set a goal to complete business and population health certificates through TAFE while still at school, which he really enjoyed.

Rhona says that the BOOST-A supported Ethan to see the big picture: 'At the start of BOOST-A, Ethan didn't really understand that one day he would leave school and wouldn't just walk into a fantastic job in a fantastic area, maybe making a movie or writing a book and getting paid a lot of money for it. It was an abstract concept – that one day this world that he lives in, that security, wouldn't be there. With BOOST-A, he really started to understand that he needed to build his skillset that would one day help him to leave school and get employment or go on to further study'. Rhona also talks about the importance of being strengths-based: 'I think it can sometimes be quite easy, particularly for a kid who's on the autism spectrum, to focus on what they are not great at. But BOOST-A really focused on what he's good at and what his strengths are'.

Ethan says, 'It's definitely a great thing to do, BOOST-A helped me a lot, and I would definitely tell someone else to use it if they're thinking about doing something like it'. He reflects that through 'using BOOST-A, I've gained a lot more confidence talking to people I don't really know, doing activities, helping out with things and I feel like I'm doing a lot better now at school and I'm less stressed when doing activities'. Rhona's recommendation to parents is to give the BOOST-A a go with your child, as 'you've got nothing to lose, you're only going to achieve a greater base of knowledge for yourself and your child'. Ethan has now graduated from high school and is studying child care and working part-time a few hours a week.
Source: Produced with permission from Ethan and Rhona

Putting the Employability Principles into practice

Teachers are in a unique and valuable position to support transition planning activities; indeed, many teachers are the 'champions' in the transition planning team. Not all teachers, however, are confident in their abilities to integrate career development content into teaching plans. This is not surprising when one considers the wide range of skills essential for successful transition planning in which teachers are expected to be proficient (Morningstar & Mazzotti, 2014). Teachers face the added challenge of supporting the transition planning process while undertaking other teaching and administrative responsibilities. In addition to teaching core academic subjects, teachers are expected to:

- Understand how to develop self-determination in students with disabilities.
- Teach self-advocacy, goal setting, and problem-solving skills.
- Know and implement evidence-based practices for student-focused planning.
- Embed opportunities for work experience, community participation, and independent living skills.
- Involve families and other agencies in the transition planning process.
  (Morningstar & Mazzotti, 2014)

In order to not overwhelm teachers or place further demands on their time, any additional resources for teachers to develop their capacity to support transition planning will likely have better uptake if aligned with school curricula. To this end, *myWAY Employability* develops students' knowledge and skills for planning a future career aligned with the Australian Curriculum's Work Studies Years 9 and 10. This resource provides students with opportunities to develop work readiness, exposure to careers, and work experience and prepare for further education or training towards a skilled occupation (Australian Curriculum Assessment and Reporting Authority [ACARA], 2015).

Transition planning is relevant to all students preparing for life after high school. Teaching practices that are appropriate for students on the spectrum and their peers without an autism diagnosis can create opportunities for an inclusive mainstream classroom. To assist teachers to use *myWAY Employability* in classroom-based transition planning, a series of practices that apply the five Employability Principles have been developed. These are called the *myWAY Employability Educator* resources and are available via the *inclusionED* professional learning platform and community of practice.[2] The *myWAY Employability Educator* resources were co-designed with an advisory group of Australian secondary school teachers who guided the choice of resources that would be feasible and acceptable to teachers, and provided feedback on the specific content within the practices. Other types of resources on the website include written and animated instructions on how to use the various features of *myWAY Employability*, including creating a personalised profile, navigating the site via the dashboard, matching strengths, linking

> To assist teachers to use *myWAY Employability* in classroom-based transition planning, a series of practices that apply the five Employability Principles have been developed.

interests and preferences to potential jobs, using the goal writing tool, reviewing progress, and communicating with the team.

Each practice in the *myWAY Employability Educator* resource kit aligns with various components of *myWAY Employability*, which are completed by students before or after the class-based practices. Each practice contains the learning objectives; preparation required (materials and equipment, including downloadable templates and activity sheets); the steps involved in applying the practice in the classroom or school environment and the estimated time required; independent tasks for students to perform out of class; and opportunities for student reflection on their achievements and learning. The practices include accommodations to meet individual students' capabilities while still being delivered as a whole-of-class learning activity.

Examples of inclusive classroom practices from the *myWAY Employability Educator* resources available on *inclusionED* that relate to each of the five Employability Principles will now be described.

Encourage the adolescent to dream big

myWAY Employability encourages students to be ambitious about their futures – to set aspirational long-term goals and to appreciate that these are often reached through smaller steps. The 'Life Skills' practice of *myWAY Employability Educator* contains activities that teach students to set and track goals and then break down their goals into smaller achievable steps. It aims to teach students to accept challenges and changes of plan as normal parts of life. These themes are explored through fictional case studies and by encouraging each student to identify and work towards achieving their own individual life skills 'challenge'. The challenge might be learning how to use public transport, how to shop for something for themselves, or cook a simple meal.

Start transition planning early

Since students commonly undertake work experience in Year 10, *myWAY Employability Educator* contains a practice on the topic of 'Work Experience Preparation' suitable for younger students to commence in Year 9. The practice is designed to complement any school's existing community-based work experience program or to be used in tandem with 'internal' work experiences offered to students within the school environment. The activities in this practice promote the preparation steps for work experience and a team-based approach to planning and undertaking the work experience – the underlying principle being that at all times the student should feel supported. The practice aims to reduce anxiety and enable work experience to be undertaken by younger students than is currently the norm. An 'internal' work experience that includes students carrying out tasks at school under the supervision of a particular staff member is particularly useful for younger students or those with higher support needs and/or greater anxiety. An example of an internal work experience may be that the student works alongside the school librarian for short periods before or after school for a term, assisting with checking books and audio-visual equipment in and out to borrowers; cataloguing resources; and shelving returned resources. Completing short periods of work experience in a familiar and trusted environment may assist the student to feel better prepared for undertaking a work experience in an external organisation at a later time.

Promote adolescent-centred planning

The *myWAY Employability Educator* resource promotes student self-determination in transition planning in many ways. For example, students are encouraged to play a central role in their transition planning meetings and to increase their career-related self-awareness. The 'Sensory/Learning profiles' practice explicitly teaches self-advocacy skills so that in their future workplaces, students are able to negotiate appropriate workplace adjustments required to be able to work safely and effectively. *myWAY Employability* contains four interactive activities that encourage students to build career-related self-awareness through exploring their career interests and strengths. *myWAY Employability Educator* provides sample lesson plans that give students time in class to engage in these career-related self-awareness activities. They are then encouraged to take the insights and knowledge learned about themselves to their transition planning meetings. These types of practices can assist students to gain confidence to play an active part and eventually lead their own career planning.

Focus on the 'big picture'

The 'Training Pathways' practice in *myWAY Employability Educator* provides teachers with resources to organise a panel presentation about post-school training pathways. Students and their parents, mentors, and other interested persons are invited to attend. Students are encouraged to take an active role in organising the event, providing an opportunity to develop employability skills such as event planning, audio-visual management, public speaking, and written communication. Invited panel speakers are graduates of the school who have taken a variety of different post-school education and training pathways to employment, such as university study, TAFE courses, apprenticeships, or on-the-job training. The panel presentation event promotes school–parent–community partnerships and provides students with real-life stories and first-hand accounts of pathways to employment; in other words, it helps them see the 'big picture' about employment.

Have a champion on the team

Each student should have a champion in their transition planning team who takes the role of assisting students to set and track career-related goals. The *Educator* resource provides a practice that supports students to identify their own champion, by thinking about a trusted adult who can help them achieve their transition planning goals.

DONETTE – A TEACHER'S PERSPECTIVE

Donette was Ethan's teacher at high school. She says that, as a teacher, the best part about using the BOOST-A was that 'it was a collaboration between the school, the home, and the student. And that was what made it perfect'. Donette also found the program easy to use because it was structured and had clear steps to follow: 'It's very easy. It's not time consuming at all. Most teachers will say, "I've got so much work on my plate" but really this isn't anything extra'.

Donette says that she has seen other parents struggle with their child's transition from school when they hadn't thought about it early enough. She really recommends starting early as it 'takes away some of the shock factor'. She also said that starting transition planning with the BOOST-A in Year 9 helps with subject selection in Year 10 and encourages the development of real-life, practical skills which are needed after students leave school.

Donette reflects that 'before Ethan did the BOOST-A program he tended to be friendly but shy and lacking direction'. She says that the BOOST-A helped him improve his organisation skills, become more confident, and take more initiative. It also helped him shift his focus to life after school: 'It brought him to the realisation that there is more to life than being in a classroom. Thinking about life beyond school, and using your strengths in a practical way'.

Source: Produced with permission from Donette

Conclusion and practitioner reflection

Transition planning is an important tool to prepare adolescents for the looming and often very intimidating transition out of secondary school. However, evidence has shown that adolescents on the spectrum benefit from a tailored approach to transition planning to ensure they feel engaged and supported to work towards their dreams. The five Employability Principles can be used to overcome the common difficulties experienced in transition planning by adolescents on the autism spectrum. BOOST-A and *myWAY Employability* were developed with the Employability Principles as the central pillars to all aspects of the program. In addition, the principles are communicated to users using visual infographics and short animated videos. Teachers are often the champions in transition planning; however, they are not often provided with the training or the support they need to carry out this important role. The Employability Principles can be easily translated into the classroom environment and be used to guide teachers in this process.

Secondary school is often the setting in which an individual develops their sense of self. Students' experiences in high school and how they are supported to process these life events have a profound impact on how they view themselves into adulthood. Broader to this, we live in a culture where people on the spectrum are often viewed as disabled, and this identity conferral can lead to adolescents perhaps internalising the messages that they are a problem and a burden. This is of particular concern in secondary school, as adolescents often become more cognisant of differences, coinciding with the process of individuation that occurs at this life stage. It is at this juncture that we have the opportunity to support students to embrace who they are, and feel they can leverage their unique attributes into skills that make them highly employable and stand out from the crowd.

Alternatively, without practical support, or perhaps more importantly the right philosophy, they could learn and believe that they do not have much to contribute to society. With their confidence and resilience lessened, they may go on to feel that they should not aim for employment as they may fail, and that failure would be catastrophic. The importance of a strengths-based transition planning process cannot be understated in this regard. When teachers and parents come from a philosophy of dreaming big, having high expectations, and encouraging a 'growth mindset', this can have ripple effects not only on tangible outcomes like success in employment, but also in how that individual views themselves and their worth in society. This should be our goal of transition planning: to support the adolescent through the individuation process to develop a strong sense of self, pride in their uniqueness, and resilience to go out into the big wide world and give it their best shot.

> *… we have the opportunity to support students to embrace who they are, and feel they can leverage their unique attributes into skills that make them highly employable and stand out from the crowd.*

Acknowledgements

The authors would like to acknowledge the contribution of the following people in the development of the BOOST-A, *myWAY Employability*, and the *myWAY Employability Educator* resources:

The hundreds of Australian young people on the autism spectrum, parents, and professionals who have shared their lived experiences and perspectives with the authors to co-design and trial BOOST-A and *myWAY Employability*.

Adie Wilmot, a psychology honours graduate, who developed key content for the information resources and articles for *myWAY Employability* and collaborated with an advisory group of teachers to develop the practices in the *myWAY Employability Educator* resource.

Brendan James, the Digital Product Manager at the Autism CRC, who coordinated the build of the *myWAY Employability* platform.

myWAY Employability has been delivered through a collaboration between Autism CRC and its participants. The project was co-led by Curtin University and supported by Aspect and the Queensland Department of Education; along with technology development partner – The Project Factory, and research partner – CSIRO e-Health Institute. *myWAY Employability* is proudly supported by the Telstra Foundation, funded under the Tech4Good Challenge initiative.

Notes

1 www.mywayemployability.com.au
2 www.inclusioned.edu.au

References

Ankeny, E. M., & Lehmann, J. P. (2010). Journey toward self-determination: Voices of students with disabilities who participated in a secondary transition program on a community college campus. *Remedial and Special Education*, 32(4), 279–289. doi:10.1177/0741932510362215.

Australian Bureau of Statistics (ABS). (2014). *Australian social trends – Paid work: Young people in employment* (cat. no. 4102.0). Canberra: Australia. Retrieved from https://www.abs.gov.au/ausstats/abs@.nsf/10204 92cfcd63696ca2568a1002477b5/40070b718b1c9acfca256e9e0028808c!OpenDocument.

Australian Bureau of Statistics (ABS). (2018). *Disability, ageing and carers Australia: Autism in Australia* (cat. no. 4430.0). Canberra: Australia. Retrieved from https://www.abs.gov.au/AUSSTATS/abs@.nsf/Lookup/ 4430.0Main+Features102018?OpenDocument.

Australian Curriculum Assessment and Reporting Authority (ACARA). (2015). *Work studies Years 9–10*. Retrieved from https://www.acara.edu.au/curriculum/foundation-year-10/learning-areas-subjects/ work-studies-years.

Bartholomew, L., Parcel, G., Kok, G., Gottlieb, N., & Fernandez, M. (2011). *Planning health promotion programs: An intervention mapping approach*. San Francisco, CA: Jossey-Bass.

Bayat, M. (2007). Evidence of resilience in families of children with autism. *Journal of Intellectual Disability Research*, 51(9), 702–714. doi:10.1111/j.1365-2788.2007.00960.x.

Blackwell, L. S., Trzesniewski, K. H., & Dweck, C. S. (2007). Implicit theories of intelligence predict achievement across an adolescent transition: A longitudinal study and an intervention. *Child Development*, 78, 246–263. doi:10.1111/j.1467-8624.2007.00995.x.

Cameto, R., Levine, P., & Wagner, M. (2004). *Transition planning for students with disabilities. A special topic report of findings from the National Longitudinal Transition Study-2 (NLTS2)*. Menlo Park, CA: SRI International.

Cederlund, M., Hagberg, B., Billstedt, E., Gillberg, I., & Gillberg, C. (2008). Asperger syndrome and autism: A comparative longitudinal follow-up study more than 5 years after original diagnosis. *Journal of Autism and Developmental Disorders*, 38, 72–85. doi:10.1007/s10803-007-0364-6.

Chandroo, R., Strnadová, I., & Cumming, T. M. (2018). A systematic review of the involvement of students with autism spectrum disorder in the transition planning process: Need for voice and empowerment. *Research in Developmental Disabilities*, 83, 8–17. doi:10.1016/j.ridd.2018.07.011.

Cobb, R. B., & Alwell, M. (2009). Transition planning/coordinating interventions for youth with disabilities: A systematic review. *Career Development and Transition for Exceptional Individuals*, 32, 70–81. doi:10.1177/0885728809336655.

Duffy, S., & Murray, P. (2013). Transition and integration – Changing our starting point. *Journal of Integrated Care*, 21(6), 306–314.

Foundation for Young Australians. (2018). *The new work reality*. Melbourne: Foundation for Young Australians. Retrieved from https://www.fya.org.au/wp-content/uploads/2018/06/FYA_TheNewWorkReality_ sml.pdf.

Fullerton, A., Stratton, J., Coyne, P., & Gray, C. (1996). *Higher functioning adolescents and young adults with autism*. Austin, TX: Pro-ED, Inc.

Green, L., & Kreuter, M. (1999). The PRECEDE-PROCEED model. In L. Green & M. Kreuter (Eds.), *Health promotion planning: An educational and ecological approach* (3rd ed., pp. 32–43). Mountain View, CA: Mayfield Publishing Company.

Hagner, D., Kurtz, A., Cloutier, H., Arakelian, C., Brucker, D., & May, J. (2012). Outcomes of a family-centered transition process for students with autism spectrum disorders. *Focus on Autism and Other Developmental Disabilities*, 27(1), 42–50. doi:10.1177/1088357611430841.

Hatfield, M., Ciccarelli, M., Falkmer, T., & Falkmer, M. (2018). Factors related to successful transition planning for adolescents on the autism spectrum. *Journal of Research in Special Educational Needs*, 18(1), 3–14. doi:10.1111/1471-3802.12388.

Hatfield, M., Falkmer, M., Falkmer, T., & Ciccarelli, M. (2017a). Effectiveness of the BOOST-A™ online transition planning program for adolescents on the autism spectrum: A quasi-randomized controlled trial. *Child and Adolescent Psychiatry and Mental Health*, 11(54), 1–12. doi:10.1186/s13034-017-0191-2.

Hatfield, M., Falkmer, M., Falkmer, T., & Ciccarelli, M. (2017b). "Leaps of faith": Parent and professional viewpoints on preparing adolescents on the autism spectrum for leaving school. *Journal of Research in Special Educational Needs*, 17(3), 187–197. doi:10.1111/1471-3802.12377.

Hatfield, M., Falkmer, M., Falkmer, T., & Ciccarelli, M. (2018). Process evaluation of the BOOST-A™ transition planning program for adolescents on the autism spectrum: A strengths-based approach. *Journal of Autism and Developmental Disorders*, 48(2), 377–388. doi:10.1007/s10803-017-3317-8.

Hendricks, D. (2010). Employment and adults with autism spectrum disorders: Challenges and strategies for success. *Journal of Vocational Rehabilitation*, 32(2), 125–134.

King, G., Baldwin, P., Currie, M., & Evans, J. (2005). Planning successful transitions from school to adult roles for youth with disabilities. *Children's Health Care*, 34, 195–216. doi:10.1207/s15326888chc3403_3.

Kirby, A. V., Diener, M. L., Adkins, D. E., & Wright, C. (2020). Transition preparation activities among families of youth on the autism spectrum: Preliminary study using repeated assessments across a school year. *PloS One*, 15(4). doi:10.1371/journal.pone.0231551.

Kohler, P. (1996). *Taxonomy for transition programming: Linking research and practice*. Champaign, IL: University of Illinois at Urbana-Champaign, Transition Research Institute.

Lamb, S., Jackson, J., Walstab, A., & Huo, S. (2015). *Educational opportunity in Australia 2015: Who succeeds and who misses out*. Melbourne: Mitchell Institute. Retrieved from www.vu.edu.au/centre-for-international-research-on-education-systems-cires.

Lee, G. K., & Carter, E. W. (2012). Preparing transition-age students with high-functioning autism spectrum disorders for meaningful work. *Psychology in the Schools*, 49, 988–1000. doi:10.1002/pits.21651.

Martin, J., & Williams-Diehm, K. (2013). Student engagement and leadership of the transition planning process. *Career Development and Transition for Exceptional Individuals*, 36, 43–50. doi:10.1177/2165143413476545.

Mazzotti, V. L., Test, D. W., & Mustian, A. L. (2014). Secondary transition evidence-based practices and predictors: Implications for policymakers. *Journal of Disability Policy Studies*, 25(1), 5–18. doi:10.1177/1044207312460888.

Mithaug, D. E., Mithaug, D. K., Agran, M., Martin, J. E., & Wehmeyer, M. L. (2003). *Self-determined learning theory: Construction, verification, and evaluation*. Mahwah, NJ: Lawrence Erlbaum.

Morningstar, M., & Mazzotti, V. (2014). *Teacher preparation to deliver evidence-based transition planning and services to youth with disabilities* (Document No. IC-1). Retrieved from http://ceedar.education.ufl.edu/tools/innovation-configurations/.

Mottron, L. (2011). Changing perceptions: The power of autism. *Nature*, 479(7371), 33–35. doi:10.1038/479033a.

Murray, N., Hatfield, M., Falkmer, M., & Falkmer, T. (2016). Evaluation of career planning tools for use with people with autism spectrum disorders: A systematic review. *Research in Autism Spectrum Disorders*, 23, 188–202. doi:10.1016/j.rasd.2015.12.007.

Patten Koenig, K., & Hough Williams, L. (2017). Characterization and utilization of preferred interests: A survey of adults on the autism spectrum. *Occupational Therapy in Mental Health*, 33(2), 129–140. doi:10.1080/0164212X.2016.1248877.

Roberts, K. D. (2010). Topic areas to consider when planning transition from high school to postsecondary education for students with autism spectrum disorders. *Focus on Autism and Other Developmental Disabilities*, 25(3), 158–162. doi:10.1177/1088357610371476.

Ryan, R., & Deci, E. (2000). Self-determination theory and the facilitation of intrinsic motivation, social development, and well-being. *American Psychologist*, 55(1), 68–78. doi:10.1037110003-066X.55.1.68.

Shogren, K., & Plotner, A. (2012). Transition planning for students with intellectual disability, autism, or other disabilities: Data from the National Longitudinal Transition Study-2. *Intellectual and Developmental Disabilities*, 50, 16–30. doi:10.1352/1934-9556-50.1.16.

Shogren, K., Wehmeyer, M., Palmer, S., Soukup, J., Little, T., Garner, N., & Lawrence, M. (2008). Understanding the construct of self-determination. *Assessment for Effective Intervention*, 33(2), 94–107. doi:10.1177/1534508407311395.

Stewart, D. (2013). *Transitions to adulthood for youth with disabilities through an occupational therapy lens.* Thorofare, NJ: SLACK Incorporated.

Synergies Economic Consulting. (2011). *Economic costs of autism spectrum disorder.* Retrieved from https://www.synergies.com.au/reports/economic-costs-of-autism-spectrum-disorder-in-australia/.

Test, D., Fowler, C., Richter, S., White, J., Mazzotti, V., Walker, A., … Kortering, L. (2009a). Evidence-based practices in secondary transition. *Career Development for Exceptional Individuals*, 32(2), 115–128. doi:10.1177/0885728809336859.

Test, D., Mazzotti, V., Mustian, A., Fowler, C., Kortering, L., & Kohler, P. (2009b). Evidence-based secondary transition predictors for improving postschool outcomes for students with disabilities. *Career Development for Exceptional Individuals*, 32, 160–181. doi:10.1177/0885728809346960.

Test, D., Smith, L., & Carter, E. (2014). Equipping youth with Autism Spectrum Disorders for adulthood: Promoting rigor, relevance, and relationships. *Remedial and Special Education*, 35, 80–90. doi:10.1177/0741932513514857.

Wehmeyer, M., & Schalock, R. (2001). Self-determination and quality of life: Implications for special education services and supports. *Focus on Exceptional Children*, 33(8), 1–16.

Wei, X., Wagner, M., Hudson, L., Yu, J. W., & Javitz, H. (2016). The effect of transition planning participation and goal-setting on college enrollment among youth with Autism Spectrum Disorders. *Remedial and Special Education*, 37(1), 3–14. doi:10.1177/0741932515581495.

Weidenthal, C., & Kochhar-Bryant, C. (2007). An investigation of transition practices for middle school youth. *Career Development and Transition for Exceptional Individuals*, 30, 147–157. doi:10.1177/08857288070300030401.

Westbrook, J., Fong, C., Nye, C., Williams, A., Wendt, O., & Cortopassi, T. (2015). Transition services for youth with autism: A systematic review. *Research on Social Work Practice*, 25(1), 10–20. doi:10.1177/1049731514524836.

10

A CREATIVE STRENGTHS-BASED POST-SCHOOL TRANSITION PROJECT FOR YOUNG ADULTS ON THE AUTISM SPECTRUM

Super Conductor and the Big Game Orchestra

Michael Whelan, Sofia Mavropoulou and Yanto Browning

The imposing front doors of the university sector are a challenge to enter, even for neurotypical young people equipped with school and family support to navigate the higher education system. For young people on the autism spectrum, these challenges can be insurmountable. Super Conductor and the Big Game Orchestra was a strengths-based creative technologies pilot project designed to establish a creative transition pathway model for young people on the autism spectrum from secondary school to university study. A cohort of 11 young people on the autism spectrum were invited onto a university campus for two weeks to design, build, and present a multi-player computer game with live music. This chapter will report on research findings that explain how the strengths-based project supported transition to university for young people on the spectrum. Youth on the spectrum perceived the overall creative project as an enjoyable experience stimulating their interest in university study, and creative mentors developed an understanding of the learning preferences, social challenges, anxieties, and coping strategies of people on the spectrum. The chapter illustrates the potential of creative post-school transition programs to provide a sustainable framework which supports cohorts of diverse young people to engage with the university sector in a way that embraces their unique expert knowledges in a safe and inclusive environment. It also provides an innovative strengths-based model for young people on the autism spectrum to express their values, needs, capacity, and contribution as potential university students.

Young people on the autism spectrum are statistically underrepresented in post-secondary study (Alverson, Lindstrom, & Hirano, 2019; Anderson, Carter, & Stephenson, 2018; Wei, Wagner, Hudson, Yu, & Javitz, 2016) and experience a higher than average fail and/or drop-out rate (Anderson et al., 2018; Hees, Roeyers, & Mol, 2018; Shattuck et al., 2012). However, the past decade has seen a rise in students on the autism spectrum moving into tertiary study (Cullen, 2015; Gobbo & Shmulsky, 2014; Hendrickson, Woods-Groves, Rodgers, & Datchuk, 2017; Pinder-Amaker, 2014).

The post-secondary education experiences of students on the spectrum is still a relatively new field of study, with more than half of all research only published within the past decade

(Gelbar, Smith, & Reichow, 2014). Gelbar et al. (2014) also highlight the paucity of research, noting that 'the current literature base contains fragmented descriptions of programs, experiences, and theoretical suggestions for effective programs' (p. 2599). However, the six years following this publication saw an increase in research, including studies on the challenges faced by young people on the autism spectrum attending college (Alverson et al., 2019; Hees et al., 2018; Hewitt, 2011), the benefits associated with greater on-campus neurodiversity (Hendrickson et al., 2017), the difficulties students face in transitioning between secondary and tertiary study (Anderson & Butt, 2017), and the key components of successful higher education transition programs (Elias & White, 2018; Mitchell & Beresford, 2014; Zeedyk, Bolourian, & Blacher, 2019).

Support for autistic students in secondary education

While tertiary study may not be a viable or the preferred option for all young people on the autism spectrum, those who choose tertiary study now have access to an increasing number of support and transition programs. Parents and educators have diverse views on the key components of successful transition programs for young autistic people transitioning into higher education. One finding endorsed by both parents and practitioners is that campus visits and meeting with disability and support services staff are helpful in obtaining a successful transition to the university setting (Dymond, Meadan, & Pickens, 2017). Another finding shared by both groups is the use of special interests during transition programs to facilitate confidence and reduce the amount of anxiety experienced by participants (Hatfield, Ciccarelli, Falkmer, & Falkmer, 2018). In comparison, findings endorsed by young people on the autism spectrum suggest opportunities to experience educational options/settings and gain information about study options prior to choosing a pathway are deemed important (Mitchell & Beresford, 2014) and that young people on the autism spectrum value repeated or extended visits to the same institution prior to enrolment (Dymond et al., 2017). Mitchell and Beresford (2014) also conclude that practitioner support is most effective when students on the autism spectrum are well acquainted with the practitioner, that the practitioner has a thorough knowledge of the manner in which the student's autism manifests, that practitioners are reliable and follow through with all verbal promises, and the practitioner has some knowledge of autism.

> ... findings endorsed by young people on the autism spectrum suggest opportunities to experience educational options/settings and gain information about study options prior to choosing a pathway are deemed important

Achieving this degree of familiarity with the individual profiles of young people on the spectrum, however, is frequently difficult for support staff and practitioners, with one primary issue being disclosure. Understandably, some students on the autism spectrum may be reluctant to disclose their diagnosis, both out of fear of stigmatisation (Anderson et al., 2018; Cox et al., 2017), and as a desire to transition into the college/university setting as a form of social life 'clean slate' (Hees et al., 2018). Social support programs must straddle students' contrasting requirements; on one hand, they may wish to not disclose to avoid social stigmatisation, while on the other hand, they are transitioning into adulthood, which may involve their autistic identities (Hees et al., 2018). Issues related to tensions between public and private identities, and the effect this has on disclosing diagnosis within a college setting, are echoed by Brune and Wilson (2013) and Cox et al. (2017), who found that autistic students frequently take a pragmatic approach to disclosure and reveal diagnoses only as needed to access formal academic accommodations. Newman et al. (2011) quantify this lack of disclosure, with 37% of students on the autism spectrum in the US National Longitudinal Transition Study-2 not disclosing to their educational institutions.

Research has indicated that students on the autism spectrum can 'often have difficulty in traditional extracurricular activities and may not enjoy or experience the same levels of success as their neurotypical peers in these activities' (Diener, Wright, Wright, & Anderson, 2016, p. 97), suggesting that specifically tailored programs grounded in research will have a better chance of successfully engaging students. The importance of building socialisation into transition programs is highlighted by Dolyniuk et al. (2002), who criticise existing transition programs that neglect social experiences and focus on work settings, the consequence being students 'rarely practice social skills within appropriate vocational or educational contexts' (p. 236). The challenges that autistic adults confront in both finding and maintaining employment are related more to social and communication issues than skill deficiencies (Hurlbutt & Chalmers, 2004). Successful program design must therefore focus on strategies for effectively facilitating social participation, grounded by strengths-based learning and common areas of interest (Ashburner, Bobir, & van Dooren, 2017) and these strategies formed the foundation of our project design. The Super Conductor and the Big Game Orchestra (hereafter called 'Super Conductor') project sought to nurture social interaction and friendships in a participant-guided project environment where shared interests in gaming, design, and music were the lingua franca. By combining the group's special interests, and in an extended on-campus experience, we sought to establish an evidence-based model of strengths-based inclusion that supported this cohort in the transition to higher education.

> *Successful program design must therefore focus on strategies for effectively facilitating social participation, grounded by strengths-based learning and common areas of interest*

Background: An evolving Model of Practice

The Super Conductor project grew from the first author's experience as the designer and director of Autism Queensland's Studio G program. Studio G is a post-school transition program that invites young people on the autism spectrum to participate in twice-weekly creative technology activities in a peer mentor-led workshop environment. Grounded in constructivist principles and engagement theory (Kearsley & Shneiderman, 1998), Studio G was designed as an interactive creative workshop supporting young people on the autism spectrum to develop social skills, life skills, and ultimately job skills, and the target group was this invisible tribe of hibernating digital natives.

After moving from Autism Queensland to Queensland University of Technology (QUT), and building upon the successful social participation model and strengths-based framework (Ashburner, Bobir, & van Dooren, 2016; Hill, 2008), the first author developed a creative project titled Altered States. Altered States was an on-campus strengths-based transition program designed to capitalise upon the emerging creative skills and ambitions of young people on the autism spectrum in the Studio G program. Creative staff from QUT commenced the project by establishing relationships of trust with participants by visiting them at the Studio G workshops at the State Library of Queensland. Once these creative and working relationships were established over a number of visits, the Studio G participants completed the project on campus at QUT Creative Industries each fortnight.

In addition to demystifying the university environment for these young people, the project was also an excellent opportunity to challenge the preconceptions held by some university staff regarding young autistic people and their potential as successful participants in university programs. The Altered States project combined a 3-D animated film written, designed, and built by Studio G participants and peer mentors, with a live orchestra playing the soundtrack in real time

FIGURE 10.1   Altered States – Performance at QUT, 2016.

for the live audience. Altered States was a hit at QUT's 2016 CreateX Festival with four public performances to full houses in a campus theatrette. Anecdotal feedback from participants and their families was that the project achieved its goals to build confidence and self-esteem.

Following the success of the Altered States project, the Super Conductor project was developed and implemented, building upon the principles developed in both the Studio G program and the Altered States project.

Super Conductor explained

Super Conductor was a creative project involving 11 young adults on the autism spectrum, four creative peer mentors, three university student ambassadors, two university disability advisors, and two university academic supervisors. In the context of collaboratively developing a computer game, the project participants contributed to game narrative, storyboard development, character and level design, music and sound design, and player journey. Participants combined morning creative project work with afternoon career development and post-school transition workshops conducted by university Equity Services staff.

Over the two weeks of the Super Conductor project, the team built a live audience-driven computer game, where players from the audience play a computer game on a big screen. Through the game controllers, players conduct a group of live musicians through Digital Audio Workstation in-ear instructions. The music flows with the twists and turns of the game itself. No game is ever the same, no performance is ever the same. It is a piece of music where the music score evolves in real time with the game action. The Super Conductor project provided a creative space where participants' established special interests in computer gaming and visual-spatial and technological strengths could be nurtured and extended.

The Super Conductor project applied an established community cultural development model where artists work with communities using processes that enable participants to express their needs, aspirations, skills, and identity. Community arts methods vary widely depending upon the aims, methods, and participants of an individual project; however, the unifying feature of work in this domain is the acknowledgement of the creativity of all people and their right to express their values, experiences, and potential. The creative project was designed and implemented in three distinct phases of preparation, process, and performance.

Phase 1: Preparation

The preparation phase of the project combined participant recruitment, artist recruitment and briefing, technical and resource preparation, and venue and logistics management.

An expression of interest to participate flyer was published and disseminated using the social media networks of previous project collaborators, Autism Queensland, and The State Library of Queensland. The flyer invited young people on the autism spectrum to participate in a two-week intensive creative project designing, building, and presenting a computer game. The flyer contained a link to an online enrolment form which solicited not only personal contact details but a range of strengths-based provocations to be completed by the participant or parent/carer. These prompts included questions such as:

- What are your hobbies?
- What do you like doing?
- What are you good at?
- What do your friends and family say you're good at?
- What sorts of jobs would you like to do when you are older?

The answers to these questions gave the creative team insights into the cohort's interests and the formation of sub-groups that worked well together throughout the project.

In addition to a one-on-one enrolment meeting with young people who had expressed interest in the project, a number of relationship-building social activities were scheduled for participants and their families prior to the intensive. These included a group tour of the QUT Creative Industries Campus facilities, a presentation from the creative mentors and project leadership team introducing themselves and their areas of creative practice, followed by a casual social gathering with soft drinks and snack food. Equipped with a background on each of the participants, the creative mentors introduced themselves and also introduced participants with similar interests to each other and their families.

The broad aims of the game development elements of the creative project were to co-design and create a multi-player computer game in which live musicians played the soundtrack live, and we had invited the cohort to join us in realising these aims. Areas of creative practice that participants could explore included game coding, music programming and performing, film making, creative writing and story line creation, character design, animation, and game environment artwork. Participants could choose an area of creative practice at the commencement of the project or to migrate between the activities and choose one at a later stage in the process once they had experienced a wide range of activities.

Based upon our knowledge of the participants' interests and skills, and in order to prepare a range of seeding resources to commence the workshop program, a range of creative and technical materials were prepared to provide a platform for the workshop activities to use on day one of the program.

The content resources prepared included:

- Basic 2 controller game architecture was coded using game design platform Unity (freeware).
- Three generic music cues (fast energetic, slow reflective, and ambient uncertain) were created and rehearsed with orchestra members.
- Three physical environments based upon Australia's three signature wilderness ecosystems (barrier reef, desert, and rainforest) were proposed as locations for the narrative to unfold and for characters to inhabit.

The tools provided included:

- Music technology resources including several Apple Mac Laptops with Ableton Live software, music keyboards, portable recorders with microphones, and hand percussion instruments.
- Art tables with digital tablets, sketching, and drawing materials.
- Video resources including Sony HandiCam video cameras, video lights, and Premier Pro video edit software.
- Two stand-alone PCs with Unity Game development software installed.

Phase 2: Process

In addition to the sequence of creative activities used to co-design and build the game, all of the cohort participated in group show and tell sessions, meals and breaks, and a series of career development workshops. The two-week workshop program followed a structured daily routine of group activities, each led by different members of the project creative and counselling team, and is outlined in Figures 10.2 and 10.3.

Time:	Monday	Tuesday	Wednesday	Thursday	Friday
9:00 9:10	Check-in	Check-in	Check-in	Check-in	Check-in
9:10 10:30	Creative Session 1	Creative Session 3	Creative Session 5	Creative Session 7	Creative Session 9
10:30 10:45	Morning Tea	Morning Tea	Morning Tea	Morning Tea	Morning Tea
10:45 12:15	Creative Session 2	Creative Session 4	Creative Session 6	Creative Session 8	Creative Session 10
12:15 1:00	Lunch	Lunch	Lunch	Lunch	Lunch
1:00 1:30	Whole Group Show & Tell	Whole Group Show & Tell	Whole Group Show & Tell	Whole Group Show & Tell	Whole Group Show & Tell
1:30 2:45	Career Counselling Session 1 (Individual)	Student Ambassador 1 Personal Stories	Career Counselling Session 2 (Family)	Career Counselling Session 3 (Individual)	Student Ambassador 2 Personal Stories
2:45 3:00	Check-out	Check-out	Check-out	Check-out	Check-out
3:00 4:00	Creative Team De-brief	Creative Team De-brief	Creative Team De-brief	Creative Team De-brief	Creative Team De-brief

FIGURE 10.2 Workshop program – Week 1.

Time:	Monday	Tuesday	Wednesday	Thursday	Friday
9:00 9:10	Check-in	Check-in	Check-in	Check-in	Check-in
9:10 10:30	Creative Session 11	Creative Session 13	Creative Session 15 (Meet the Orchestra)	Creative Session 17 Bug Fixing The Game	Creative Session 19 Prepare for Public Presentation
10:30 10:45	Morning Tea	Morning Tea	Morning Tea	Morning Tea	Morning Tea
10:45 12:15	Creative Session 12	Creative Session 14	Creative Session1 6	Creative Session 18 Bug Fixing The Game	Creative Session 20 Prepare for Public Presentation
12:15 1:00	Lunch	Lunch	Lunch	Lunch	Lunch
1:00 1:30	Whole Group Show & Tell	Whole Group Show & Tell	Whole Group Show & Tell	Whole Group Show & Tell	Whole Group Show & Tell
1:30 2:45	Career Counselling Session 4 (Individual)	Student Ambassador 3 Journey Stories	Tour of the Campus	Practicing the Game	Rehearse Public Presentation
2:45 3:00	Check-out	Check-out	Check-out	Check-out	Check-out
3:00 4:00	Creative Team De-brief	Creative Team De-brief	Creative Team De-brief	Creative Team De-brief	Creative Team De-brief

FIGURE 10.3 Workshop program – Week 2.

Each discrete component of the workshop program was designed to nurture an aspect of individual confidence, creative voice, self-esteem, and group belonging. Check-ins were a brief contact between individual creative mentors and their group of three to four participants at the commencement of each day. The check-in acted as a mood, health, and energy check to quickly assess student readiness for participation in creative practice sessions. If mentors felt that a student might not be ready for a planned activity, the mentor either exercised their own discretion and encouraged the student to join in when they were ready, or escalated the matter to supervising academic staff. Check-in provided valuable transition from the life-world of participants to the supported creative world of Super Conductor.

The creative sessions were the core element of the workshop program and were based upon a practice of student-led, strengths-based play. Creative mentors invited participants to join in one of the range of activities ranging from story line development, character design, environment or level design, sound effects design and recording, music performance, and coding. The work in each of the individual groups was discussed and showcased at daily show and tell sessions and played a key role in planning creative sessions for the following day. Students with multiple areas of interest were free to migrate between groups as they chose and often made substantial contributions in a number of creative disciplines.

The career development workshops involved individual goal setting and aptitude activities, university student ambassador presentations, and family member/carer participation. The project's career counsellor used standard career development and aptitude instruments such as career interest quizzes, quizzes that identified career aptitude, and online tools such as the Bullseye Career Information posters, designed and produced by the Federal Education Department.

Self-awareness was a key ingredient of the career development sessions and helped participants to make links between personal interests, subject area choices, and career choices. The career development sessions also showcased the personal journeys of current QUT students through 'My Story' presentations. Each of the QUT student ambassadors were chosen to deliver autobiographical presentations based upon their non-traditional pathway to university study due to lived experience of access obstacles such as disability, cultural and linguistic diversity, or a socioeconomic barrier. The final session of the career workshops focused upon scholarship opportunities for applicants experiencing a disability, and other information in the form of a resource kit of brochures, contacts, and post-school pathways.

FIGURE 10.4 Creative session – Super Conductor, 2017.

The check-out session at the end of the day allowed participants to reflect on the experiences, achievements, and obstacles of the day and help shape priorities and activities for the following day. The creative mentor debrief session gave the creative team an opportunity to discuss program participation, individual participant opportunities, and group planning for resources and logistics.

Phase 3: Performance

On the Saturday following the final session, our game was presented and performed to a live audience as a part of the 2017 Queensland Music Festival Umbrella Program. Mentors and participants had successfully created Super Conductor: a live audience-driven computer game, where players from the audience use controllers to play a computer game on a big screen which becomes a discreet conductor for a group of live musicians (through in-ear instructions). Audience members were invited to come up onto the stage and play the game using the controllers provided. The game was projected onto a cinema screen for players and audience, audience members were invited to play the game, and the participants joined the orchestra as live sound effects operators delivering atmospheric and character sounds live to the game.

Autistic participants

Of the 11 young people on the autism spectrum who participated in the creative project, nine also joined the research phase of the project as participants and of these (eight males, one female, mean=18.37 years, 16–22 years), three of them had prior experience with Studio G and with the creative project mentors.

FIGURE 10.5 Super Conductor – Queensland Music Festival, 2017.

FIGURE 10.6 Super Conductor – Queensland Music Festival, 2017.

Creative peer mentor participants

All four creative mentors (one of whom was on the autism spectrum) had prior experience with the Studio G program and were therefore already acquainted with several of
the mentees. One mentor had participated in the animation group in the Altered States
project and there was also one musician who acted as a liaison between the orchestra and
mentees. On behalf of the university, two members from Equity Services and three student
ambassadors (two with personal lived experiences of autism) coordinated and ran parallel
activities aimed at providing information to the mentees and their parents about tertiary
education and university life.

Research procedure

Following ethics clearance from the Research Ethics Committee at QUT, documentation with information about the research was sent to all participants, and, where necessary, their parents. Written and oral consent was obtained from each participant or parent prior to the start of the first interview. To ensure consistency across the two interviews, all the individual interviews were conducted by the same research team (2nd author and the research assistant), using the same equipment arrangements and room, which was situated on the same floor level as the workshop venues at the university campus. Prior to the interviews, mentees and mentors had access to hard copies of the interview guides. Additional field notes were taken to facilitate data interpretation and the duration of each interview ranged from 20 to 30 minutes.

Research interviews

In alignment with the research design, two semi-structured interview guides (Creswell & Poth, 2018) were developed for each participant group for each research phase. Prior to the creative project, mentees and mentors were asked questions about their expectations from their participation in the creative workshops. At the completion of the project, participants were asked about the challenges they had encountered throughout the creative process and what they felt they had gained as a result of their work on the project. In addition, mentors were asked about their prior and new understandings of autism, and both groups were encouraged to provide their recommendations for future iterations of the creative project.

Data analysis

All interview audio recordings were transcribed verbatim and checked by all participants prior to the thematic analysis. Two members of the research team independently read all the transcripts, and, following a series of discussions, co-developed a codebook with the themes for each set of transcripts. Themes and sub-themes were refined and consolidated in three whole-team meetings.

Findings

Mentees' views of their experience

Prior to their engagement with the project, participants were asked about their potential contribution to the project and the majority (72%) of them shared their expectation that they would be provided with opportunities to apply their own skills such as drawing, music production, gaming, programming, script writing, and character development. Fifty percent expressed a genuine interest in the project, with two specifically identifying the potential to express their individual spin and create space for featuring individual work. In addition, three mentees shared their expectation to develop attributes such as confidence for their own work, open-mindedness, and sense of responsibility. Only one student reported their expectation to meet persons who are like-minded. The majority (66%) of students shared a sense of enjoyment and satisfaction with their anticipated contribution to a creative project. When asked about anticipated challenges, mentees referred to a mix of factors that were expected to cause discomfort. These included sensory sensitivities with sound and certain lights, emotional issues related with their social anxiety, sensitivity to physical contact, and concerns about their capacity to apply technical skills required for the project.

Before commencement of the creative project, mentees reported a variety of expected outcomes pertaining to their learning and personal development. The majority (55%) of students viewed this experience as an opportunity for skill development (such as independence in transportation, game development, problem solving for technical issues, mentoring skills), while other (33%) students mentioned that they expected to develop personal attributes such as self-confidence, open-mindedness, and an awareness of responsibility. Two students anticipated that they would gain more experience in group work and project development. Only one student referred to gaining knowledge about university studies through his participation in the project. Three students expressed uncertainty about what they would gain from their participation in the project.

Following their involvement in the creative program, mentees were asked about their actual contribution to the project, and their responses showed a variability which reflected both their diverse strengths and interests, as well as the range of opportunities available within the project (i.e., music production, coding, art design). It became apparent that the mentees had used the project to showcase their skill/talent and/or build their knowledge and skills in an area of their personal interest. Interestingly, one mentee expressed interest in becoming a mentor for other students in the future following his participation in this collaborative creative project.

Four students reported project-related concerns, including technical issues, achieving productivity, skill level standards, intense work pace, and coping with requests for changes in their own creative work. Mentee comments such as 'Big day, the day is a bit longer than the average school time' and 'You could say the challenge was trying to be productive as much as possible' suggest that work on the project was taxing at times; however, the demands were tempered by the supportive network of peers and mentors. Notably, only one student revealed experiencing interpersonal conflicts that needed to be resolved.

On balance, the cohort perceived the overall creative project to be an enjoyable experience that stimulated an interest in university study, but nevertheless the group found the intensive pace of work rather challenging. A preference for greater structure in the setup of the project was expressed by several mentees. In regards to specific benefits associated with participation in Super Conductor, four mentees reported that they had increased their creative and technical skills, while three of them emphasised their social gains following the intensive, collaborative experience. One of the students shared his high enthusiasm about his participation in the project:

> I learnt game design and how animation roughly works … We were just learning all the new things that I didn't know before so I can improve on things that I want to do because before – I've always wanted to do sound and music but at school I can't do that.

Regarding mentees' interest in tertiary education, two participants explained how the project had influenced their thinking about university study, while five of them expressed their interest to pursue studies in creative arts (animation, game design, technology, manga art). Three students reported still feeling uncertain about the prospect of post-secondary education, while two students referred to newly acquired knowledge relating to university operational issues and alternative pathways to tertiary study. Interestingly though, two students identified their personal learning difficulties as well as financial issues as barriers to any potential university study.

Overall, mentees were satisfied with the program, with an overall sense that the project had been a fun, enjoyable, and interesting experience for them (66%). Several (33%) referred to the constructive social aspects of the experience (i.e., building relationships with mentors and other young people on the spectrum). Three students were positive about an extension or a repetition of the program in the future.

However, five participants expressed their dissatisfaction with technical and structural aspects of the program, with a lack of organisation, problems with transportation, noise levels, and the monotony of food all recurring themes. Two students elaborated on perceived weak features in the creative component of the project, criticising an ambiguity surrounding the overall theme of the game, a lack of coherence in game design features, and an overall simplicity in the demonstration of technical concepts.

Mentors' perceptions of their experience

Prior to their participation in the creative project, all mentors referred to their professional development as the most anticipated personal outcome. Only one mentor communicated a desire to develop deeper knowledge of working with students on the autism spectrum through engagement in the project. Following their participation, creative mentors expressed their experience as enjoyable and satisfying and elaborated on deep insights into the learning preferences, social challenges, anxieties, and coping strategies of people on the autism spectrum. Three mentors pointed out that it had been an enjoyable experience for them; they felt a lot of personal satisfaction participating in an innovative project and were happy to see the mentees also enjoying the project. It is worth noting that two mentors shared their strong feelings of self-pride for accomplishing a large project within a short time frame with this group of mentees.

I think we made a cool bit of art and I think it was a pretty cool performance.

Regarding their perception of their role, before the start of the project, three mentors had perceived their role as mentors, offering guidance and hands-on help to scaffold the skills of the mentees to support them in completing a large creative project. After their participation, one

FIGURE 10.7 Super Conductor and the Big Game Orchestra – Queensland Music Festival Performance, 2017.

mentor described her role as a combination of supervision and guidance, while also acting as a mediator between mentees with similar skills and high expectations of themselves, whereas another mentor was heavily focused on game development and did not interact with the mentees as much as the other two mentors.

In the first interview, all mentors had mentioned practical issues as anticipated challenges in their mentoring role, including giving clear directions, handling competing demands from mentees, variable levels of ability, and the nature of intensive work mode. Three mentors elaborated on expected emotional and stress issues in relation to mentees. Specifically, they expressed their uncertainty about the strength of mentees' skills, their motivation and focus, and lack of confidence. Following their participation, mentors described their efforts to resolve social emotional issues (i.e., anxiety, low stress tolerance, tendency for distraction, no request for help) between mentors and mentees and a few mentors stressed the challenge of responding to different personalities and levels of ability, as well as negotiating intense passions on special interests.

Recommendations for the future

Mentees were encouraged to offer suggestions for improvement of future iterations of the program, and the majority (89%) of them offered ideas for improving technical aspects of the program (time length, background music, grouping, task structure, game design, sensory equipment) while a few emphasised the need for making changes to sensory aspects (such as greater food variety). They also highlighted their preference for greater task and group choice, and a better sense of agency, as key components of a successful future project.

Mentors described aspects of the game design which could be improved, including music adjustments, game extension, or embedding this project into a university module in future iterations. Two mentors underlined the importance of having several technical issues resolved before the start of the project to allow more time for educating mentees on game development and rehearsing with the orchestra. They emphasised how important it is to plan for greater participant integration into the whole project. Three mentors stressed the importance of having a network of colleagues in the team from whom to draw support. One of the mentors, who was also on the spectrum, described his own resilience and lived experience as the source of his self-maintenance.

Conclusion

Super Conductor was an ambitious project on a technical level alone. There is no precedent for any previous creative work where game players, invited from a live audience, play a live two-player game projected onto a cinema screen with a live chamber orchestra and sound effects crew performing the music and sound live. Players controlled the game controllers of a Unity game engine which displayed the game on screen and also sent Open Sound Control (OSC) cues to another computer running Ableton music software. Ableton simultaneously played pre-recorded samples and sequences and also wirelessly sent conductor messages in the form of music cue names, tempos, and dynamics (intensities) to the ear-pieces of the musicians and sound effects performers. Musicians had learned by rote a range of music cues and played them when instructed via their earpiece commands from the computer. This complex coding and concept design were combined with story lines, characters, environments, and animation and was completed in an intense two-week workshop period.

On reflection, and with the benefit of hindsight, a creative project of this scale and complexity would have been a semester-long challenge for final year undergraduate students in the Creative Industries Faculty here at QUT. Super Conductor was successfully realised by our group of 11 young autistic people and a team of four creative mentors in ten days and then presented flawlessly to a live audience as part of the Queensland Music Festival. The uncertainty expressed by participants prior to the project commencement about their ability to meet the technical challenges of the project was not founded, and they rose to the challenges of the project in a spectacular fashion. The most consistent negative message for us as project creators from the participants was linked to the long days, the high-pressure environment of the project, and the boring sandwiches!

> Creative post-school transition programs such as Super Conductor provide a framework which supports cohorts of diverse young people to engage with the university sector in a way that embraces their unique expert knowledges in a safe and inclusive environment.

Strengths-based models of practice such as those applied in the Super Conductor project create Huss, Kaufman, Avgar, and Shouker's (2015) indirect symbolic space that fosters inclusion and excellence where applicants from diverse backgrounds can celebrate their unique skills and aptitudes. Creative post-school transition programs such as Super Conductor provide a framework which supports cohorts of diverse young people to engage with the university sector in a way that embraces their unique expert knowledges in a safe and inclusive environment. The ways in which universities engage diverse cohorts require an understanding that capacity building is not just for prospective students, it is also required by universities. Recognising and acknowledging the contribution diverse student populations can make is crucial for universities to be willing and able to shift their current practices and procedures, which otherwise can act as barriers for young people on the autism spectrum to engage.

Tara Simmons (1984–2019) was a musician, research assistant, and B.Psych (Hons) graduate who contributed to the data collection and analysis for this chapter and the co-authors dedicate this chapter to her memory.

References

Alverson, C., Lindstrom, L., & Hirano, K. (2019). High school to college: Transition experiences of young adults with autism. *Focus on Autism and Other Developmental Disabilities*, 34(1), 52–64. doi:10.1177/1088357615611880.

Anderson, A., Carter, M., & Stephenson, J. (2018). Perspectives of university students with autism spectrum disorder. *Journal of Autism and Developmental Disorders*, 48(3), 651–665. doi:10.1007/s10803-017-3257-3.

Anderson, C., & Butt, C. (2017). Young adults on the autism spectrum at college: Successes and stumbling blocks. *Journal of Autism and Developmental Disorders*, 47(10), 3029–3039. doi:10.1007/s10803-017-3218-x.

Ashburner, J., Bobir, N., & van Dooren, K. (2016). *Studio G multimedia program for young adults on the autism spectrum: Examining the impact on social participation, well-being, and post-school transition. Full report.* Brisbane: Cooperative Research Centre for Living with Autism.

Ashburner, J., Bobir, N., & van Dooren, K. (2017). Evaluation of an innovative interest-based post-school transition programme for young people with autism spectrum disorder. *International Journal of Disability, Development and Education*, 65(3), 262–285. doi:10.1080/1034912X.2017.1403012.

Brune, J., & Wilson, D. (2013). *Disability and passing: Blurring the lines of identity*. Philadelphia, PA: Temple University Press.

Cox, B., Thompson, K., Anderson, A., Mintz, A., Locks, T., Morgan, L., & Wolz, A. (2017). College experiences for students with autism spectrum disorder: Personal identity, public disclosure, and institutional support. *Journal of College Student Development*, 58(1), 71–87. doi:10.1353/csd.2017.0004.

Creswell, J. W., & Poth, C. N. (2018). *Qualitative inquiry and research design* (4th ed.). Thousand Oaks, CA: Sage.

Cullen, J. (2015). The needs of college students with autism spectrum disorders and Asperger's syndrome. *Journal of Postsecondary Education and Disability*, 28(1), 89–101.

Diener, M. L., Wright C. A., Wright S. D., & Anderson, L. L. (2016). Tapping into technical talent: Using technology to facilitate personal, social, and vocational skills in youth with autism spectrum disorder (ASD). In T. Cardon (Ed.), *Technology and the treatment of children with autism spectrum disorder* (pp. 97–112). Cham, Switzerland: Springer. doi:10.1007/978-3-319-20872-5_9.

Dolyniuk, C. A., Kamens, M. W., Corman, H., Dinardo, P. O., Totaro, R. M., & Rockoff, J. C. (2002). Students with developmental disabilities go to college: Description of a collaborative transition project: On a regular college campus. *Focus on Autism and Other Developmental Disabilities*, 17(4), 236–241. doi:10.1177/10883576020170040601.

Dymond, S., Meadan, H., & Pickens, J. (2017). Postsecondary education and students with autism spectrum disorders: Experiences of parents and university personnel. *Journal of Developmental and Physical Disabilities*, 29(5), 809–825. doi:10.1007/s10882-017-9558-9.

Elias, R., & White, S. (2018). Autism goes to college: Understanding the needs of a student population on the rise. *Journal of Autism and Developmental Disorders*, 48(3), 732–746. doi:10.1007/s10803-017-3075-7.

Gelbar, N., Smith, I., & Reichow, B. (2014). Systematic review of articles describing experience and supports of individuals with autism enrolled in college and university programs. *Journal of Autism and Developmental Disorders*, 44(10), 2593–2601. doi:10.1007/s10803-014-2135-5.

Gobbo, K., & Shmulsky, S. (2014). Faculty experience with college students with autism spectrum disorders: A qualitative study of challenges and solutions. *Focus on Autism and Other Developmental Disabilities*, 29(1), 13–22. doi:10.1177/1088357613504989.

Hatfield, M., Ciccarelli, M., Falkmer, T., & Falkmer, M. (2018). Factors related to successful transition planning for adolescents on the autism spectrum. *Journal of Research in Special Educational Needs*, 18(1), 3–14.

Hees, V., Roeyers, H., & Mol, J. (2018). Students with autism spectrum disorder and their parents in the transition into higher education: Impact on dynamics in the parent–child relationship. *Journal of Autism and Developmental Disorders*, 48(10), 3296–3310. doi:10.1007/s10803-018-3593-y.

Hendrickson, J., Woods-Groves, S., Rodgers, D., & Datchuk, S. (2017). Perceptions of students with autism and their parents: The college experience. *Education and Treatment of Children*, 40(4), 571–596. doi:10.1353/etc.2017.0025.

Hewitt, E. (2011). Perspectives on support needs of individuals with autism spectrum disorders: Transition to college. *Topics in Language Disorders*, 31(3), 273–285. doi:10.1097/TLD.0b013e318227fd19.

Hill, K. (2008). A strengths-based framework for social policy: Barriers and possibilities. *Journal of Policy Practice*, 7(2), 106–121.

Hurlbutt, K., & Chalmers, L. (2004). Employment and adults with Asperger syndrome. *Focus on Autism and Other Developmental Disabilities*, 19(4), 215–222. doi:10.1177/10883576040190040301.

Huss, E., Kaufman, R., Avgar, A., & Shouker, E. (2015). Using arts-based research to help visualize community intervention in international aid. *International Social Work*, 58(5), 673–688. doi:10.1177/0020872815592686.

Kearsley, G., & Shneiderman, B. (1998). Engagement theory: A framework for technology- based teaching and learning. *Educational Technology*, 38(5), 20–23.

Mitchell, W., & Beresford, B. (2014). Young people with high-functioning autism and Asperger's syndrome planning for and anticipating the move to college: What supports a positive transition? *British Journal of Special Education*, 41(2), 151–171. doi:10.1111/1467-8578.12064.

Newman, L., Wagner, M., Knokey, A.-M., Marder, C., Nagle, K., Shaver, D., … Schwarting, M. (2011). *The post-high school outcomes of young adults with disabilities up to 8 years after high school. A report from the National Longitudinal Transition Study-2 (NLTS2)*. Menlo Park, CA: SRI International.

Pinder-Amaker, S. (2014). Identifying the unmet needs of college students on the autism spectrum. *Harvard Review of Psychiatry*, 22(2), 125–137. doi:10.1097/HRP.0000000000000032.

Shattuck, P., Narendorf, S., Cooper, B., Sterzing, P., Wagner, M., & Taylor, J. (2012). Postsecondary education and employment among youth with an autism spectrum disorder. *Pediatrics*, 129(6), 1042–1049. doi:10.1542/peds.2011-2864.

Wei, X., Wagner, M., Hudson, L., Yu, J. W., & Javitz, H. (2016). The effect of transition planning and goal-setting on college enrollment among youth with autism spectrum disorders. *Remedial and Special Education*, 37(1), 3–14.

Zeedyk, S., Bolourian, Y., & Blacher, J. (2019). University life with ASD: Faculty knowledge and student needs. *Autism*, 23(3), 726–736. doi:10.1177/1362361318774148.

PART 5

Conclusion

Art is My Strength (by Alice Pegler, aged 16 years)

'I used strong things like trees and deer. Art is my strength.'

11

SUMMARY AND PROPOSITIONS

Keely Harper-Hill, Suzanne Carrington, Beth Saggers and Michael Whelan

The need for effective evidence-based teaching practices that support Australian students on the spectrum to thrive in inclusive school settings has never been greater. In this concluding chapter, a series of eight propositions are presented. Each of these propositions speaks to key themes that have been woven throughout the book chapters. The authors call for greater understanding of genuine inclusion and encourage individuals and school communities to challenge their own beliefs about the rights of all students to educational and social opportunities equivalent to those of their peers. Effectiveness relies on practices which are flexible and responsive to the diverse nature of the classroom, and teachers cannot be expected to do this alone. Researchers call for school-wide pedagogies and resourcing to assist teachers to shape and personalise their teaching to meet the diverse needs of their students. An inclusive approach to curriculum which allows teachers to address student belonging and connectedness alongside their participation and learning is critical to achieve that goal. This chapter highlights the importance of effective planning for post-school transition for all students, including those on the autism spectrum. Success in life after school is grounded in authentic participation and inclusion in their school communities.

The Cooperative Research Centre for Living with Autism (Autism CRC) research on evidence-informed educational practices reported in this book is transformational. Internationally, educators are expected to respond to diversity in a way that views individual difference as a reflection of our society and not as a 'problem' (UNESCO, 2005). Viewing diversity simply as a variation in the ways of perceiving and interacting with the world means that it is embraced rather than seen as a deficit in need of remediation. Certainly, the diverse, unique, and sometimes complex needs of students on the autism spectrum (Woronko & Killoran, 2011) can challenge educators working inclusively in schools and in partnership with families and carers. It is access to appropriate inclusive educational environments, practices, and approaches which

> *It is access to appropriate inclusive educational environments, practices, and approaches which will provide students on the autism spectrum with the best chance of social, behavioural, and academic success.*

will provide students on the autism spectrum with the best chance of social, behavioural, and academic success. It is important to consider how knowledge of evidence-informed inclusive practice is shared with respect to the competing demands on educators' time. Educators working in schools need support to develop the skills to implement these practices in order to effectively support students on the autism spectrum.

Accordingly, the purpose of the teaching approaches and practices described in this book is to support the work of teachers and specialists in inclusive school settings with students on the autism spectrum and, ultimately, all learners. Educators who engage with the contents of this book will broaden their understanding of evidence-informed inclusive practices in order to advance the behavioural, social, and learning achievements of their students and support their learning, participation, and engagement with educational contexts.

The narratives in each of the chapters present up-to-date research and elucidate the challenges inherent in translating research into classroom practice. They have been driven by a commitment to collaborate with educators in schools to work out how best to enact inclusive changes and improve inclusive education for all students. The purpose of this approach is straightforward: to support educators to have the knowledge and skills, and to use available partnerships with specialists, to confidently and competently practice in inclusive school settings. This final chapter provides an opportunity to reflect on the collective wisdom imparted throughout the preceding ten chapters and presents the essence of contemporary inclusive practice.

In the following discussions, a series of eight propositions will be presented. These propositions represent a summary of some key considerations when enacting change in practice in inclusive school settings.

1. **School communities that understand the difference between inclusive education and special education are well placed to interrogate their own beliefs, values, and practice with regards to inclusion. Understanding the belief and value systems of their members and how they inform practice will support education communities to move from good intentions towards sustained and committed inclusive school practices.**

From the outset of the book, we have proposed that it is not possible to realise and sustain a commitment to inclusive practice without the often-confronting interrogation of the beliefs and values of all members of the school community. As discussed by Cologon (2019), such interrogations are not about blame, but about understanding how they have arisen in order that they can then be reframed and addressed. The impact of applying a medical model of disability to education permeates school systems, leadership teams, and school communities across Australia today. The medical model which conceptualises diverse learners as requiring *remediation* to become closer to 'normal' is at odds with schools as institutions tasked with the *education* of their learners in order that they may live the most fulfilling of lives. Rather than encouraging schools to broaden their capacity to meet the needs of all students, the medical model has enabled schools to view diverse needs as being 'outside of their scope'. This is not to underplay the needs of diverse learners, some of which are considerable. It is, however, to lay the responsibility for meeting these needs at the foot of all teachers and schools – not a select few. This requires capacity building and school systems which prioritise this above the continuation of a one-size-fits-all model.

Including students with diverse learning needs in school settings which espouse the values of inclusion but where school leaders, classroom teachers, or student support workers subliminally perceive some learners as 'other' with needs that are 'additional' and 'burdensome' in equal parts, when compared to the needs of their peers, cannot lead to inclusion. It is only with a deeper understanding of true inclusion that school communities can begin to understand the work that lies ahead of them to achieve true inclusion. The historical journey from segregation by location (i.e., special schools) through segregation by practice (e.g., 'integration' of students located in local schools but considered to be 'other'), through to 'inclusion' where all learners are equally valued, continues to play out in Australian schools today. It has been the purpose of the research into practices to support students on the autism spectrum detailed in this book to assist school communities to move forward with their inclusive practice but with an understanding that it is their values which will determine their success.

2. **In order for evidence-informed practices to be adopted by classroom teachers, these practices must be a good 'contextual fit' within different teaching contexts and applicable for use with a range of diverse students. Achieving a 'good fit' is reliant on collaborations between researchers and teachers to tailor these practices for inclusive school settings.**

Current methods for mobilising evidence-informed practices into school settings have a poor rate of success and take too long. Throughout this book, researchers have repeatedly described methods to address these shortcomings by engaging teachers to shape and modify practices and their supporting resources. This engagement has led to practices and resources which are feasible and perceived by teachers to be both valid and valuable in inclusive school settings.

The clear need for research about evidence-informed teaching practices to be designed and completed in collaboration with classroom teachers – as per the Structured Teaching (Chapter 6) and Models of Practice (MoP) (Chapter 5) research projects – has been addressed in a number of projects in the School Years Program. Design-based research (DBR) methodology used in the MoP chapter provided a rigorous and highly effective process through which participating teachers provided critical information on social validity, content validity, and utility of the MoPs within classroom practice. The success of the process, evidenced by the viability of the MoPs, strongly positions DBR as a research method that promotes uptake of research findings into Australian classrooms.

> *Recognising teachers as unique contributors, with expertise in understanding the classroom context, firmly places them as respected colleagues rather than research subjects.*

Recognising teachers as unique contributors, with expertise in understanding the classroom context, firmly places them as respected colleagues rather than research subjects. This puts researchers in a stronger position to gain deep insights into classroom practice, leading to conclusions and recommendations which are more nuanced and relevant. In turn, by acting on these insights, researchers increase the potential for schools and teachers to more broadly and successfully adopt evidence-informed practices.

Of course, responsibility for successful collaborations between teachers and researchers does not lie only with researchers. Recruitment of teachers across the projects of the Autism CRC was challenging and no doubt reflects the competing demands that teachers must balance. However, the greater the number of teachers who participate in research, the more informative the outcomes. Extending on the importance of teacher participation, it is well established within the teacher professional learning literature that a teacher's decision to adopt new teaching practices, or adapt existing practice, requires both confidence and self-efficacy (Damschroder et al., 2009; Fixsen, Naoom, Blase, Friedman, & Wallace, 2005). Successful uptake by teachers of the findings from the Autism CRC School Years Program of research reflects the value placed on partnerships with schools and teachers.

3. **Addressing student wellbeing and connectedness with school is critical for student outcomes while at school as well as into adulthood.**

Perhaps it has been the myth of the autistic child wanting to be alone that has distracted from the universal need to be a part of something. The evidence, however, is unequivocal. Inclusion, and the sense of belonging and value that comes from it, is critical for wellbeing and as a protective factor for good mental health. Within inclusive education, genuine appreciation of a student as a member of the school community provides a sense of connectedness to school. Amidst ever increasing demands to deliver all learning areas of the curriculum, it can be challenging to prioritise the personal and social capabilities of students. Yet, as a manifestation of these capabilities, student wellbeing is an important determiner not only of academic attainment but in the lifelong legacy of mental health and resilience and post-school success.

Students who experience challenges understanding the social and communicative elements of contexts they engage in can experience additional risks successfully connecting and feeling a sense of belonging within their school community. Students with diverse social and communication abilities are less equipped to establish and maintain reciprocal relationships with others that often support a sense of belonging. Having the opportunity to consolidate relationships can be further threatened when emotional regulation is difficult.

Adolescence, in particular, is a time when: i) many students are at greater risk of poor mental health; and ii) their relationships with peers are powerful and defining influences. The chapters in Part 2 present strengths-based approaches to establishing school connectedness for all members of an inclusive school community. Values-led capacity building of the school community enables them to flexibly respond to the needs of students in order to foster a sense of school connectedness. A whole-of-school approach is responsive to the calls that it is the school environment which must adapt to enable the student to participate, not that the student must adapt in order to be accepted within the school community. This focus on developing the school environment and the actions of those therein is in contrast to a special education approach which aims to remediate the social and communication 'deficits' in order that students will participate according to predetermined conventions.

To establish positive connections with teachers and peers alike, students with diverse learning needs may require higher levels of scaffolding than that of their age peers. This requires that educators have the support and skills required to provide appropriate scaffolding. Effective working collaborations between schools, multidisciplinary support, and specialist staff are necessary in order for the upskilling of teachers in the delivery of appropriate and timely support to all students across the course of the school day. Accordingly, school systems must address how schools can be structured and resourced in order for wellbeing to become core business for all schools.

Part 2 of the book deals directly with the positive outcomes of school connectedness for adolescent students on the spectrum. The evidence provides a strong long-term rationale for education systems to not only pay attention to schools as inclusive communities, but to adequately resource them to position wellbeing as a core tenet of the curriculum. The whole-of-school model adopted in the Autism CRC School Connectedness Project described in Chapters 2 and 3 highlights the important role played by parents in facilitating school connectedness and underscores the importance of schools and teachers to work closely with families. An inclusive school setting not only values student wellbeing but works proactively to successfully establish and maintain productive collaborations between teachers, specialist staff, and parents.

4. **School-wide pedagogical frameworks are critical to provide diverse learners with consistently equitable learning opportunities.**

Implementing an inclusive approach for students who are challenged by the social, sensory, and often unpredictable nature of the school environment can be an area of learning for teachers. This may be particularly so when students are highly anxious, often resulting in emotional dysregulation or engagement in repetitive behaviours. Teachers need to be adaptable and flexible in their role. They play a pivotal part in developing a diverse suite of actionable, workable, and sustainable inclusive practices to support the diverse and individualised range of needs within their classrooms and school communities. In inclusive settings, this requires that teachers are provided with all necessary materials and training to develop their practice to be responsive to the full breadth of their students' needs. They will need to be provided with the opportunities and resources to be able to adjust their practices to a range of different and diverse learning needs and to suit their contexts and through a tiered approach to support. They also need opportunities to work collaboratively with each other. This includes working with students, families, specialised staff, and multidisciplinary teams.

5. **In order for students to experience success after school, they must be at the centre of their own learning. Students must understand and own those adjustments which have supported their successful learning and participation in order for them to advocate for the use of these adjustments as they move into adulthood.**

We believe that all students must be deliberately positioned to understand their own needs, to help to orchestrate their best learning, and to advocate for the adjustments which facilitate this. Orchestrating the conditions which lead to their best learning can occur in many different ways and we are not suggesting that all students are able to articulate needs based on metacognitive processes. However, most students can be supported in a range of diverse ways to be able to recognise and voice some of the preferred adjustments and approaches which make participation less stressful, more enjoyable, and leads to learning for them.

Many students can make choices and indicate preferences as an initial step towards a life where they are able to exercise a degree of agency. As an example, it is often the case that a student who needs visual supports and understands written words is given a written schedule. However, given the opportunity, the same student may express a preference for photographs on their schedule so that they can 'see' where they need to be. At the start of each school year, this student can be involved in taking photos which will be used in their personalised schedules and visual supports. As the student progresses through school, an ongoing dialogue about the type of visual support they need places them at the centre of this process. Opportunities and processes by which adjustments can be reviewed and students can suggest changes to their adjustments foster the ability to advocate for their needs to be met. It is often the case that if advocacy skills are targeted, it is frequently at the behest of a small number of teachers. Changing this ad hoc approach requires school leadership teams and teachers to have a shared vision of students who are able to advocate for their needs. School processes that enable teachers and students to undertake this shared work must be planned and not left to chance or goodwill alone. Also,

> *... most students can be supported in a range of diverse ways to be able to recognise and voice some of the preferred adjustments and approaches which make participation less stressful, more enjoyable, and leads to learning for them.*

teachers must be supported to understand the power of asking students 'Tell/show me what I can do that will help you'.

6. **Effective planning for post-school transition and a commitment to teaching the skills necessary for students' success in life after school are crucial for improving post-school outcomes for students on the autism spectrum and many diverse learners.**

Appropriate post-school transition planning, and close attention to teaching life skills, must become a priority if the unacceptably poor post-school outcomes for students on the spectrum are to be effectively addressed. Dedicated, well-resourced transition is essential in order to equip young people with an appropriate, feasible, and positive vision for their future.

Students on the autism spectrum and many of their peers with diverse learning needs require more than the transition planning activities that are typically carried out in inclusive school settings. The need for explicit teaching, repeated opportunities for rehearsal and role-play, deliberate generalisation strategies, and prolonged and varied work experience all speak to the importance of transition planning commencing in middle school rather than senior school.

Strong parallels can be drawn between the findings from the Better OutcOmes for Student Transitions for students on the autism spectrum (BOOST-A) reported in Chapter 9 and the lived experience of the first author in Chapter 8. There is a very real need for curriculum content to include capabilities to find and use available resources such as Internet searching. Paired with attention to practical skills (e.g., those required to use a range of transport options and understanding dress codes), these capabilities must be addressed in a concerted manner. For students seeking employment, the social complexity inherent in entry level positions also places an emphasis on the requirement to foster social emotional competence and problem-solving abilities. Never will successful collaboration between teachers, special educators, and specialists be more critical.

Further, explicit commonalities between these chapters include, but are not limited to, strengths-based, student-centred planning. In Chapter 8, the authors specify that there is a very real need to learn how to prioritise, break down, and sequence tasks, and to organise routines and possessions. Set against competing demands of a national curriculum, the need to teach these skills may be easily overlooked. However, not fostering students' understanding of their own executive function needs renders transition planning to a mostly tokenistic endeavour. Critically, it compromises students' abilities to effectively self-advocate.

> *For students seeking employment, the social complexity inherent in entry level positions also places an emphasis on the requirement to foster social emotional competence and problem-solving abilities.*

7. **The delivery of multi-tiered support systems in inclusive schools is bound on respect and requires shared values, common goals, and open communication and partnerships between schools, teachers, specialist staff, and families.**

The relevance of interrogating the beliefs and attitudes of the broader school community, including allied health specialists, has also highlighted the importance of collaborative and inclusive partnerships and the need to develop and provide multi-tiered systems of support to meet the diverse needs of the school community. This tiered approach would be founded on collaborative partnerships that support mutual respect and work to achieve shared values and goals among all stakeholders including the students on the spectrum. It is important that collaborative partnerships form the foundation of a multi-tiered system whereby all stakeholders including families, teachers, the student, and a multidisciplinary team have the opportunity to work together to devise the approaches taken at every level. Such partnerships need to be given the time and opportunity to nurture the collaborative relationships and the shared vision and are an important commitment when implementing an inclusive approach. In addition, a multi-tiered system of support is going to be founded on a supportive leadership and whole-school approach.

8. **With the best will in the world, values alone cannot lead to successful inclusion. School systems that advocate for inclusive practice must also resource schools and build their capacity to meet the needs of all of their students.**

Pivotal to the success of inclusive practices and inclusive schools is the need to adequately provide our school communities with the physical, human, and material resources to support inclusive practices. In addition, there is a need to focus on a whole-school inclusive approach, ethical leadership, knowledgeable staff, multidisciplinary support, a multi-tiered system of support, collaborative partnerships, open communication, a sense of belonging, and inclusive practices that meet the needs of all students.

References

Cologon, K. (2019). *Towards inclusive education: A necessary process of transformation*. Melbourne: Children and Young People with Disability Australia.

Damschroder, L., Aron, D. C., Keith, R. E., Kirsh, S., Alexander, J. A., & Lowery, J. C. (2009). Fostering implementation of health services research findings into practice: A consolidated framework for advancing implementation science. *Implementation Science*, 4(1). doi:10.1186/1748-5908-4-50.

Fixsen, D. L., Naoom, S. F., Blase, K. A., Friedman, R. M., & Wallace, F. (2005). *Implementation research: A synthesis of the literature* (FMHI publication No. 231). Tampa, FL: University of South Florida, Louis de la Parte Florida Mental Health Institute, National Implementation Research Network.

UNESCO. (2005). *Guidelines for inclusion: Ensuring access to Education for All*. Paris: UNESCO.

Woronko, D., & Killoran, I. (2011). Creating inclusive environments for children with autism. In T. Williams (Ed.), *Autism spectrum disorders: From genes to environment* (pp. 213–226). Rijeka, Croatia: InTech.

INDEX

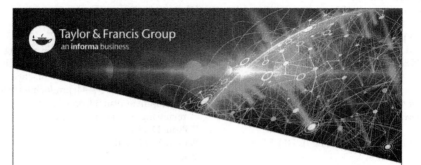